INSIDE *the*

CANBERRA

PRESS GALLERY

Life in the Wedding Cake of Old Parliament House

INSIDE *the*
CANBERRA
PRESS GALLERY

Life in the Wedding Cake of Old Parliament House

Rob Chalmers

Edited by Sam Vincent and John Wanna

ANU
THE AUSTRALIAN NATIONAL UNIVERSITY

E PRESS

ANU

E PRESS

Published by ANU E Press
The Australian National University
Canberra ACT 0200, Australia
Email: anuepress@anu.edu.au
This title is also available online at: http://epress.anu.edu.au

---

National Library of Australia
Cataloguing-in-Publication entry

Author: Chalmers, Rob, 1929-2011

Title: Inside the Canberra press gallery :
                life in the wedding cake of Old Parliament House / Rob Chalmers ;
                edited by Sam Vincent and John Wanna.

ISBN: 9781921862366 (pbk.) 9781921862373 (ebook)

Notes: Includes bibliographical references and index.

Subjects: Australia. Parliament--Reporters and
                Government and the press--Australia.
                Journalism--Political aspects--
                Press and politics--Australia.

Other Authors/Contributors: Vincent, Sam.
                             Wanna, John.

Dewey Number: 070.4493240994

Cover design and layout by ANU E Press

Back cover image courtesy of Heide Smith

Printed by Griffin Press

Contents

Acknowledgments

My first thanks must go to my wife, Gloria, for transcribing a number of interviews (which sometimes, on the tape, sounded like a conversation among illiterate, drunken professional footballers). Gloria closely edited the text many times and picked up some howlers. So many people have assisted me that I do not dare try to list them for fear of leaving one or more out. Generally, they are mentioned in the text. I must give particular thanks to Senator John Faulkner, Eric Walsh and Jeff Townsend for, among other things, passing a practised and knowledgeable eye over the text and for some great material. Michael Delaney was an invaluable source of much material and an instant guide to how things worked in government. Justin Stanwix constantly nagged me to hurry up and write the book. I drew material from many authors listed in the bibliography and they are generally acknowledged as the source in the text. Finally, I thank my late father, Bobby, for the care and attention he devoted to this selfish only child during its upbringing—and my late mother, Janet, for marrying him. Finally, I thank the Federal Parliamentary Press Gallery for just being there to join.

Foreword

If the Canberra Press Gallery is an institution, Rob Chalmers was an institution of that institution. His career spanned 60 years and 12 prime ministers, 24 federal elections and five changes of government. There is not a member of Parliament today who can remember a Press Gallery before Rob Chalmers joined it in early 1951, moving up from Sydney as a young journalist. As a result, his insight was as unique as his experience. At a time when politicians and political correspondents alike have become simply talking heads on televisions for most Australians, scrutinised and judged on the same terms as minor (and not very interesting) celebrities, Rob has written the story of the men and women of the Australian Parliament and the Australian Press Gallery from the perspective of one who knew them: knew their foibles and their frailty, knew their strengths and weaknesses and their sometimes unexpected kindnesses. At a time of great cynicism about the political process, not just in Australia but around the world, this book provides an acute and timely reminder that politicians, and the journalists who report them, are not the semi-fictionalised figures flattened to ten second sound bites or thirty second direct-to-camera feeds that our modern media so often makes them appear to be, but instead are men and women frequently doing their best, and sometimes doing their worst, in complex circumstances and faced with huge dilemmas. Arriving in the Gallery just a few years after the Second World War, Rob had a front row seat and a backstage pass for both dramatic political crises and subtle policy changes for more than half-a-century, and in this book he has collected the most memorable. His observations are pointed – there are no free passes in this book, as there were none in *Inside Canberra*, the political junkie's must-read newsletter he published for well over 30 years – and his sharp eye and sharper pen capture and sketch politicians from Billy Hughes to Bob Hawke and beyond. For many of us in Parliament House, losing Rob from the Gallery corridors was very much the end of an era. We are all lucky that he recorded so many of his experiences – a lasting record of a time past and of an extraordinary career.

John Faulkner, September 2011

Preface

Ben Chifley occupied the Opposition Leader's chair and, opposite him, across the table of the House of Representatives, sat the recently elected Prime Minister, Robert Gordon Menzies, when I first reported Question Time. Here were the two giants of Australian politics: 'Chif', revered by my father, and 'Ming', whom he loathed. Menzies was often referred to as 'Ming' after a comic-book character, Ming the Merciless, an evil Chinaman dressed in robes and with long fingernails. (Another explanation was that 'Mingees' was the Scottish pronunciation of Menzies.) I was overawed and apprehensive on this day, 7 March 1951. Behind Chifley sat household names: Bert Evatt, Eddie Ward, Arthur Calwell, Reg Pollard, and Cyril Chambers. Behind Menzies on the front bench were Harold Holt, Artie Fadden, Jack McEwen, Earle Page, Richard Casey and Larry Anthony (father of Doug). On the back bench of the Government side sat the wizened figure of Billy Hughes, who was then aged eighty-nine. The public galleries, occupying two sides of the square chamber, were packed, as was the press gallery, occupying the other two sides—one above the Speaker's chair (where I sat), and the other on the opposition side. Some of the best-known political journalists sat in the press gallery: Alan Reid (Sydney *Sun*), Harold Cox (Melbourne *Herald*), and Ian Fitchett (*The Age*). The Speaker, Archie Cameron, read prayers and everyone stood.

Prayers over, we all sat down and Menzies announced 'with deep personal regret' he had received a letter of resignation from the Cabinet of Dame Enid Lyons, the widow of Joseph Lyons, Prime Minister for most of the 1930s. An extraordinary woman, mother of 12, she was only seventeen when she married the thirty-five-year-old Lyons, who was then the Tasmanian Labor Government's Treasurer. Dame Enid was the first woman elected to the House of Representatives and, as Vice-President of the Executive Council, the first woman to gain cabinet rank. After Menzies' announcement, the Speaker, craggy-faced Archie Cameron, revealed he had received a letter from M. Spaak, President of the Consultative Assembly of the Council of Europe, inviting representatives of the house to 'certain proceedings' in Strasbourg. Cameron also announced he had received a letter from the President of the Knesset, 'the Parliament of Israel', as he put it, together with a resolution of the Knesset 'concerning the proposed re-armament of Germany'. The letter, said Cameron, was in Hebrew and French and he tabled it. Then Question Time began. In contrast with current practice, on this day, the Leader of the Opposition, Chifley, did not ask a question. Evatt led off, asking Menzies if he would intervene in retrenchments in the Legal Service Bureau, which provided advice to ex-servicemen. Menzies' reply was brief and courteous: 'I cannot undertake to intervene in one sense of the word, but I shall be very glad to discuss the matter with the Attorney-General, with a view to ascertaining what the position is and what he has in his mind.' No attempt at point scoring, or a smart reply: just a simple, straight answer to a straight question. For an hour, the Opposition asked about hides, sulfur, immigrant labour, defence, dollar loans, Commonwealth diplomatic services and currency.

All of this marked a milestone in my years as a journalist. Still only a cadet, I found myself at the very centre of political life in Australia and it had not taken all that long. I had no idea whether I would last in political journalism. I did know, however, that it was enjoying and satisfying. As it turned out, I remained in the press gallery at the Old Parliament House until May 1988—37 years—when the move was made to the new and permanent Parliament House on Capital Hill, directly behind the Old Parliament House. I remain a member of the press gallery and, at the time of writing, the journalist with by far the longest continuous membership, with more than 58 years on the clock and still ticking.

This book is in part a political history, and in part a biography. One objective is to give the reader some flavour of politics before television, radio and later the Internet came to dominate the dissemination of political news and comments. Giving the outsider an inside look at how the gallery operated and its place in the body politic is another objective. Such are the number of years covered by the book that many of the major dramas played out in the old Parliament are not even mentioned. Yet a majority of the main actors are assessed. Mainly, the book consists of events and people who have stuck in my memory.

Rob Chalmers

1. Youth

I was born in Concord West in Sydney's western suburbs on Bastille Day, 14 July 1929, and duly christened Robin Donald Chalmers at Chalmers Presbyterian Church in Chalmers Street, Sydney. My mother, Janet (nee Smith), was a country girl from Grenfell, NSW. Her father was Isaac (Ike) Smith, a friend of Billy Hughes in the early days of the Australian Workers' Union when they both organised for the union, riding bikes around New South Wales for the cause. My father, Robin (Bobby), was born in Wellington, New Zealand, and his father, John ('old Jack' to the family), was born in Scotland. Bobby's mother, Louise (nee Seager), a handsome woman, was born on the Isle of Wight. Her father, an engineer, played a big part in the development of the wharves in Wellington Harbour. Jack's father had a successful cooperage (barrel-making) business in New Zealand, and, according to family legend, a savage fist fight between Jack and his father ended in Jack smashing a prized miniature model ship in a bottle over his father's head. This led to the estrangement for life of Jack and his father. Jack was cut out of the will and successive generations have mourned this fist fight. Jack was a champion cyclist in New Zealand, and when he came to Sydney, he competed in the six-day bike races, sponsored by the notorious John Wren, who built a fortune on illegal starting price (SP) bookmaking in Melbourne, where he bribed coppers and politicians with aplomb (he was later immortalised in the Frank Hardy classic *Power Without Glory*). At the turn of the century, professional bike racing was a popular sport and at one stage the Sydney Cricket Ground had a bike track around its circumference. The African-American champion cyclist Major Douglas was a friend of Jack's and there is a family picture of my father, Bobby, sitting on the athlete's knee. In New Zealand, Jack built, and raced, his own 18-footer skiff on Wellington Harbour—a sport later taken up by his son, John (young Jack), on Sydney Harbour. Before World War I, the family—old Jack, Louise, young Jack, daughter, Leah, and my father, Bobby, the youngest of the tribe—moved to Queensland. Another daughter died when only about five.

Old Jack, Louise and the three children took up a prickly pear selection near Gayndah. Prickly pear from South America had overrun much of Queensland's good faming country and leases were available to those brave enough to take one on the basis that the land be cleared of this noxious weed. A 'peppercorn' secured a lease and the family laboured long hours in the struggle against the pear. They would start burning clumps of it at the bottom of a paddock, working their way up and, by the time they got to the top of the paddock, the burnt pear at the bottom had re-emerged. Prickly pear plants were brought to Australia on the First Fleet when Captain Arthur Phillip collected a number of cochineal insects from Brazil en route to Botany Bay. The red dye derived from cochineal insects was important to the Western world's clothing industries, and was the dye used for British soldiers' red coats. The cochineal insects fed off the pear, which was also brought from Brazil. Prickly pear began to cause concern from about 1870 and, by 1925, was completely out of control, infesting some 25 million hectares in New South Wales and Queensland and spreading at the rate of 250 000 ha a year. Finally, the answer came with the cactoblastis moth, which biologically controlled and stopped the amazing spread of prickly pear in eastern Australia and is still regarded as the outstanding example of such control around the world. Six years after the release of the moth, most of the original thick stands of pear were gone and properties previously abandoned were reclaimed and brought back into production, but this was far too late for the Chalmers family; old Jack had finally given up and moved to Sydney well before World War I.

When World War I broke out, young Jack enlisted in the Australian Imperial Force (AIF) and sailed for Egypt, where most of the AIF trained before heading for France or Gallipoli. One of the more demanding training regimes was a race to the top of the Great Pyramid of Khufu—the tallest of the pyramids. Young Jack was the first of his battalion to reach the top and he won his division of the battalion's boxing tournament. After Egypt, Jack was a stretcher-bearer in the hell of trench warfare on the Western Front. The stretcher-bearer heroes had the most arduous and dangerous of jobs: going out into 'no-man's land' and bringing back the dead and wounded. Bobby, who was younger than his brother, Jack, enlisted in the war but, fortunately, by the time he reached France, hostilities had ceased.

Jack married Marjorie, an English girl, and brought her back to Sydney to start a family. He and Bobby joined the North Bondi Surf Club and were excellent swimmers. Jack was the Australian champion belt swimmer at one stage and Bobby won the NSW breaststroke championship. Both were involved in separate and heroic episodes of lifesaving, which electrified Australia.

The weather at Coogee Beach on 4 February 1922 was cloudy, with a southerly blowing and the surf choppy; lifesavers from most parts of Sydney had come for a surf carnival. That day, prior to the carnival, young lifesaver Milton Coughlan was body surfing ('shooting the waves', in those days) when suddenly he cried: 'Shark! Shark!' This is a description of the shark attack based on Ray Slattery's *Grab the Belt*, a book about epic Australian rescues. Slattery describes the events at Coogee that day:

> Following his warning cry, Coughlan, struck out for the beach but moments later the shark struck, attacking him savagely. It was a terrible fight, Coughlan struggling desperately, while the sea around him developed a widening red stain. Jack ran for the belt, found a reel and

the line all right but the belt was missing. This didn't stop him. Chalmers hastily knotted the line about his waist and ran into the sea while other lifesavers grabbed the reel. The shark kept returning to attack Coughlan whose resistance was waning. The grey shape swirled under water as Jack approached. Reaching the stricken youth he was shocked at what he saw. Coughlan's hands were gone, his arms badly mauled. At this stage, Frank Beaurepaire also from the North Bondi Club, rushed to give the beltman assistance. By then the shark swam parallel to the beach in a gutter a few metres from the shore. According to my father, Beaurepaire waited until the shark swam past him by only a few feet, before he plunged into the gutter and swam out to join Jack. Jack and Beaurepaire yelled and splashed as the shark kept circling its victim. The shark gave them some anxious moments before it turned and swam seaward. Many hands helped the group out of the water and Coughlan was laid on the sand. He was beyond help and died within a few minutes.

Slattery records how the tragedy shocked Australia: 'Jack Chalmers' courageous act fired the public imagination and he became a National hero overnight.' My uncle was awarded the Albert Medal—named after the Consort to Queen Victoria—the highest award for valour available to a civilian. Only a few seasons earlier, the Surf Life Saving Association of Australia had instituted a system of awards to recognise outstanding deeds of valour by its members. The Meritorious Award in Gold was the highest award and, until then, it had not been awarded. Jack Chalmers received the first and Frank Beaurepaire was awarded the second. Sean Brawley has a slightly different account of the rescue.[1] He says the rescue took place from the rocks at the southern end of the beach and that Jack slipped and fell off the rocks several times, lacerating his leg and at one stage dashing his head against a rock, sustaining mild concussion as a consequence. Nevertheless, he staggered on, found the reel had no belt and tied the line around his waist—a dangerous practice as it could tighten and constrict the swimmer. Brawley says when he got to Coughlan, Jack discovered too much line had been paid out and those manning the reel were still hauling in the slack. Instead of being pulled in by the lifesavers on the reel, Jack had to swim in, dragging Coughlan with him. Brawley's account of Beaurepaire assisting after Jack had begun dragging Coughlan towards the beach tallied broadly with other accounts. A Melbournian, Beaurepaire, the Olympian and Australian swimming champion, had spent the summer in Sydney and joined the North Bondi club. The national fund to reward my uncle was supported by the *Sydney Morning Herald*. Brawley says the amount Chalmers received was not known (and I cannot remember my father telling me). Brawley says Beaurepaire received £5000 from the fund and he agrees that, with others, Beaurepaire

1 Brawley, Sean 2007, *The Bondi Lifesaver: A history of an Australian icon*, ABC Books, Sydney, pp. 103–4.

used this windfall to launch his tyre empire. The Beaurepaire business became one of the best known in Australia and its founder was knighted. Beaurepaire later became Lord Mayor of Melbourne. According to my father, the fund was entirely in recognition of Jack's bravery and he voluntarily gave Beaurepaire a large amount.

The following year (1923) on 18 March, a huge sea was running at Bondi Beach. The beach was closed and my father, Bobby, was playing cards in the North Bondi surf clubhouse with some of his mates. Word came to them that three people had been washed into the sea at Ben Buckler—the northern arm of Bondi Beach. They were standing on a rock, sightseeing, and had misjudged how far they needed to be up from the sea. A monster wave grabbed all three and sucked them into the water. Only one, a youth, was a swimmer and he helped his non-swimming mate to struggle back to the Ben Buckler rock ledge. But the girl, Tui Kirby, only seventeen and a non-swimmer, was well out to sea. Her billowing gown filled with air and kept her afloat. Bobby and a group of lifesavers grabbed a reel with a long line attached to a belt and struggled around towards the Ben Buckler headland. They were buffeted and knocked over by massive waves; some suffered severe cuts and abrasions by the time they reached the rock ledge. They were then ready for someone to go into the sea. That somebody was Bobby. He got into the belt and by some miracle managed to launch himself into the sea during a lull in the waves without being washed back and smashed onto the rocks. But before he had gone far, the line attached to the belt snagged in a cleft in the rocks. Unable to go any further, he let the belt go and soon he was a long way out in a rough sea, in an area where sharks were prevalent and he could not see Kirby.

He looked around and, on the cliffs above Ben Buckler, onlookers were directing him using towels to wave signals, and finally he reached Kirby, who announced, 'I can't swim.' They were in mortal danger. They could not get back onto the rocks at Ben Buckler and Bobby decided the only course was to try to drag Kirby to the beach. This meant that they had to get clear of the Ben Buckler northern headland to get a good run to the beach. Then he would have to deal with the huge waves, when he finally reached the edge of the surf break, a long way from the safety of the beach. Meanwhile, the pilot ship *Captain Cook* had been ordered out from Watson's Bay and was steaming to pick up the two desperate people. The Doherty twins had a fishing shack on the northern headland of Bondi Beach, halfway between the beach and the Ben Buckler headland. During a lucky lull in the sea, the two brave fishermen managed to launch a small rowing boat and, with tremendous skill and courage, made it through the huge seas and picked up Bobby and Tui Kirby. The next day's *Daily Telegraph* ran a graphic account of the rescue, noting that upon returning to the clubrooms at North Bondi, 'young Chalmers was accorded a tremendous ovation by the crowd for his plucky rescue'. For his bravery, Bobby was later awarded only the third Meritorious Award in Silver by the Surf Life Saving Association—thus, of the first three of these rare awards, the two brothers had won one each. I have only recently discovered in papers kept by my daughter Susan a copy of the program for a 'Testimonial Matinee' to 'Rob Chalmers & Doherty Bros, under the patronage and in the presence of the State governor, Sir Walter Davidson'. Listed were the 'musicians and artists' and the stage manager was a 'Mr Freddy Wallace'. Whether there was a presentation of funds to my father and the Doherty brothers is not stated. My father never mentioned this honour accorded him.

Not long after my birth, we moved to more salubrious rental accommodation in the beautiful Sydney harbourside suburb of Rushcutters Bay. The Great Depression was on and Bobby had a job four days a week testing electricity meters for the Sydney County Council in a building immediately behind the Sydney Town Hall. He walked a considerable distance to and from work every day to save tuppence.

Then, about the middle of the 1930s, the Municipal Council of Granville—then a suburb regarded as 'way out west'—built the first Olympic swimming pool in the western suburbs. Bobby applied for the job as manager and won—defeating some 200 keen applicants. He was made for the job: an ex-digger, a swimming champion, a surfing hero, a licensed electrician and a fitter and turner. He established a swimming club and the baths became the social centre for young kids and teenagers during the summer, in a suburb where there was very little to do and not much money about.

After the Japanese attack on Pearl Harbor in December 1941, Bobby left Granville for a job as a fitter and turner on the Garden Island naval base in Sydney Harbour. There was a sudden surfeit of flats at Kirribilli as many residents departed for safer areas. Kirribilli was close to what were considered two prime targets for Japanese bombing: the Harbour Bridge and Garden Island. We moved to a two-bedroom flat at Studley Royal, 59 Kirribilli Avenue, close to St Aloysius Catholic Boys' School, at the opposite end of Kirribilli Avenue to Kirribilli House, where John Howard lived during his time as Prime Minister. Studley Royal—a rather grand name for what had been the grand residence of an upper-class family in earlier years—had been converted to apartments and the former stables were now two snug flats. We lived on the second floor—reached via an elegant staircase with a polished wooden handrail. The flat had a balcony with a glorious view across the harbour to the city, Circular Quay, Sydney Cove, on the right the Rocks and the towering Harbour Bridge and, to the left, Bennelong Point (later the site for the Opera House), Farm Cove and the Botanic Gardens. You could throw a stone from our balcony onto the Jeffery

Street ferry wharf below. When about to leave for the city, I could watch the little ferry leave Circular Quay and have time to stroll down to the wharf to board it.

With Australia still at war at this time, we practised rushing to the basement air-raid shelter. Bobby was on Garden Island the night the Japanese midget submarines attacked the *USS Chicago*, an American cruiser anchored on the eastern side of the island. One of the submarines fired a torpedo at the *Chicago* but the torpedo ran under the cruiser and under the ferry *HMAS Kuttabul*, moored alongside Garden Island as a dormitory for young sailors. The torpedo struck the wharf directly alongside the *Kuttabul*, totally wrecking the vessel's wooden hull and immediately causing her to sink. Nineteen sailors lost their lives. At this stage, the very nervous Americans on the *Chicago* brought their six-inch guns to bear on almost anything that moved in the harbour and it was amazing that more casualties did not result. As a volunteer fireman at Garden Island, Bobby and his mates rushed from the machine shop where they were working on the western side of the island and dashed to the scene of the *Kuttabul* to see what they could do, but there was very little that could be done. As they arrived, many much younger men were pulling the dead and dying sailors from the water. At this stage of the war, there were 'brownouts' on all over Sydney. There was further alarm when the mother ship of the midget submarines shelled Rose Bay from the sea—unchallenged. It also dispatched a reconnaissance plane, which flew over the Harbour Bridge. After the war, Bobby left Garden Island to work as an electrician with the Sydney County Council, operating from the old convict-built two-storey warehouses lining the eastern side of Sydney Cove, with Government House standing out above.

I had my sixteenth birthday and Bobby decided that I should learn how to drink in moderation, so, a few days a week, I would meet him at the Milsons Point pub, joining in rounds of beer with his working-class mates. (I regret that the lessons in moderate drinking were not fully effective throughout my life.) Frank Miller, a drinking mate of Bobby's, was a tall, gangly, languid, likeable, typical Australian who enjoyed a laugh. Frank was not enthusiastic about work. Sometimes he would come into the pub after a day at the White Bay powerhouse near Pyrmont as a fitter and turner and Bobby would inquire: 'Well, how did you go today Frank?' 'Well, I beat them, I didn't strike a blow all day,' he would say with great satisfaction. Bobby and Frank Miller travelled on the same ferry from Kirribilli each morning for work. As the ferry came into the wharf at Circular Quay, Frank would heave himself to his feet and exclaim, 'Isn't work a bastard?' Having left school at the age of twelve, my father was largely self-educated, reading two pages of the dictionary every night. He was a keen reader and a conscientious worker. Like hundreds of thousands of his generation, Bobby was convinced by the Depression years that the only way forward was Labor and socialism. He was devoted to the union movement, a supporter of Jack Lang and convinced of the theories of Douglas Credit.

Bobby was also intensely interested in international affairs. His list of heroes was diverse: Stalin (long before he was exposed as a monster), Gandhi, Nehru, Churchill, Eisenhower, Joe Louis, Don Bradman, Jack Crawford, John Curtin, Ben Chifley and Franklin D. Roosevelt. He was anti-colonialist and against racism—issues that were hardly heard of before World War II. I remember him taking me to an evening meeting in a hall near Granville when I was about twelve to hear Federal MP and Langite 'Stabber' Jack Beasley (West Sydney). My father was responsible for my interest in both politics and journalism, and encouraged me in many ways. Together, we would read the *Sydney Morning Herald*, but not *The Daily Telegraph*.

The latter was—and still is—favoured by most working men in Sydney, but my father loathed the proprietor, Frank Packer, whom he rightly regarded as anti-union. At the age of twelve, he had me reading books such as Dale Carnegie's sociological masterpiece *How to Win Friends and Influence People*. I left school in 1945 at the age of sixteen with the Intermediate Certificate and thought about what I would do. My father's encouraging words to me as I entered the workforce were simple: 'Rob, remember you have nothing to beat.' Having worked most of his life as a tradesman, he also advised: 'Don't start work at 7.30.' At that time, working-class teenagers were expected to enter the workforce and begin earning money to contribute to the family. There was no thought of a university degree, which was regarded as far too expensive before the Higher Education Contribution Scheme (HECS). There were scholarships, although it did not occur to my family that I should try for one. I did later qualify for university by matriculating at night school during my time in the reading room of the Sydney *Daily Mirror*.

My first job was hazardous. At Wynyard Station, in George Street in the city, there was a popular theatrette, running continuous newsreels as well as cartoons. A full session ran for about 1.5 hours. There was another theatrette in Market Street next to the State Theatre—both owned by the same company. The management had only one copy of whatever film was being shown so as a session finished I ferried the reels back and forth in a haversack on a pushbike. This involved frenzied riding through the cars, trams and buses up and down George Street to exchange the reels with the projectionists. Mercifully, such a hazardous occupation soon ended.

2. A Journo in Sydney

My father decided that I should do something serious about a career in journalism and, with a family contact, Roger Davis, a senior journalist on *The Daily Telegraph*, he contacted Mark Gallard, the then Editor-in-Chief of *Truth* and *Sportsman*, publishers of the *Daily Mirror*. I managed to get a job as an office boy at the Sydney headquarters in Hosking Place in the city. I was often instructed to take several bottles of champagne to the fashionable restaurant Romano's, for the *Mirror*'s proprietor, Ezra Norton, and his luncheon guests. Cigarettes were in short supply after the war and one had to be 'in the know' with a cigarette vendor. I would be sent off to a kiosk in Clarence Street on a regular basis to collect Mr Norton's cigarettes. None of this was a great learning experience, except that I got to know the Sydney CBD, before I cracked a job in the reading room at the *Truth* and *Sportsman*'s editorial headquarters in Kippax Street, Surry Hills.

John Norton was one of the most colourful figures in the history of Australian journalism. Born in 1858 in Brighton, Sussex, he migrated to Australia in 1884, settling in Sydney. Despite bouts of drunkenness, he became a successful journalist and built up the newspaper *Truth*—at various stages published in Sydney, Brisbane, Melbourne and Perth. The *Australian Dictionary of Biography* says that Norton senior introduced a sensational form of abuse of many figures in authority in the pages of *Truth*, from Queen Victoria ('flabby, fat and flatulent') to local councillors, especially the raving 'wowsers'—a word he claimed to have coined. His articles and alliteration (Lord Dudley was accused of 'libidinous lecheries and lascivious lapses') were immensely popular with the working class. *Truth*'s circulation skyrocketed.

Ezra Norton was a hands-on newspaper proprietor, as were Warwick Fairfax (later knighted by Prime Minister Harold Holt, but not by Menzies) with the *Sydney Morning Herald* and Frank Packer (later Sir Frank) with *The Daily Telegraph*. Packer even checked the expense claims of his journalists. With the death of Stalin, Packer ordered a cartoon to be published in the *Telegraph* with a crocodile shedding tears—a commentary on the standard eulogies that were being published at the time of the death of the communist monster. Norton was not a member of the Sydney establishment and when the Australian Jockey Club (AJC) committee failed to elect Norton as a member, this bastion of the establishment became the target of ferocious criticism by the *Mirror*. This criticism did bear fruit when, after constant pressure from the *Mirror*, the AJC agreed to admit journalists to hearings of racing stewards inquiring into such matters as betting frauds, jockeys pulling horses and doping.

Newspapers then—even more than now—were examples of the management of complex organisations. The process involved the text of the journalist's story first being typed onto sheets of copy paper, before going to the subeditors' room, where it would be assessed for importance, given a place on a page, edited and given an appropriate heading, type size and font noted on the copy and sent off to the composing room. Here the material was 'set' on a linotype machine operated by highly skilled tradesmen. These machines produced letters from hundreds of lead moulds moved around in the machine by operation of an elaborate keyboard. The moulds ('slugs') would then form words and sentences and were assembled in the right order by a compositor (another trade branch of printing) on a steel table (a 'stone') to make up the page. 'Galleys' were impressions of the material on the stone, which went to the reading room where the senior reader read to the junior—my job. One had to follow the words of the reader and stop him if there was an omission or mistake in his reading against the copy. There were some eight teams, working throughout the day, checking all editions. When the galleys and pages on the stone had all been checked, semicircular impressions of the pages were made and then locked onto the rollers of the huge, super-fast rotary presses. There were, from memory, at least six editions a day and a number of 're-plates' involving limited changes to pages to deal with developing stories.

Six months in the reading room provided invaluable hands-on training in the writing style expected and the way senior journalists treated their stories. It is a curious thing that today, with newspapers produced by the miracle of computers, deadlines seem to run behind the deadlines imposed in the hot-lead era. This is probably due to newspapers being much larger, with a lot more pages and, of course, colour. Apart from the actual production, there were also the complexities involved in the need for an advertising department to generate revenue. Distributing the paper across the city and State was a substantial and complex task. Paper sellers sold hundreds of papers from rent-free footpath sites on the streets of Sydney. They did a roaring trade as the evening rush hour approached and papers were bought for reading on public transport on homeward journeys.

A cadetship on the *Mirror* was not easy to get in the late 1940s. Under the Chifley Government's postwar reconstruction legislation, priority rightly went to journalists returning from the war. But finally, I was promoted to a cadetship after six months and I began my journalistic career. A cadetship was normally spread over four years and, on its completion, a journalist went on to the lowest level applying in the award: 'D' grade. From there, one would expect to be graded 'C', 'B', 'A' and 'A plus'.

Training on the *Mirror* for a cadet was not comparable with the intense training and instruction given in other trades to apprentice carpenters, electricians, fitters and turners and plumbers. I had already achieved some ability as a touch typist. While in the reading room, I went to East Sydney Technical College for touch-typing courses and one of my co-students was well-known journalist (Sydney's) 'Won' Casey—as opposed to (Melbourne's) Ron Casey. One of the agreeable features of this course was that we were the only males in a room full of young ladies. The typing course was taken in the boss's time and, having abandoned Pitman's shorthand as too difficult, I decided to take up Summerhayes' Shorterhand—an Australian invention. Bobby helped me at the kitchen table at home, testing my memory for the correct shorthand symbols for contractions of common words and phrases. In later life in the press gallery, if I found it difficult to work out an outline or interpret my shorthand, I would go to Gough Whitlam's office and there Carol Summerhayes, a granddaughter of the creator, would easily read my outlines and solve my difficulties. Shorthand courses are a slow slog in many ways, so to relieve the boredom, we cadets would nick down to the Metropolitan Snooker Saloon rather than business college on occasions. Even so, we finally got through the course.

The *Mirror* did not 'train' its cadets. Essentially, you relied on your own initiative and learned from others—the more senior cadets and other journalists. At first, work was nothing but low-grade clerical duties: putting together lists of radio programs and shipping movements. The NSW lottery results for the cable edition were a major challenge for cadets. The cable edition contained material flowing in overnight by cable from overseas news agencies. Generally, this edition ran at about 10.30 pm, when the last number was drawn, and the page containing the lottery results was locked up on the stone in the composing room. The lottery was drawn from a large wooden barrel in an office just off George Street, near Wynyard, with the draw beginning about 9.30 pm. Each winning number from first prize down to the lowest £5 was read aloud by a government official. The cadets had to get all these numbers down in a hell of a hurry and get them to the *Mirror*'s office.

The hardest to get accurate were the numbers of the final draw: 1500 prizes of £5 read rapidly. At the end of the draw, the official results would be transmitted to the *Mirror* from the lottery office and we would find that, on average, there were half a dozen or so incorrect numbers of £5 prizes in the paper. Pensioners and other needy people expressed bitter disappointment after reading the *Mirror*. Full of hope, they expected to collect the handy sum of £5 only to find that it was a mistake. Every week, we would receive groans and moans from the news editor and the chief of staff asking us to lift our game. The winner of first prize in the NSW lottery was known by mid-morning, and we competed with the *Sun* to get an exclusive interview with the lucky winner. We were sent off with a photographer, a radio car and a driver; the aim was to get to the winner before the *Mirror*'s competitor, the *Sun*. If we were successful, the idea was to entice the winner away from his or her home or workplace, so the opposition would not get an interview. One driver often with me was George, who was probably about thirty, a sixth-division veteran not all that long back from the war. It struck me later that here I was, an inexperienced kid, telling a knockabout bloke like George what to do and how to do it. But George was (fortunately) smarter than me. If we could not find our target at his/her residence, George had the nous to suggest we try some of the pubs. That often worked.

The Saturday edition was all about sport, and the permanent sporting journalists were supported by cadets who did the dogsbody work of assembling racing results. These had to be absolutely accurate: the correct placing of horses in each race, the odds for the various runners, tote odds, and so on. Any cadet who made a mistake with these details was in trouble. Punters not at the races could only 'get on' with illegal SP bookmakers who, unlike the on-course bookies and the on-course tote, paid no taxes to the State Government, and therefore, every effort was made to wipe out the SPs. It was a vast and crooked industry supervised by corrupt coppers. My cousin Don Smith ran the biggest SP in Yass, NSW, in the 1950s. The local police sergeant tipped him off when a visit from 'the flying squad' was expected. The flying squad was composed of senior vice squad detectives from Sydney who were supposed to swoop on SPs. Don was invariably given a warning enabling him to set up a dummy SP operator to be arrested by the flying squad. As the dummies had no previous offences, they would receive a light fine—paid by Don—and life got back to normal in the SP business.

The last edition of the *Mirror*—the country edition—went to press in the late afternoon and was delivered to Central Railway Station for distribution all over the State. Cadets put the nuts and bolts of this edition together. For example, we covered the wool sales at the Royal Exchange Building off Bridge Street. Each bid was noted in the day's catalogue and the auctioneer would let us know what were the more significant bids and whether or not it had been a good day for the sellers. These were the essential details for the story to accompany the table of bids. The graziers were to be seen sitting at the back of the auction room waiting to hear the outcome of a year's work on their property. It was the same story at the stock sales at Homebush, where we would carefully notate the prices fetched at auction for two-tooth wethers, finished bullocks, and so on. The stock and station agent would give journalists a rundown on what was happening in the market. With this information, a story would be phoned through for the country editions.

During my cadetship, I was intrigued by the new ballpoint pen, which had just come onto the market. It was claimed the pen could write under water—something I never actually needed to do, but it was an interesting thought. The original biro was too expensive for me to buy straight out so I put one on lay-by, but when I got my hands on this treasure it was an absolute dud. The original biro was hopeless for shorthand, as it could not make a thick or thin stroke. Worse—it leaked hopelessly all over one's fingers.

One of the tasks assigned to cadets and more to my liking was a 5 am departure by launch from Bennelong Point—then the site of a tram depot and later the Opera House. Accompanied by a photographer, we travelled to Sydney Heads where we would scramble aboard one of the great P&O ships coming into Sydney Harbour. The ship's purser met us and, after a lavish breakfast, we were given the cabin numbers of VIPs and other interesting people onboard. There were pop stars and other entertainers, whom we interviewed as the ship steamed up to dock at Darling Harbour. Cadets were also sent to interview people of note arriving via plane at Mascot Airport. This was before the jet age and passengers came to Australia on the long-range piston-driven planes of the time such as the Lockheed Constellation.

The Sydney *Sun* had an aviation correspondent, John Ulm, son of the famous Australian airman Charles Ulm, stationed permanently at the airport. He helped inexperienced cadets and could recite some wonderful 'bloopers' made by young journalists doing interviews at Mascot. One hopeful interviewed Cardinal Gilroy who was departing for Rome to participate in some solemn event. The journalist asked this question: 'Will the Cardinal's wife be accompanying him?' Another keen young reporter would ask visiting celebrities who had just cleared customs: 'Now this is your first visit to Australia; how do you like it?'

Police rounds were exciting, as they covered accidents, murders, muggings, robberies and general mayhem in the city and suburbs. There was a specialised police-rounds group but cadets were used on occasions when a big story broke requiring extra manpower. The *Mirror*'s police roundsman, Bill Jenkins, kept in sweet with police as a generous shouter in the pubs and would boom up his best contacts in the *Mirror* for the wonderful work they were doing. These were the days of relative innocence and police corruption was confined to minor industries such as brothels and SP bookmaking. The curse of drugs had yet to arrive.

Cadets did a lot of court work, from suburban magistrate's courts through to the High Court at Darlinghurst and the Supreme Court and Equity Court off Queens Square. The Equity and Supreme Courts were beyond our understanding in most cases, but we got by with the assistance of barristers involved in the cases. They would give us a rundown on what each judgment meant. With nobody to assist or tell us how to put together a story, we learned from the subeditors who handled our copy before it appeared in the paper. For the afternoon editions (often up to five), speed was the key and one had to keep a keen eye on the clock since we were competing at that time with the Sydney *Sun*, the other afternoon paper in Sydney. A lot of copy was simply dictated over the phone, maybe from a hot and dirty public phone box, to wizardly women copytakers back at the *Mirror* office. They were excellent spellers and corrected our halting grammar as they typed.

At the Magistrate's Court in Paddington, the police prosecutor and the magistrate would drink together at the pub opposite the court at lunchtime and sometimes the journalists would join in. I thought this was a cosy sort of an arrangement but not too good for the accused. A 'surfie' teenager had been found guilty of some sort of homosexual charge at the Bondi Beach dressing sheds and at lunchtime the magistrate remarked to the prosecutor, 'Oh, you could tell he was guilty by his long hair.' That says a lot for justice from police and magistrates in New South Wales at that time. The *Mirror* put heavy responsibilities on cadets in court work. We covered murder trials lasting for a week or more, alone and unaided, having to sit through these trials and follow the proceedings very closely. High accuracy was required, particularly with the names and addresses of those charged, various witnesses and exactly what was said. And one had to have the ability to work out what was the big news story of each half-hour to an hour, then head for the phones for *Mirror* copytakers to re-lead stories, changing them as the trial developed. When back in court, hopefully another journalist from another paper would fill in on happenings in the interim. It was a demanding job.

I was sent to Nyngan, way out west in New South Wales, on the overnight sleeper train to report the trial of a local grazier, Edward Ronald Backhouse (twenty-nine), accused of attempted murder. It was alleged he had sent a box of chocolates laced with strychnine to another young man, who was a local involved in a love triangle with a young woman. The only advice the chief of staff gave me was to buy an expensive box of chocolates, take it down to the Nyngan telephone exchange and ask the girls to put me through to the *Mirror* office as soon as I came on the line. This did the trick over the week I spent covering the trial. After arriving in Nyngan and booking in to the pub, I asked for a key to my room. 'Oh, no key, you'll be in number six sharing with Jack. He's a shearer', was the publican's reply. I was somewhat taken aback, but as it turned out, the shearer and I never met in the bedroom. There were reporters there from the *Sun*, *TheDaily Telegraph* and the *Sydney Morning Herald*, and we were overnight celebrities—newspaper reporters from the big smoke. At the end of the week, the defendant was found not guilty, mainly because of a lack of direct evidence connecting him with the poisoned chocolates.

An aspiring journalist had to sink or swim: you either got the hang of it quickly or you did not, and if you did not then, too bad, you were no longer required. One afternoon, the chief of staff, without any notice, told me to get myself to the NSW Art Gallery and phone in a story on the awarding of the Archibald Prize for portraiture. I told him that I did not know the first thing about art. 'When you get to the gallery, find somebody who does,' he snapped. I did. That was the way it worked and, if you were not worldly wise when you began working at the *Mirror*, it did not take long to learn a lot about the seamy side of life. Cadets were required to cover what was called 'dirty day' at the Redfern Magistrate's Court—generally once a month. This was a closed court and the most awful charges of various descriptions were heard: bestiality, buggery, assaults on children and the like. Journalists were allowed in the court but the text of their stories had to be read and approved by the magistrate.

I was getting plenty of experience in day-to-day journalism, but had not thought much about specialising in any aspect of it. What I did not want was to end up permanently in police rounds. Nor did I relish years covering courts. Someone soon made up my mind for me.

3. Inside the Canberra Press Gallery

Soon after Christmas 1950, the chief of staff told me I would be going to Canberra for the upcoming session of Parliament. I was excited and anticipated seeing household names such as Menzies, Chifley, Evatt, Fadden and Calwell in action on the floor of Parliament. To serve in the press gallery in Canberra was one of my ambitions, but I feared I was far too junior to be selected for such a job. My father congratulated me. I was twenty-one and still in my cadetship. With another young journalist, Tony Ferguson, who was later to have an illustrious career with the Australian Broadcasting Commission (now Corporation: ABC) including as executive director of *This Day Tonight*, I arrived at Canberra Airport in a Trans-Australia Airlines (TAA) DC3. The terminal was a wooden building, not much bigger than two decent farm sheds. Our home away from home was the Hotel Civic in the heart of Civic Centre. The basis of our stay was all expenses paid by the *Mirror*: taxis when required, laundry, meal payments, and so on. Like the majority of Australians who had not visited the national capital, I could not visualise what it was like, yet it was only some 320 km from Sydney—then a five-hour drive. Was it a smaller version of Sydney without the harbour? Was Parliament House in the middle of the city? I soon realised that Canberra was a country town without a clearly defined centre.

Civic Centre was not and still is not the heart of Canberra. The square footage of the total number of retail establishments and offices in Civic Centre would hardly have equalled those of Queanbeyan, just over the ACT border to the east. Apart from the police station and the Canberra Club, 'Civic' consisted of two colonnaded buildings: the Melbourne and the Sydney Buildings. There were two other 'centres', both south of the Molonglo River: Kingston and Manuka. Both were smaller than Civic. There were picture theatres at Civic and Manuka. Although Canberra was the site of the new Parliament, for many years, the city's development was halted—first by the Depression, then by the war and again by the problems of the postwar placement of literally thousands of returned servicemen back into civilian life. The Chifley Government believed priorities for spending were postwar reconstruction and the avoidance of unemployment, not the development of 'the Bush Capital', as Jack Lang contemptuously referred to Canberra in his newspaper, *Century*. At the beginning of the war in 1939, there were only 13 000 residents, and, on my arrival in 1951, that number had grown to only 25 000. The population is now heading for 350 000. In 1951, the boundary of Canberra north of the Molonglo River was the pine break cutting through Northbourne Avenue, and south of the river, Griffith, Narrabundah, Kingston and Forrest. Deakin had not been built, the Woden Valley had not been developed and Belconnen, Tuggeranong and Gungahlin town centres were still many years away.

The 'provisional' Parliament House in Canberra was nothing like the NSW Parliament House I was familiar with in Macquarie Street, Sydney, which dated back to the mid-1800s. Canberra's Parliament House stood alone, south of the Molonglo, fronting on to lawns to its north; not far beyond, sheep grazed. A market garden alongside the river was on the site where the High Court and National Gallery now stand. The Treasury building and the National Library were yet to be constructed. To the north-east, across the rose garden, the Administrative Building was the only major office in sight. The long, gleaming white parliamentary building of three storeys was flanked on either side by extensive lawns and garden areas enclosed by a high hedge. It was later referred to as 'the wedding cake' because, when viewed from the northern bank of the Molonglo, that is certainly what it resembled. Behind the building was a lane that provided service access for the kitchen, dining rooms and bars. On the other side of the lane running parallel with the parliament building and almost as long was a dense ground-hugging hedge—the habitat of feral cats. Just beyond the lane, Queen Terrace connected Commonwealth Avenue with Kings Avenue—the major thoroughfares connecting the parliamentary precinct with the northern side of the Molonglo. Directly behind Parliament House and on the other side of Queen Terrace was a dusty paddock (Camp Hill), which was used as a car park for those who worked in Parliament House.

John Smith Murdoch, the first Commonwealth Government architect, was asked to design the building to serve as the Parliament for 50 years. He also designed two office buildings in the same style—both white—200 m from Parliament House. East Block overlooked Kings Avenue and West Block overlooked Commonwealth Avenue. For symmetry, their roofs were about the same height as Parliament House, and Queen Terrace linked them to Parliament House. The central axis—a key feature of Walter Burley Griffin's prize-winning design for the national capital—is a unifying concept for the city. It is a straight line running from the top of Mt Ainslie, through the centre of the Australian War Memorial at the foot of Mt Ainslie, down the centre of Anzac Parade, the ceremonial avenue, across the Molonglo (now Lake Burley Griffin), through the centre of Old Parliament House and (now) through the centre of the permanent Parliament House, to Bimberi Peak—the highest mountain in the Brindabella Ranges 25 km to the south. A large statue of King George V stood over King George Terrace—the road running past the front of Old Parliament House. Nobody could miss this imperial monstrosity, slap bang on the central axis.

Whatever Doug Anthony's achievements for the Country Party and later the Nationals, the standout for the nation was his effort in 1964 when only a junior minister with the Interior portfolio. He had the statue moved some 50 m west, so it no longer interrupted the view from Parliament to the War Memorial. Before he could get Cabinet approval, he first had to convince Menzies—the country's leading monarchist. Anthony explained:

> I raised the ticklish issue with him one afternoon after there had been a good question time in Parliament. Menzies stood silent for a while, looking out the window. Then he said, 'I suppose you're right'. Moving the monument restored the magnificent openness of Griffin's central vista.[1]

There was also a life-size statue of King George V in King's Hall, unveiled by his son, the Duke of York, when opening the parliament building in May 1927. The statue stood on a marble plinth—handy for resting drinks on during royal balls and similar gay times. Having opened the door of Parliament House at 11 am with a 15-carat gold key, the Duke and Duchess then joined the official party for a lunch of turtle soup, poached salmon and Canberra pudding. At the time, alcohol was not allowed in the national capital, so the drink of the day was non-alcoholic fruit punch.[2] What the Duchess thought of the non-alcoholic fruit punch is not recorded. In later life, as the much-loved Queen Mother, she was known for her wit and fondness for gin and tonic. A London story told of how she was at a function attended by Noel Coward and Louis Mountbatten. When drinks came on, she is reputed to have said to them, 'I don't know what you old queens are having but this Queen is having gin and tonic.'

Construction of the building began in 1923 with workers drawn from all over Australia. In 1924 there were 1400 labourers working in Canberra and a similar number of tradesmen. Many of them would have worked on the Old Parliament House and East and West Blocks. A majority would have come from outside Canberra, Queanbeyan and Yass. Most of them were accommodated in makeshift camps of tents and other temporary structures scattered across Canberra. Timber was sourced from the various States to symbolise the federal roots of the building. Bricks came by light rail from the nearby brickworks at Yarralumla. The cost of the building and furnishings totalled more than £600 000—almost three times the original estimate. Two flights of stairs are climbed to reach the front door of Old Parliament House and then another flight inside to get to King's Hall—the heart of the building.

Everyone in the building—from the Prime Minister to the cleaner—crossed King's Hall at some stage in a week. With a highly polished parqueted floor and light flooding in from expansive skylights, it is an impressive space, the walls filled with historical paintings, the major subjects of which are prime ministers, speakers and presidents of the Senate. Great occasions were celebrated here,

---

1 Sparke, Eric 1988, *Canberra: 1954–1980*, AGPS, Canberra.
2 A source for much of the material is the management of Old Parliament House.

including royal balls. The House of Representatives chamber is alongside King's Hall to the east and the Senate chamber is to the west. Lobbies run from King's Hall around both chambers. The press gallery offices were on the second floor on the house side and directly above the lobby, one floor down running past the Cabinet room, with the Speaker's suite at one end and the Prime Minister's office at the other. The government and opposition party rooms were off the main lobbies on the first floor. Two large courtyards, one on the western side of the building and the other on the eastern side, are each dominated by a poplar tree—grown to enormous size by the time I arrived in the building.

The non-members' bar, opening on to the eastern courtyard, was the centre of social life. The Marquis of Salisbury and Arthur Henderson (a former leader of the British Labour Party and Home Secretary in McDonald's 1924 government) planted the poplars when they visited Canberra in 1926 with the delegation from Westminster of the Empire Parliamentary Association. During the visit to the still unfinished provisional Parliament House, the delegation presented a gift from the British Parliament: the Speaker's chair for the House of Representatives, which was modelled on the Speaker's chair in the House of Commons. The House of Commons burned down during the war after an attack by German bombers and the old chair was lost. When the Commons was rebuilt, the new speaker's chair was modelled on the chair in the House of Representatives. The Australian chair was constructed partly from oak from the roof of Westminster Hall—more than five centuries old—and oak from Nelson's flagship, *HMS Victory*. There were spirited debates in the Parliament about leaving the chair behind when Parliament moved to the new building. Traditionalists wanted it in the new chamber, but the argument against it going was that it would look out of place in the quite different architecture of the new chamber. This argument carried the day and was undoubtedly correct.

The space limitations of the building imposed an egalitarian rule in the lavatories. Ministers, MPs, staffers, journalists and cleaners all used the same lavatories. Years after the move to the permanent parliament building, Mick Young returned to the House of Representatives chamber of Old Parliament House to speak at an event. I cannot remember what the occasion was, although I was present, when Young spoke of his liking for the old building. He remarked upon the fact that the egalitarian use of the lavatories also ruled in the House of Commons at Westminster. He told the story of how, after the war, the British Labour Prime Minister Clement Attlee was standing at a urinal when Churchill entered and stood at the urinal at the opposite end from the Prime Minister. Attlee remarked: 'You're a bit stand-offish this morning, Winnie.' 'I won't stand near you,' said Churchill. 'Every time you see something big, you want to nationalise it.' Mick got a good laugh out of the audience.

For decades after the opening of the provisional Parliament House in 1927, most parliamentarians saw very little of Canberra, and from their point of view there was not much to see. There were few restaurants of any note in the 1950s, and, for most parliamentarians, the sitting week consisted of arriving at the Canberra airport at the beginning of the week, spending all day and most of the evening in Parliament House before going to a fairly lonely room at the Hotel Kurrajong. Some MPs invested in small apartments. The mortgage would be covered by the Canberra travel allowance, and, at the end of their parliamentary life, they would sell up for a capital gain. Despite the capital-gains tax later introduced, financing apartment mortgages from the Canberra travel allowance is still a good deal. Billiards was a popular pastime at which Labor MPs of working-class background were the superior players.

The Parliamentary Library was and still is a wonderful resource for not only MPs but also journalists with a research bent. The newspaper room then and now has all the significant Australian newspapers available and an impressive collection of international English-language papers. The members' and non-members' dining rooms were the best eating establishments in Canberra. The menu was *à la carte*, there were white tablecloths and linen napkins with service by waitresses in crisp white uniforms. Subsidised by the takings from the non-members' bar, the dining rooms were well patronised and cheap. Because parliamentarians stayed in the Parliament during the sitting week, so would the journalists. At the end of the sitting week, the parliamentarians would go directly to the airport, each occupying a chauffeured government car (as they do today) and that was all they saw of Canberra.

Although the politicians did not see much of Canberra and did not get away from Parliament House, for ministerial staffers, parliamentary staff and public servants, Canberra was home. It was not regarded as a hardship post, although for many years it was so regarded by the Government. The residents of Canberra from the 1920s certainly up to the 1960s had their nature strips mowed by the Parks and Gardens Branch of the Interior Department and every new resident was entitled to a generous free handout of shrubs and trees for their gardens from the Government Nursery. The Interior Department provided cheap rental housing, which could be purchased at the low interest rate applying to the returned servicemen and women's housing schemes.

In his masterful small book *Parliament and the Press*, C. J. (Clem) Lloyd chronicled the tenuous position of the Federal Parliamentary Press Gallery from its establishment in 1901 until 1988. I have drawn extensively on Lloyd's book. Clem was an interesting character, a member of the gallery and later a staffer to Labor politicians, before beginning a distinguished career in academia. For many years, he was a member of a Friday luncheon group, of which I was also a member, together with a half-dozen or more characters such as Mungo

MacCallum, Eric Walsh, Russell Parkes and Alan Wood. When the Whitlam Government came to power, Lloyd was involved in a power struggle with the lofty mandarin Sir Arthur Tange, who headed the Defence Department (see Chapter 14). In the first chapter of his book, Lloyd quotes Sir Alan Turner, former Clerk of the House of Representatives:

> The [Press] Gallery seems to be here because it is here. The Federal Gallery probably inherited the status and privileges of the Victorian, when Federal Parliament occupied the State Parliament building in Melbourne. And I suppose the State Gallery simply carried on the tradition of the House of Commons when the Victorian Parliament was formed on the Westminster mode. The gallery has no formal right to exist and it owes its privileges and access to the chambers of the House of Representatives and the Senate and to its occupancy of rooms in the Parliament entirely to practice and tradition.

There has inevitably been tension between parliamentarians and the gallery. In the long history of Westminster parliaments, a minority of MPs loathed journalists. The majority of MPs, however, regard the gallery as part of the Parliament and recognise its vital function of informing Australia and the world of the work of the Parliament, the executive government and the opposition. Nevertheless, a breach of privilege—real or perceived—is something that has to be guarded against by members of the gallery. Even though rent is paid for the occupancy of offices in the gallery in the present Parliament House, this does not guarantee access or tenure.

The Speaker and the President of the Senate may eject any member of the gallery from the premises temporarily or permanently. Claims of breach of privilege against journalists produced some notable struggles between the Parliament and the press. Lloyd recounts an event in 1942 when Richard Hughes (later to have a distinguished career as a foreign correspondent) launched in *The Daily Telegraph* a colourful attack on the Senate and senators for rejecting a regulation to lift a ban on the sale of beef from the sewage farm at Werribee in Victoria. The ban had been applied when it was claimed tapeworm disease could be contracted from this beef. The ban was to be lifted as an urgent wartime measure. The President of the Senate, Senator Cunningham, described the article as a 'deliberate attempt by the newspaper concerned to discredit the Senate in the regard of the people and bring it into contempt'.

The Senate voted to expel the four representatives of *The Daily Telegraph* and *The Sunday Telegraph* from Parliament House. An apology was sought from the proprietor, Frank Packer, without success. House Speaker Nairn applied a similar ban of his own volition, despite the article not reflecting on him. Nor did he seek the advice of the Clerk of the House, the legendary Frank Green—a friend of Hughes—who believed only the house could deal with alleged breaches of privilege. The offenders from *The Daily Telegraph* established themselves in the nearby Hotel Canberra, where they were supplied with sufficient material from gallery colleagues and Frank Green to continue reporting the parliamentary proceedings and the doings of the executive government. The deadlock continued for four months until Packer assured Cunningham that Hughes had not meant to disparage senators or the Senate (though he clearly did).

The *Mirror*, like other papers represented in the press gallery, sent a small team of journalists to Canberra to help the permanently stationed journalists handle reporting Parliament when it was in session. This was a major undertaking and each paper devoted a lot of attention to Question Time and debates in the Parliament. Newspapers from the smaller States tended to focus their attention on parochial issues. For example, the Brisbane morning paper, *The Courier-Mail*, and the afternoon paper, *The Telegraph*, concentrated generally on debates or questions relating to Brisbane and Queensland. Similarly, Adelaide's *Advertiser* and the afternoon paper, the *News*, gave a lot of attention to SA issues. Until the 1970s, the Australian Journalists' Association (AJA) had resolutely fought attempts by the newspaper proprietors to syndicate the coverage of parliamentary proceedings to all newspapers and the ABC through the services of Australian Associated Press (AAP).

Not all proprietors were in favour. Ezra Norton, proprietor of the *Daily Mirror*, insisted on retaining his independent gallery staff for both chambers. The proprietors kept up the pressure and finally the AJA ended its resistance. In the early 1970s, AAP opened its own bureau in Canberra, providing coverage not only of parliamentary proceedings but also of political and departmental news. I met Kevin Power when the *Mirror* reinforcements for the 1951 autumn session arrived at the *Mirror*'s Parliament House office, which consisted of just two rooms. Power was known in the gallery as 'Kewpie', no doubt because he resembled a Kewpie doll: short and dumpy with a shiny, round face. He was the headman of the *Mirror* and Les Love ('the Lapper'), who turned out to be quite a character, was his number two.

Between the two of them and the sessional staff, we covered not only the Parliament, but also the whole of Federal Government activities. Neither Kewpie nor the Lapper gave the newcomers to the *Mirror*'s gallery office an introduction to anyone, not even the Prime Minister's press secretary, let alone their much-cherished contacts on both sides of the Parliament and in the Public Service. We had to make our own way. Apart from Menzies, Country Party leader, Artie Fadden, and, for some curious reason, Sir Wilfred Kent Hughes, who was Minister for the Interior and, in effect, ran Canberra, ministers did not have press secretaries.

The ministers had to handle the press themselves—a great way for junior reporters to get to know them. Unlike present-day ministers, they were not shielded by spin doctors, and ministers such as Harold Holt were adept at press relations and knew nearly everyone in the gallery on first-name terms. I got to know Holt very well. Ezra Norton was a racist—as so many Australians were at the time—and appeared to have a particular aversion to Chinese. Kevin Power would receive instructions from the news editor to ask Holt, as Immigration Minister, why a certain Chinese cook or waiter in Sydney's Chinatown should not be deported. Power avoided doing this himself and frequently passed the query on to me. I was well known to Holt's staff and would be ushered into Holt's office to put the nasty racist query directly to him. He would not enter into a debate about the issue, undertaking to inquire. That got me off the hook. Frequently, we heard no more about the matter from our Sydney office.

In a reflective mood one morning after my mission to have another Chinese deported, Holt told me of the efforts to end his political career by Sir Keith Murdoch, when he was head of The Herald and Weekly Times newspaper empire. Holt enlisted in the Second AIF in May 1940 and, as a former Acting Air Minister, he was offered a senior commission in the Royal Australian Air Force (RAAF). He sought no favours and preferred to be a private soldier.[3] He was nearing the end of his artillery training at Puckapunyal, Victoria, and was preparing to depart for the Middle East when tragedy intervened.

On the morning of 13 August 1940, a RAAF plane crashed just beyond Canberra airport, killing all passengers and crew, including Minister for the Army, Sir Henry Gullett, Minister for Civil Aviation and Air, James Fairbairn, and Brigadier Geoffrey Street, Vice-President of the Executive Council. (The site is marked by a plaque in a pine forest at the southern edge of the airport.) Prime Minister Menzies appealed to Holt to leave the Army and return to the Cabinet, where he was now sorely needed. Holt agreed. He won his seat of Fawkner in the September 1940 election and the Government was returned, but only because of the support of the two Victorian independents, Arthur Coles (founder of the G. J. Coles retail empire) and Alex Wilson. His colleagues in 1941 dumped Menzies, and Arthur Fadden, leader of the Country Party, became Prime Minister. His government staggered on for just more than a month before Curtin became Prime Minister when the two independents crossed the floor against Fadden to support Labor.

Out of government, Holt considered re-enlisting, but decided against it. As the 1943 election neared, there were rumours Holt was under pressure to stand aside for Murdoch. Nothing came of this but Holt told me Murdoch had put up an independent against him in Fawkner. This was William Edward Cremor, who

---

3   Frame, Tom 2005, *The Life and Death of Harold Holt*, Allen & Unwin, Crows Nest, NSW, p. 20.

served in World War I and World War II as a lieutenant colonel in the Middle East and led his regiment in the Greece and Crete campaigns. The obvious motivation of Murdoch (a notable war correspondent in the First War) was to provide an independent with a notable war record—in contrast with Holt's brief army experience. Cremor, backed by Murdoch, polled well in the election, with 15 958 votes, reducing Holt's primary vote to 23 931, yet Holt won easily when preferences were distributed.

Holt told me, with considerable passion, he would support the continuing broadcasting of Parliament even if it had only one listener. He had certainly changed his views on parliamentary broadcasts, which were introduced in 1942. According to Tom Frame,[4] Holt initially opposed their introduction, saying it would encourage politicians to grandstand and prolong parliamentary proceedings. The broadcasts remain popular today. For many years, the supervision of absolute fairness of parliamentary broadcasting was absurdly restrictive on the team of experienced radio announcers. When a division was being counted and the result of the division announced, nothing went to air. All the listeners could hear was the background noise of papers being shuffled and faint voices away from the microphones on the floor of the chamber. Later presenters of the broadcast explained what a particular division was about, what business had taken place and what was coming up. ABC news items are broadcast to fill in the silence.

One of the gallery traditions was the morning round. Each morning, we were given a list of queries, which *The Mirror* office in Sydney had for stories. About 9 am, journalists—mainly representatives of the afternoon newspapers— gathered in the press gallery; frequently, others from the evening papers would join in. We would agree on which ministers we would visit and what queries we had and then we would set off. We would see seven, eight or nine ministers in any one morning. On our arrival at a minister's office, the minister's secretary would go into the boss's office with the statement: 'The press is here, Sir.' Rarely were we refused. We were then ushered into the minister's office where he was asked what he was going to do about this or that. Josh Francis, the blustering Minister for the Army, was one who was frequently asked to answer questions. As ever, one way or another, the Army would frequently have some sort of stuff-up—someone would drown or guns would go off accidentally, wounding or killing someone. Asked why these events happened and what was being done about it, Josh had the perfect comment: 'I'll have an immediate inquiry.' Satisfied, we would go on to the next minister.

A serious weekly chore was filling in the expenses claim—otherwise known as the 'swindle sheet'; the funds thus acquired would help defray the substantial

4   Ibid., p. 31.

costs of alcohol consumption. Using whatever cunning we had, we worked the swindle sheet to the maximum, doubling the actual laundry costs, falsifying taxi fares, and it was amazing how many MPs were allegedly entertained at lunch by the *Mirror* staff. It was flagrant theft. These sheets had to be OK'd by Kewpie Power before dispatching them to Sydney. Kewpie did not have much argument with our claims because, as he was rorting the system himself, we were all in the same boat.

When I arrived in Canberra, the leading journalists in the press gallery were Harold Cox (Melbourne's *Herald*), Kevin Power (*Daily Mirror*), Alan Reid (Sydney's *Sun*), and Leo McDonald (Brisbane's *Telegraph*)—all afternoon papers. The evening papers were represented by Frank Chamberlain (*The Sun News Pictorial*, Melbourne), Ian Fitchett (*The Age*), Ray Maley (*The Argus*, Melbourne), Ken Schapel (*The Daily Telegraph*), plus Jack Commons of the ABC, Jack Allsop of the Australian United Press (AUP), Stan Stevens (Adelaide's *The Advertiser*) and Oliver Hogue (Sydney's *Sunday Sun*). There were no representatives from the *West Australian*, Perth's *Daily News* or *The News* of Adelaide. The majority of the 42 journalists who then made up the gallery in that year did not hold university degrees.

All the journalists in the gallery were members of the AJA, the journalists' union, and there were no photographers; casual outside photographers were hired for pictures. The gallery committee liased with the Parliament, the Government and the Opposition on matters such as access to various parts of the building, the Parliamentary Library and the newspaper room. The other important group was the bureau heads—the journalists who headed the various bureaus. As representatives of the newspaper proprietors, they decided the most hotly contested of all issues in the gallery at the time: which organisations and individuals were allocated what space.

Ian Fitchett, smartly dressed, a Falstaffian figure, bureau head for *The Age* and later the *Sydney Morning Herald*, was one of the great gallery characters. A member of the Melbourne Cricket Club and from a well-known Victorian family, Fitchett had a law degree and had been a war correspondent. He had an acerbic, often cruel wit and was a first-class journalist with good contacts. Fitchett was also a snob and cruelly put down many of his contemporaries in the gallery. For example, he dubbed Eric Walsh, then heading the *Mirror* bureau and just as likely to turn up for work in a cardigan as a suit, as 'leader of the cardigan set'. Frank Chamberlain, an earnest journalist on *The Sun News Pictorial* and a successful radio commentator, was of somewhat dumpy appearance and had smooth skin; he was 'grease ball'. Fitchett was a member of the Victoria Racing Club (VRC), with its headquarters at the famous Flemington Racecourse. He came back from a Melbourne Cup meeting looking down in the mouth and I asked him, 'How did you go, Fitch?' He replied, 'Bloody awful. Thank Christ I was too pissed to punt on the nod'—a reference to VRC members being able to book on credit with rails bookmakers adjoining the members' enclosure.

I am obliged to Graham Freudenberg[5] for the following wonderful story of a Fitchett joust with Menzies. Fitchett's grandfather, the Reverend W. H. Fitchett, founding Principal of the Methodist Ladies' College in Melbourne, was also a noted author who extolled the deeds of Nelson, Wellington and Gordon. His most famous work, *Deeds that Won the Empire (1897)*, inspired Menzies, and Sir John Monash carried his copy to Gallipoli. At a press conference after Menzies' role in the Suez fiasco, Menzies took to Fitchett over a piece he had written in *The Age*. Said Menzies: 'You may fancy yourself as a journalist, but you will never write anything as good as your grandfather's *Deeds that Won the Empire*.' 'No', huffed Fitchett, 'but I'm working on the sequel: *Deeds that Lost the Empire*'.

In the non-members' bar one night, Fitchett was holding forth on the Tasmanian Liberal Senator Peter Rae, an ambitious young man who was chairing a senate committee inquiry into Australian capital markets, particularly stock exchanges, at the height of the Poseidon boom. Rae was always trying to squeeze the maximum publicity from this exercise. In the drinking group was psephologist Malcolm Mackerras, who could go on for hours dissecting election statistics in every seat in Australia, hence Fitchett referred to him as 'an algebraic arsehole'. Fitchett was denouncing Rae as a mug and Mackerras broke in: 'No, Fitchett, he is quite a smart operator. I went to university with him in Hobart.' Fitchett pondered this for a second or so before his response: 'Oh, he may be Hobart smart.' From then on, among the young cognoscenti of the non-members' bar, a reference to anyone as 'a bit Hobart' meant not smart at all.

Menzies held press conferences in his office, which heads of the press gallery bureaus attended. Because there were no methods of recording these conferences, the bureau heads would be accompanied by a junior to take notes. The latter were somewhat derisorily referred to as 'pencillers'. Following the death of Churchill, in January 1965, Menzies was immensely honoured by the British Labour Government of Harold Wilson putting forward his name, to the Queen, as the successor to Churchill as Warden of the Cinque Ports. The five towns of the Cinque Ports were Hastings, Romney, Hythe, Dover and Sandwich, covering a stretch of the English coast closest to the Continent and the landing place for almost every invasion since Neolithic times. This wardenship was, for a number of centuries, one of the realm's key defence posts, to which the King made all appointments.

---

5   Freudenberg, Graham 2005, *A Figure of Speech: A political memoir*, John Wiley & Sons, Milton, Qld, p. 20.

For a man with Menzies' veneration for tradition, to hold this post would be a great honour, especially when he was the immediate successor to Churchill. That it no longer had any practical significance was not, from Menzies' point of view, important.[6] Menzies called a press conference to discuss the honour bestowed upon him. It was made clear to us that we were not to ask questions other than those relating to the lord wardenship of the Cinque Ports. At the conference in his office, Menzies went on for some time about details, such as how he would handle the job, how he was entitled to wear an antique uniform and to a stake in Walmer Castle, built by Henry VIII. As the questions became more desultory, Ian Fitchett, who invariably sat at the back of the Prime Minister's office, interjected:

'Sir, will you be entitled to the flotsam and jetsam?'

Menzies: 'Yes, Fitchett.'

Fitchett: 'What about mermaids, Sir?'

Menzies: 'Yes, Fitchett.'

At this stage, the Australian ports were in the grip of a damaging wharfies' strike. As the conference wound down, Fitchett said to Menzies, 'Well, we've heard about your ports, Sir, what about our ports?' Menzies shot back: 'See the Minister for Transport about that, Fitchett.' Following his induction as Lord Warden, Menzies took to flying the Cinque Port flag on his official car.

Fitchett had an exclusive, leaked story in *The Age* of Cabinet discussions concerning splitting the Reserve Bank from the Commonwealth Bank. Menzies hated Cabinet leaks and warned his ministers about the need for absolute Cabinet confidentiality. Fitchett ran into Menzies in King's Hall on the morning *The Age* ran the story. Menzies said, 'I'll make you eat crow, Fitchett.' Fitchett replied: 'And I'll eat it, Sir, providing it's garnished with the sauce of your embarrassment.'

In the 1950s, the George Sorley variety show appeared a couple of times a year in a tent set up in a vacant paddock in Civic Centre. It was a popular, bawdy show. Any form of entertainment was very much appreciated at a time when there was nothing much on but the movies at Manuka and Civic and dances at the Albert Hall. On the death of George VI, Menzies made a major ministerial statement to the House of Representatives—a maudlin affair, dripping with pathos and bathos. At its conclusion, Menzies slumped into his chair and cradled his great, leonine head in his hands—a picture of despair. Fitchett, at this stage, rose from his seat in the press gallery, declaring, 'I can't stand any more of this. I've seen better acts under canvas at George Sorley's.'

---

6   Martin, A. W. 1999, *Robert Menzies: A life. Volume 2: 1944–1978*, Melbourne University Press, Melbourne.

Helga Sundstrup (*The Daily Telegraph*) was the only woman in the gallery and the first stationed on a permanent basis. She joined us in the morning-round calls on ministers. She was married to Bernie Freedman, then on *The Argus* in the gallery and later to have a long and successful career in the public relations section of the Immigration Department. When the new Parliament House opened in 1988, Bernie, who had retired from the Public Service, returned to the gallery as the representative of *The Jewish News*. He retired from that role in 2005. Nowadays, there would be at least as many female journalists in the gallery as men and not just in junior positions. For example, at one stage about 2005–06, three women headed the three Fairfax bureaus: Michelle Grattan (*The Age*), Laura Tingle (*Australian Financial Review*) and Louise Dodson (*Sydney Morning Herald*). Grattan is the veteran among the women. She joined *The Age*'s Canberra bureau in 1971, when the late Alan Barnes headed it; the legendary editor the late Graham Perkin appointed Michelle. Perkin had earlier served in *The Age* bureau under Ian Fitchett and knew what was needed in Canberra. Michelle has been at one time or another head of all the Fairfax bureaus and had a stint out of the gallery as editor of *The Canberra Times*.

Old Parliament House was already crowded in 1951 with the gallery absolutely chock-a-block; MPs shared small offices and ministers' offices were scattered all over the building. Despite the squeeze, the gallery maintained its common room, equipped with a table-tennis table. It was in this room that Archie Cameron, the Speaker of the day, climbed through a window from the roof and nabbed a poker school in action attended by Alan Reid and Oliver Hogue. They were given a severe dressing down as Cameron had brought down an edict that no gambling was allowed in Parliament House (or at least those parts under his direct control). He suspected the parliamentary barber, Cec Bainbrigg, was running the illegal SP book, but failed to get the evidence.

Cec cut the hair of all comers from Ben Chifley down. Cec would take our bets over the phone at his home on Saturday race day and come Monday morning was the settlement—mostly in Cec's favour. An unmarked envelope would appear in your mailbox setting out how much was owed, or hopefully won. Cec was in the news when Cameron ordered him to take down a magnificent picture of the champion horse Phar Lap from his barbershop wall. This made headlines all over Australia. Archie was a blue-nosed Presbyterian who converted to Catholicism, yet his conversion did not mean he abandoned his views of the sinfulness of gambling. He was an eccentric character and in the summer could be seen walking around the house in a Jackie Howe singlet, featuring the name of some champion shearer on the back.

At the centre of the gallery were 'the boxes'. Each bureau had a shelf space with the bureau name marked on it. Press releases from all over the house— government and opposition as well as from lobby groups—were deposited in these boxes. Anyone putting a press release in the boxes pushed a button to ring an electric bell to alert the gallery to a new release. We were all one big family, though not always harmonious. Crowded together, we had to put up with cramped conditions. Journalists who work in busy newsrooms are accustomed to dealing with distractions, with lots of other people around, phones ringing, constant conversations, and activity everywhere. Hence, the crowded *Mirror* office in the gallery did not present a problem. When the house was sitting, many journalists—to get away from cramped offices—spent a lot of time in King's Hall, which was one of the larger spaces in Parliament House. From here, one could watch the comings and goings of ministers and MPs. The library and the government and opposition lobbies ran off King's Hall. Senators had to cross the space to attend party meetings.

The easy informality of relations between the gallery and parliamentarians existed until Parliament made the move to its permanent home on Capital Hill in 1988. This was illustrated by a story Don Whitington told me. Chifley, when in Canberra, lived in one room in the Hotel Kurrajong, close to Parliament House. When he became Prime Minister in July 1945, the Lodge was opened only when he had VIPs to entertain. He walked between Parliament House and the Kurrajong, often accompanied by other Caucus members, but just as often he would be alone, whether walking home at midnight or going to Parliament at 8 am. There was not a policeman or security officer in sight. Nobody thought anything about security until the Hilton Hotel bombing in Sydney in February 1978.

One frosty winter night, Jack Allsop (AUP) and his number-two, Les Teece, after a day's work in the gallery, were about to climb into Teece's bull-nosed Morris immediately outside the House of Representatives' side entrance. At this moment, Chifley emerged from the side door of the building, which led directly from the Prime Minister's office. The two journalists offered Chifley a lift; he accepted and climbed into the front passenger seat. The car refused to start and no matter how hard the crank handle was turned it would not go. Chifley then took the driver's seat, pushing in the clutch while the two journalists pushed the car. 'Let her out, Chif', they yelled as they got up a bit of speed. Still no start. Then they had another go and another and another. In the end, they pushed the car all the way to the Kurrajong.

Question Time, regarded as the most lively event of a sitting day, began at 3 pm, with journalists reporting for 15-minute 'takes' before leaving the gallery to dictate a story over the phone to a copytaker, or via the telex machine linked directly to the Sydney office. Once the *Mirror* missed a story of an apple falling from a child's hand in the public gallery onto the head of an MP in the house. Unfortunately, as the *Sun* featured it, our Sydney office demanded to know why we had missed the story. As bureau head, Kevin Power was anxious to pin the blame on an underling. In the end, we all managed to wriggle out of responsibility. The probable reason was that this happened in the few seconds while the *Mirror* journalist had his eyes on his notebook and other gallery members around him had not realised he missed the incident.

Reporting Question Time and parliamentary debates was not easy, particularly if edition deadlines were tight and copy had to be produced in a hurry. Most of the older gallery journalists, who had not entered the newspaper business through a cadetship, had no shorthand. Mine, while not high speed, was enough to get down fairly sizeable chunks of direct quotes. The trick was to transcribe the notes immediately after leaving the chamber, while they were still fresh in the memory. Some journalists without shorthand simply wrote keywords in longhand, relying on their memory to then turn the words into sentences.

With more experience, I discovered a lot of background information and important leaks could be extracted from ministers and senior public servants by assuring them the material would not be attributed to them. I took no notes during these conversations, as the appearance of a notebook and pen would tighten up the information flow from your informant. Far better to appear relaxed, concentrate hard on what was being said, and, on departing, get down as much of the conversation as you could remember. Journalists then, as now, under no circumstances would attribute background material to the source. Apart from the ethics involved, to go back on an undertaking would dry up the source forever. Protecting the source is fundamental to reporting—investigative or otherwise. The only equipment we had for covering proceedings in the chamber was a notebook and a pen. For many years, it was forbidden to record parliamentary proceedings broadcast by the ABC, and we had no recording equipment to do so, even if we had wanted to. When small dictaphone machines did become a standard part of a reporter's gear, the gallery furtively recorded proceedings and could then check the accuracy of notes taken in the chamber.

When I first came to the gallery, Question Time produced more stories than it does now. The era of television and radio news and talkback shows has a far greater influence on politics. Ministers then could not get away with blatantly ducking questions because they did not like them, and the Standing Orders, as interpreted by speakers, required answers to be relevant to the question. Now an answer is considered relevant if the minister in reply at least uses a phrase from the question. For example, an opposition MP may ask a question on government policy on, say, industrial relations. The minister is then free to avoid answering the question asked and regale the house with a lecture on the faults of the Opposition's industrial relations policy. This certainly did not happen in Menzies' day, and probably not until the Parliament moved to the permanent Parliament House in 1988. Menzies, in particular, treated all questions put to him as requiring a reply.

The following Question Time exchange from 1956 gives the reader something of the flavour of Menzies' style and also of the problem of the shortage of space in the old parliamentary building. Note that the building of a permanent Parliament House is also raised:

Mr CLYDE CAMERON (Labor, SA): I direct my question to the Prime Minister. Is the right honourable gentleman aware of the fact that six members of the Liberal Party, six members of the Australian Country Party, and ten members of the Australian Labor Party are obliged to do all of their work in their respective party rooms because there is no separate accommodation available for their use? Does he know, also, that many of the honourable members who have office accommodation outside party rooms are crowded three to each small room, whilst most ministerial secretaries and typists are provided with rooms to themselves? Does he know that certain members on the Government side of the House recently were forced to take basement accommodation, because the accommodation previously occupied by them had been handed over to ministerial staff? Does he know that the secretary of the Opposition, and his secretary, have been forced to work in one tiny basement room instead of being given accommodation on the main floor level? Does he agree that Members of Parliament have stronger rights to Parliament House accommodation than have the members of ministerial staff? Is it a fact that in the days of the Bruce–Page Government and of the Scullin Government, only the Prime Minister had his office and staff situated in Parliament House? Finally, will the Prime Minister state what he intends to do about the suggestion that was put forward by the Leader of the Opposition that an all-party committee or body of inspection should be appointed at an early date to inspect the whole of the accommodation at Parliament House in order to ascertain at first-hand the amount of accommodation that is being monopolised by Ministers and their staffs, and the conditions under which members of Parliament have to do their work, with a view to taking steps to find accommodation for ministerial staffs, other than that which they are now monopolising in this building?

Mr MENZIES: It requires a singular feat of memory to remember all the bits in that question, but no doubt it will be in Hansard, and I can have a look at it. I quite agree that the problem of accommodation in this building is very serious, but when I look back to the time when I first came to this place 22 years ago, I recall that private members, badly off as they may be to-day, were much worse off then, because I do not recall that there was private room for any private member at all.

In 1952, I was instructed to interview William Morris Hughes, the former Prime Minister, who was usually interviewed on his birthday by one of our more senior reporters, John O'Hara; on this occasion, however, the latter was away and I was not looking forward to the meeting. Hughes had a small office on the House of Representatives side of the building and I entered with great trepidation. There was this gnarled, gnome-like little figure, aged ninety, deaf as a post, but one of the giants in the history of Australian politics. He was born in Pimlico, England, founded the Australian Waterside Workers' Federation, and was a Labor wartime prime minister, until 1916, when he split the Australian Labor Party (ALP) because of his unsuccessful insistence that there should be conscription for service on the Western Front. Hughes formed a government by switching to the conservative side of politics, and was—and still is—regarded as the number-one Labor rat. Dubbed 'the Little Digger', Hughes toured the World War I battlefields, insisting on Australian control of Australian forces. He led the Australian delegation to the Paris Peace Conference in 1919 and secured an Australian mandate for New Guinea and other German colonies in the Pacific. Hughes was a remarkable and quick-witted orator, notable for his energy and often-unscrupulous opportunism.

As a former prime minister, he was entitled to a private secretary and he chewed these up at a great rate. His temper was more than even the strongest young men could handle over a protracted period as his secretary. One of his well-known quotes was: 'If there was an aristocracy of bastards, Menzies would be a prince.' My interview with Hughes did not go well. I found it difficult to get any humorous touches—the essence of the interviews O'Hara put together on each of Hughes' birthdays. It was a less than funny encounter. Worse still, Hughes insisted on editing my copy. This is a demand journalists should not agree to, but I was young and easily browbeaten by the great man. When I returned with the copy for Hughes' inspection, for some reason, this enraged him. He sat with the copy in front of him and angrily swept everything off his desk with his arm with a huge clatter. He scribbled furiously and finally said, throwing the copy at me: 'You wouldn't have done this to that bastard Menzies.' I hastened from his office and ignored the Hughes' editing. His funeral later that year was probably the biggest ever seen in Sydney until then, with tens of thousands of people lining the streets. Few who watched the coffin pass by would have known of his hatred for Menzies—then at the zenith of his political career.

4. Menzies: The giant of Australian politics

Menzies' presence matched his political dominance: an imposing figure, he was tall, well proportioned, although with an ample girth, with a good head of greying hair, offset by jet-black, bushy eyebrows. And in 1951 he was a mere fifty-seven years of age. He was a born orator with a compelling, but never hectoring, style of delivery. The blue-rinse ladies of Sydney's North Shore and Melbourne's Toorak 'liked Mr Menzies because he spoke so nicely'. Menzies was the dominant figure in Australian politics in the twentieth century. He was Australia's longest-serving Prime Minister, serving from April 1939 until August 1941 and then from December 1949 until January 1966. Above all, after World War II, he transformed the conservative side of politics—then uncoordinated and weak—into the most successful postwar political party.

Although the hero of conservatives, Menzies did not have many close friends outside Parliament. Many claimed to be his friend, yet Menzies did not spend much time with them. Jack O'Sullivan, a journalist of solid Irish-Catholic working-class stock, a big man, was responsible, in the days when few ministers had press secretaries, for promulgating ministerial press releases. Jack was a steady customer of the non-members' bar and at first glance he would not have seemed to have much in common with the erudite leader of Australian conservatives. Yet he told me he often spent time with Menzies at Kirribilli House—just the two of them. They both liked the corned beef served at Kirribilli House, and would spend hours together yarning and watching the ever-changing scene on Sydney Harbour. Menzies was also accompanied at Kirribilli by his press secretary, Hugh Dash, and later Tony Eggleton. The city's leading socialites would have feted Menzies on every visit to Sydney had he sought it. Unlike one of his successors, John Howard, Menzies was not interested in social gatherings and the adulation of the rich and famous. Menzies served a ministerial apprenticeship in the Victorian Parliament and was elected to the House of Representatives in 1934, going immediately into the Lyons United Australia Party (UAP) ministry. Prime Minister Joseph Lyons, who had been ill for some time and was exhausted (some said by the effort to stave off what he perceived as the prospect of a challenge from Menzies), died in April 1939. Earle Page was sworn in as Prime Minister, but announced he would step down for whomever the UAP elected as its leader. He added that if that leader was Menzies, the Coalition with the Country Party would end, and end it did. Menzies was not universally liked within the UAP. Certain members, including ministers, resented his sometimes overbearing manner and sharp wit, and during his absence abroad he received more than one warning of plots against him. Some thought he lacked leadership skills; others maintained that he was unpopular in the electorate and that the Government could not carry its wartime responsibilities with him as head. After complex internal manoeuvres, and Labor's refusal to agree to the formation of a British-style national wartime government, Menzies had the galling experience of losing majority support in his own Cabinet. He resigned both the prime ministership and, later, the leadership of his party. 'It was the most humiliating personal collapse in the history of federal politics in Australia.'[1]

Throughout his political career, Menzies was dogged by the slur of cowardice for failing to enlist in the AIF in World War I. It was claimed he had resigned his commission (he rose to the rank of lieutenant) in the Melbourne University Rifles during the war. For the facts on this, I rely on *Robert Menzies—A Life*.[2] Menzies was a member of the Rifles between 1915 and 1919 and served the necessary stint of compulsory military training required of his age group to provide a militia for the *domestic defence of Australia*. He did not resign his commission to avoid war service. He held his commission until his mandatory period of service was over. This still did not explain why he failed to enlist in the AIF, as had Menzies' two older brothers, Frank and Les, with their parents' approval. Frank later explained (in an oral history contribution to the National Library of Australia) that for the family to have two out of three boys at the front seemed 'a pretty good contribution'. It was decided one grown man was needed at home to stand by his parents, who were ageing, not well off and had just been through what they regarded as a trauma and a disgrace. They had lost their daughter, Belle, who eloped with a soldier 'deeply disapproved of' by other members of the family.

When Menzies was Prime Minister in 1939, the Country Party leader, Earle Page, subjected Menzies to a bitter attack in the house. Page had served on the Western Front as a doctor (his field instruments are on display at the Australian War Memorial in Canberra). Page told the Parliament that he and his party were no longer prepared to serve in a Menzies government and, with war threatening, he did not believe Menzies had the right attributes to bring about 'a united national effort'. Page said, based on Menzies' record, he had no confidence the Prime Minister had what was required: 'the maximum courage, or loyalty or judgments.' After numbering what he believed were faults in Menzies' record, he devoted particular attention to Menzies' war record. Page is responsible for fostering the falsehood—still widely held to be true—that Menzies resigned his commission. Page continued:

---

1   Martin, *Robert Menzies*, vol. 2, pp. X11 and X111.
2   Martin, A. W. 1993, *Robert Menzies: A life. Volume 1: 1894–1943*, Melbourne University Press, Melbourne.

I am not questioning the reasons why anyone did not go to war. All I say is that if the right honourable gentleman cannot satisfactorily and publicly explain to a very great body of people in Australia, who did participate in the war, his failure to do so, he will not be able to get that maximum effort out of the people in the event of war.

All this was greeted with cries of 'shame'. Menzies immediately replied and was heard in silence. On the charge of not serving in the war, there was real, if dignified, bitterness in Menzies' response. He said the charge was not a novelty and represented 'a stream of mud through which I have waded at every election campaign in which I have participated'. Menzies explained that on the issue of enlistment he had to answer the supremely important question '[i]s it my duty to go to the war or is it my duty not to go? The answer to that question is not one that can be made on a public platform.' Menzies went on to say the question related to 'a man's intimate and personal family affairs and in consequence, I, facing these problems of intense difficulty, found myself, for reasons which were and are compelling, unable to join my two brothers in the infantry with the A.I.F'. In the political uproar following the Page attack, two Queensland Country Party MPs, Arthur Fadden and Bernie Corser, disassociated themselves from Page's speech, saying that henceforth they would sit as independent Country Party members. (It is somewhat ironic that after Menzies resigned as Prime Minister with so many in his party room opposed to him, Fadden became Prime Minister.)

In 1949 Fadden became Country Party leader and Deputy Prime Minister to Menzies. During Menzies' second period as Prime Minister, it was not unusual for Labor MPs to attack Menzies' military record. I was in the house when Eddie Ward, the Member for East Sydney (who was frequently referred to in the writings of gallery journalists as a 'Labor firebrand'), dredged up the Melbourne University Rifles falsehood and attacked the Government for not providing sufficient funds for defence. Sir Wilfred Kent Hughes (a Rhodes Scholar who had served in both wars and was a prisoner-of-war of the Japanese in the Second) rose to speak. Kent Hughes, who once saw himself as a rival to Menzies, came to the latter's defence. He attacked Ward and questioned what he would know about defence. 'The Member for East Sydney has never even learned to stand to attention,' said Kent Hughes. Like a flash, Ward interjected: 'The Prime Minister has learned to stand to attention, but he never learned to charge.'

Another cross Menzies carried was the sneering reference to him as 'Pig-Iron Bob'. (Again, I rely on much of the work of Martin.) In late 1938, waterside workers at Port Kembla, NSW, refused to load the steamer *Dalfram* with pig-iron produced in the BHP blast furnaces. Tom Roach, the union secretary, explained that pig-iron should not be sent to Japan because 'success to the Japanese Fascist militarists in China will, according to their own statements, inspire them to further attacks on peaceful people, which will include Australia'. This turned out to be remarkably prescient. Menzies, as Attorney-General, received Cabinet endorsement to use the *Transport Workers Act*, passed by the Bruce–Page Government in 1929—the so-called 'dog-collar act', much hated by unions. This required workers on the wharves to receive a licence and, as anyone could apply, it obviously encouraged 'scab' labour. Menzies said the issue was not whether the shipment of pig-iron was right or wrong, but rather preventing Australian foreign policy being set by industrial action. (John Howard, who years later in his WorkChoices legislation outlawed political strikes and, indeed, made a strike for any reason difficult, would approve of this.)

The Menzies Government's position was dubious. It had banned the export of iron ore because of what were then considered limited deposits in Australia. Yet it was prepared to export the more valuable product of pig-iron to Japan—after the Rape of Nanking. Menzies showed courage in agreeing to visit Wollongong at the invitation of the Labor MP for the area, Bert Lazzarini, to confer with union officials. Some 4000 South Coast miners went on strike for the day and thousands of men and women lined the streets from Bulli Pass to Wollongong waving anti-Menzies placards and hissing as his car went past. By mid-January, BHP had closed its Port Kembla plant because its products could not be dispatched and some 7000 people were out of work. Menzies met the unions in the town hall for discussions, achieving nothing. There was no violence on the day. Martin believed union infighting did not help settlement of the dispute. It finally ended on 21 January after Menzies offered to lift the 'dog-collar act' and agreed to talks with the union on future government policy relating to exports.

More than two decades later, the Pig-Iron Bob label meant Menzies' sensitivity impeded the abolition of the longstanding ban on iron-ore exports. The ban was imposed because it was believed the nation had only limited reserves of iron ore. Yet following discoveries by Lang Hancock in the Pilbara of high-quality iron ore, other vast deposits came to light. Harold Raggatt (later Sir Harold), the head of the Department of National Development, was the key to lifting Menzies' persecution complex about the Pig-Iron Bob tag. Bill Spooner, Minister for National Development, was a major power in the NSW branch of the Liberal Party and unsuccessfully contested the deputy leadership of the Liberals against Harold Holt. He was tall, bulky, slow moving—a menacing figure. Raggatt sent Spooner a ministerial minute giving detailed information about iron-ore production, consumption in Australia and the bright outlook for exploration, proving Australia had an enormous resource. Raggatt's aim was to persuade Menzies to lift the export embargo. Raggatt told me Menzies was resisting because it brought back unpleasant memories of the Pig-Iron Bob tag. The cautious Spooner scribbled a note on Raggatt's minute—'Who says?'—and returned it to his departmental head. Raggatt returned the minute to Spooner and, under the minister's note, he had carefully written: 'See page — of *Who's Who.*' On turning to this page, Spooner discovered it was Raggatt's entry, listing his impressive technical expertise as a geologist. This ended correspondence on this particular Raggatt minute. The ban was lifted.

Spooner had a habit, when interviewing senior officials in his Parliament House office, of swivelling on his office chair and gazing out the window. One meeting included the then head of Treasury, Roland Wilson. Raggatt told the author that, after this meeting, Wilson told Raggatt he used to think Spooner was thinking when he gazed out the window, but Wilson no longer believed this. He was, said Wilson, 'just…just…err…just looking out the window'. Raggatt deserves the praise of later generations for winning the argument to export iron ore.

William Charles Wentworth, who represented the Sydney seat of Mackellar, was one of the most interesting of the 1949 Liberal recruits. He had inherited a considerable chunk of the fortune of the redoubtable capitalist and legislator of the nineteenth century in colonial Sydney, the first William Charles Wentworth. The Wentworth family home, Vaucluse House, at Watsons Bay in Sydney, is a popular tourist spot. The first William Charles Wentworth was born on Norfolk Island, the son of D'Arcy Wentworth and a convict mother. D'Arcy Wentworth came to Sydney, made a fortune, became a large landowner and conducted a long-running feud with Governor William Bligh. Wentworth supported the Rum Rebellion and was finally acquitted on charges and restored to his position. Regarded by many of his colleagues as an eccentric, Bill Wentworth MHR was a foaming-at-the-mouth anti-communist who bridled at Menzies alone deciding who should be a minister. In founding the Liberal Party, Menzies was careful to ensure that all power resided in the parliamentary leader of the party. In government, Menzies, as leader of the parliamentary Liberal Party, selected the Liberal MPs for the ministry and allocated their portfolios. Wentworth sought to follow the Labor tradition of the party room electing ministers to the ministry and led an unsuccessful party-room revolt against Menzies' despotism. Wentworth received no promotion while Menzies was leader.

Wentworth, a backbencher and a rebel, was viewed by most of his colleagues as a genuine eccentric—fixated by his fervent pursuit of all things communist. At the same time, he was a determined and capable MP. It was no small thing that he persuaded the Parliament to lift its game on the frequency of publication of Hansard—then in a bound edition once a week. Wentworth led a committee that managed to convince Menzies there should be a daily copy of Hansard available each morning on the day after a sitting. This is still a valuable tool for all those who work in Parliament, particularly the media. Wentworth's greatest gift to Australia was to preside over a committee that recommended the standardisation of railway gauges in Australia. Colonial governments had been unable to agree on a standard gauge for the nation in the 1800s. In Victoria the gauge was 5 ft 3 in (1600 mm), in New South Wales it was the British or standard gauge of 4 ft 8.5 in (1435 mm) and in Queensland, 3 ft 6 in (1067 mm). On the busy Sydney to Melbourne line, passengers had to disembark at Albury to change trains. The movement of freight was even more tedious.

As a result of Wentworth's determination, we now have a standard-gauge railway running from Brisbane through Sydney to Melbourne and from Melbourne to Adelaide and on to Perth as well as a link running from Sydney through Broken Hill and joining the standard gauge at Adelaide. Menzies believed Wentworth was far too erratic for a portfolio, but finally, in the Gorton Government, Wentworth was appointed Minister for Social Services and Minister in Charge of Aboriginal Affairs. He was the first federal minister with direct responsibility for Aboriginal Affairs and is now highly regarded for his groundbreaking work to bring the plight of Aborigines into political discussion. He spent many months each year visiting Aboriginal settlements and missions throughout Australia and particularly in northern Australia. Mungo MacCallum, a senior gallery journalist, was a nephew of Bill Wentworth and had a political bent well to the left of his uncle.

When uranium was discovered in the Northern Territory, Wentworth believed this would be worth a fortune for Australia and, when interviewed by Oliver Hogue for the *Sunday Sun*, he declared that uranium would outstrip wool as Australia's top export (all these years later, uranium still has a long way to go to equal wool exports). Wentworth pestered Menzies to allow him to question Harold Raggatt, head of the National Development Department, about what was being done to hasten the development of uranium mining. Raggatt had played a significant role in the development and encouragement of the oil search industry in Australia. Menzies finally agreed to allow Wentworth to question Raggatt at a Cabinet meeting on the pace of development of the uranium industry. Raggatt told me of the encounter. In the Cabinet room, Wentworth demanded to know how many exploratory shafts were being dug in the Northern Territory and Raggatt gave him an approximate number. Then he wanted to know how many men were digging each shaft. Raggatt replied, 'Well, only two; they are digging them with pick axes.' Wentworth demanded to know why there were not four men down each shaft. Raggatt answered coolly: 'Mr Wentworth, how would you stop them shoving the pick axes up one another's arses?' At this stage, Menzies said, 'Well, that will do Mr Wentworth'.

For the gallery, 1951 was a very big year, with the High Court decision in March by a majority of six to one rejecting Menzies' legislation to dissolve the Communist Party of Australia. Then came the double-dissolution election of 28 April 1951, an election that followed the Labor majority in the Senate blocking banking legislation. To the disappointment of Labor leader, H. V. Evatt, the Governor-General, Sir William McKell (former Labor Premier of New South Wales, whose appointment to the job by the Chifley Government was denounced by Menzies), gave the Prime Minister his double-dissolution election. The outcome was a loss of five seats by the Government but it still finished with a handsome 17-seat majority. Menzies decided to hold a referendum to give the Government power—denied it by the High Court—to dissolve the Communist Party. There was no stomach within the State Labor parties to resist the referendum, coming after the April election. Evatt fought for the 'no' case single-handedly and 'no' won narrowly with 50.56 per cent of the total vote and three of the six States— New South Wales, Victoria and South Australia—returning a 'no'-vote majority.

The death of Ben Chifley, a former engine driver, in his room at the Kurrajong Hotel marked the end of an era, when Labor had a powerful connection to working men and women and many of the ALP's top politicians came from the shop floor. The Commonwealth Jubilee Celebrations were also in 1951, culminating in a state dinner at Parliament House on 12 June, which was attended by Chifley, although he was not well. Chifley did not attend the state ball held the next night in King's Hall. About midnight, Menzies called for silence and solemnly announced the death of Chifley to the assembled guests. The ball ended at that point and people silently made their way out of the building. I was staying at the Civic Hotel that night and was awoken by *Mirror* colleague John O'Hara, who shared a room with me. John, like Chifley, was a Bathurst boy and, between sobs, he told me of Chifley's death. Chifley's body lay in state in King's Hall for some days, before the state funeral in Bathurst.

Apart from the busy year of 1951, a rush of news did not particularly overstretch the gallery for some years. Despite the failure of Menzies to ban the Communist Party of Australia, it was still a background issue to the continuing Cold War. The power of the communists in the unions was linked to damaging strikes, involving communist-led unions. Inflation and unemployment—measures of the Government's ability to manage the economy—were not big issues. The economy was given nothing like the prominence it is now afforded in the media. Neither Menzies nor Evatt was particularly noted for their grip on basic economics, nor were most members of the gallery tutored in the 'dark arts'. National development, such as the Snowy Mountains Hydro-Electric Scheme and other major government projects, was regarded as a worthy objective and a lot of Hansard space was devoted to it.

Menzies, like all top politicians, was keenly aware of the importance of the media. When he was opposition leader, Menzies was greatly impressed by the legendary Don Rogers, press secretary to both Curtin and Chifley, and anxiously sought to recruit someone to match him. This turned out to be a mate of Don Whitington (who later was my business partner), Charles Meeking, whom I got to know well. Compared with the television era, at that time, press conferences were rare. In the mid-1950s, Menzies' press conferences were perhaps monthly at most. If Menzies, Chifley, Evatt or any of the leading figures on either side of the Parliament wanted to speak to citizens, they would go into the house to say what they wanted to say. The newspapers extensively reported parliamentary debates and the standing of an MP had much to do with the standard of his or her oratory and debating skills in the chamber. Most MPs had considerable public-speaking experience before they entered Parliament.

Labor MPs in particular—the majority with a union background—were well versed in debating and politics before they stood for preselection for a seat. Because of the strain on office accommodation for MPs in the provisional Parliament House, they spent little time in the office—normally shared with at least one other MP. Parliamentary committee work was not nearly as intense as it is today. Many filled in time sitting comfortably in their place in the chamber listening to debates. Ministers would also attend interesting debates, or listen to the contributions of the more eloquent backbenchers from their side of the house. There were impressive orators on both sides of the house—none excelling Menzies, although Whitlam and Kim Beazley sr were his equals.

The standard of oratory and debate in the Parliament in the 1950s, 1960s and 1970s far exceeded the standards achieved in the past several decades. Menzies would sometimes leave his office—only a few steps away from the side entrance into the chamber from the government lobby—to listen to debates. The Prime Minister often would come into the chamber to listen to the Labor Member for West Sydney, Danny Minogue. Born in County Clare, Ireland, and educated in the Emerald Isle, Minogue possessed a wonderful Irish brogue, which Menzies found delightful. Minogue invariably used debates to berate the Government for its meanness to the 'poor pincheners'. Albert Thompson, the Labor MP for Port Adelaide (1949–63), was a senior Salvation Army officer and in the Caucus had picked up some colourful additions to his vocabulary. In one of his budget speeches, he declared with considerable fervour: 'Mr Speaker, if this Budget is not defeated, this country will be rooted.' The Speaker wisely decided not to pull Albert up for unparliamentary language, conscious that the Salvo did not understand its meaning.

Thompson also had the misfortune to share a two-seat bench in the house with former coalminer and colourful character Rowley James, who held the seat of Hunter (in the Newcastle area) for 30 years from his election in 1928. Rowley was a large, rotund figure, and one could observe from the press gallery Rowley's habit of leaning on one cheek of his arse to let go a roaring fart in Thompson's direction. Albert would lean as far as he could into the corridor alongside him to escape the noxious gas. Following one of James's louder farts, Eddie Ward was on his feet taking a point of order: 'Did Hansard record the Member for Hunter's interjection?' he asked. Rowley would take his walking stick into the chamber and was known to pound it on his desk in anger at contributions from the other side of house. Speaking in the debate on Arthur Fadden's 1951 'horror' budget, Rowley roared, 'This is a bludger's budget! It taxes pessaries and condoms', emphasising his point with a whack of his stick on his desk. Rowley's son, Bert, followed him into the seat in 1960 and held it for 20 years.

Menzies—rather than is the practice today of ministers commenting on policy issues in answer to Dorothy Dixers—would make a ministerial statement in the house. He would carpet any minister who made any sort of press release or comment about a new policy initiative outside the Parliament. The Opposition was keen to have parliamentary statements made by ministers since the issues could then be debated. Although press conferences were somewhat irregular, Don Whitington told me that during the war, Curtin would regularly hold two press conferences a day—one for the morning papers and one for the afternoon editions. These were subject to heavy wartime censorship and what appeared in newspapers from the Curtin press conferences was what the Government allowed to be printed. Curtin used the press conferences as a conduit to keep the newspaper proprietors up-to-date with developments in the war. Journalists at these conferences made extensive private reports not subject to censorship to their proprietors.

Melbourne for a time became the wartime capital of Australia. US General Douglas MacArthur, after a perilous journey, arrived in Melbourne on 21 March 1942 and set up his headquarters. He met Prime Minister, John Curtin, in Parliament House, Canberra, five days later—six weeks after the fall of Singapore and the subsequent Japanese air raids on Darwin, the occupation of Java and the first attacks on New Guinea. In a press statement released on 16 February, Curtin had described the fall of Singapore as 'Australia's "Dunkirk", which opens the battle for Australia'. War historian Paul Hasluck (later senior minister and Governor-General) described the meeting as having 'the air from the start of being one of the fateful meetings of history'. It was reported that at the Canberra meeting MacArthur assured Curtin, 'Mr Prime Minister, you and I will see this thing through together' and '[y]ou take care of the rear and I will take care of the front'.[3]

From then on, Cabinet met mainly in Melbourne. All the departments relevant to the war—Defence, Army, Air, Navy, Supply, Munitions, Aircraft Production and War Organisation of Industry—were in Melbourne. When a Cabinet meeting was called for Melbourne, there was an exodus from Canberra. Ministers, their staff, senior bureaucrats and gallery bureau heads were driven to Yass Junction, where they picked up the Sydney–Melbourne train. Much of the night was occupied with drinking and playing cards, interrupted at Albury for the change of trains. The 40-minute jet flights between Canberra and Tullamarine were

---

3   Essay by David Black.

decades away. Until reliable airline services began, MPs travelled by train from all over Australia to Canberra for sittings of the Parliament, as they had when the Parliament was in Melbourne before 1927.

In my first year in the gallery, I was introduced to the budget lock-up—an arrangement allowing journalists, on an embargo basis, access to the budget documents in the afternoon before the budget was brought down in the Parliament. An embargo prohibits material supplied in advance being published before a time and date stipulated by the provider of the material. Only for the budget is the embargo taken to an extreme of journalists being given copies of the budget documents in a room they cannot leave until the Treasurer stands in the house to introduce the budget that evening. In the Old Parliament House, the lock-up was conducted from about 2pm in a couple of relatively small committee rooms on the Senate side of the Parliament. The lock-ups were, and still are, watched over by Treasury officials, who also give technical advice on the meaning of the documents, or where various bits of information a journalist might be after can be found in the pile of budget papers. In the old Parliament, Treasury officials even accompanied journalists to the lavatory to ensure no budget details leaked out (no pun intended). In the permanent Parliament House, there are lavatories located within the lock-up areas.

Originally, all this secrecy was to prevent budget decisions leaking in advance of the Australian stock exchanges closing. According to Don Whitington, the lock-up was an initiative of the gallery when Chifley was Treasurer. He made his budget speech at 8 pm in the house and the budget papers were not supplied until then. This meant a frantic rush to get the details into the first editions of the morning papers. The gallery pleaded for more time and the lock-up procedure began. Subeditors are in the lock-up to subedit copy, make up pages and, with the magic of electronics, the pages can be shot to distant newspaper offices with the touch of a button. With the arrival of globalisation, the excuse that the lock-up is to avoid stock-exchange fiddles no longer applies. There are exchanges open around the world and investors can buy or sell at any hour of the day or night by email. The secrecy is all the more absurd given that the Government deliberately leaks details of the budget to the media in advance of its presentation to Parliament. The aim is to generate interest in its contents well in advance of its presentation to Parliament.

Treasurer Paul Keating introduced another dodge: holding a press conference in the lock-up about 5 pm so that the captive audience would have pro-budget propaganda sold to them hours in advance of it coming down in the Parliament. Journalists could not get adverse comments on the budget from interest groups until the Treasurer began his speech. The lock-up is now unnecessary and exists merely to allow the Government of the day to have some control over its presentation to voters via the media.

Budget papers have become more impenetrable over the years. When I first went to lock-ups, what the Government had done with taxpayers' money the previous year and the details of what it proposed to spend in the coming year were quite clear. This is no longer the case.

In 2005 the Australian Council of Trade Unions (ACTU) mounted a High Court case arguing the passage of appropriation bills authorising government spending was unconstitutional in relation to expenditure. It claimed the Government had not made clear, as was required by law, the funds it proposed spending on advertising supporting its proposed industrial relations legislation, WorkChoices. The appropriation bills of the Howard Government frequently did not reveal even outlines of how much it was spending in various areas. The High Court rejected the challenge, in effect ruling it was an issue Parliament needed to sort out. There was ample precedent for this approach. The High Court is happy to rule whether or not the substance of legislation is constitutional, but it rarely seeks to tell the Parliament how to go about the legislative process. The appropriation bills in the Labor Government's first budget in 2008 were not much better.

Menzies did not provide Christmas drinks for the gallery at the Lodge. From Malcolm Fraser's time on, prime ministers played host to a crowd of 100 or so gallery members who turned up for the free drinks and finger food, all provided by the taxpayer. In Menzies' day, such largesse was not so freely used. He did have Christmas drinks for the heads of bureaus in the cabinet anteroom. They were, however, served martinis mixed by the Prime Minister's own hand. How the martinis went down with a group of beer drinkers I never discovered. In the Menzies Cabinet and for some years after his retirement, ministers made financial contributions from their own pocket to the cabinet liquor store. Hubert Opperman, a teetotaller, objected to this although it was pointed out to him that he and other ministers could invite guests for a drink in the cabinet anteroom. Taxpayers have footed the bill on and off for cabinet liquor. Menzies and all prime ministers before him were required to pay for food, right down to milk, bread and liquor for the Lodge. Fraser, as Prime Minister, changed the system and taxpayers paid for cabinet drinks. Certainly, in the Hawke and Keating Governments, ministers were required to make a contribution to the cabinet bar. When Howard made Kirribilli House his home, taxpayers were required to provide food and liquor at both the Lodge and Kirribilli House, plus extensive renovations at the latter.

Menzies had reasonable relations with the senior gallery journalists. It was not his habit—nor that of most political leaders—to give 'exclusive' interviews to newspapers, as is now common. The senior people could see him from time to time for a background chat. Yet his relations with the Fairfax press and the *Sydney Morning Herald* were hostile. This is set out in *Robert Menzies—A Life*:[4]

> Always rocky, Menzies' rapport with the newspaper [*Sydney Morning Herald*] took a downward turn in 1958. The elegant J.D. Pringle, editor between 1952 and 1957, had espoused causes naturally antagonistic to Menzies' policies (recognition of Red China and revulsion at Britain's Suez performance were prime examples) and tension between Menzies and the management group of the paper—especially Warwick Fairfax, the owner and 'Rags' Henderson, the managing director—was long standing.

Gallery old hands explained that the antagonism between Menzies and Warwick Fairfax stemmed from an affair Menzies had with Fairfax's wife (I cannot recall anyone saying which wife—Betty, the first wife, or Hanne, the second—but government staffers and senior public servants accepted that Menzies had an affair with Fairfax's wife). I have never been given any details or evidence. David McNicoll introduced a new angle to the Menzies–Fairfax feud with the publication of his book *Luck's A Fortune*. McNicoll, a first-rate journalist from a middle-class Victorian family, mixed with and reported on Sydney society, largely because he was the right-hand man of Sir Frank Packer, proprietor of *The Daily Telegraph*. Packer's son, Kerry, and grandson, James, were the beneficiaries of Frank's brilliance in building the family fortune on *The Women's Weekly* and *The Daily Telegraph*. It was Frank Packer who secured the goldmine of a commercial TV licence and built Channel Nine into the dominant commercial network. After the war, McNicoll wrote a clever and informed daily column, on page one of the *Telegraph*. There was not much happening in the upper reaches of Sydney society that McNicoll did not know about. In *Luck's A Fortune*, he published, in full, a taped interview he had with Menzies, then aged eighty-three and with his retirement eight years behind him. In the interview, the following appears:

> McN: I tell you who I saw the other night. I went and had a drink with Hannah (then Lady Lloyd Jones).

> Sir R: Oh yes.

> McN: She was looking very well, I thought.

> Sir R: Was she?

> McN: Yes, very well, I thought. She hadn't been well.

---

4   Martin, *Robert Menzies*, vol. 2, pp. 377–8.

Sir R: No she had not.

McN: But she was in good heart. [McNicoll went on to discuss another matter.]

This exchange raises a point McNicoll might not have realised. When he mentioned he had a drink with 'Hannah', he did not say Lady Lloyd Jones. This explanation in a bracket was put there for McNicoll's readers. Menzies might well have thought McNicoll was talking about Sir Warwick's second wife, Hanne, whom he married in 1948, the year before Menzies defeated Chifley to return to the prime ministership. James Fairfax, oldest son of Sir Warwick, describes the arrival of Hanne on the Sydney scene in *My Regards to Broadway*. She was Danish and her family lived in Copenhagen. She married an Englishman, Donald Anderson, who worked for Shell in Malaya and was transferred to Bangkok and, when war broke out, Hanne and her baby son, Alan, were flown to Singapore and later, with other wives, evacuated by boat to Sydney. Anderson became a prisoner-of-war in a Japanese prison camp in Bangkok. In Sydney, Hanne became involved in the ballet set and, through this, met another ballet enthusiast, Warwick Fairfax.

There was a development on the Menzies 'affair' in the February 2007 edition of the *Sydney Institute Quarterly* (*SIQ*), published by the Sydney Institute—described by the ABC 'as an influential privately funded think tank dedicated to the principals of policy debate'. The Executive Director of the Sydney Institute, Gerard Henderson, was a staffer for Kevin Newman, a minister in the Fraser Government, and was later chief of staff to John Howard (then in opposition) from 1984 to 1986. Regular listeners to Henderson's comments on ABC's Radio National *Breakfast* know he was quick to defend Howard and his government from critics. One such critic is Mungo MacCallum, who was for some years in the gallery and now lives in semi-retirement at Byron Bay, although he still writes and commentates. *SIQ* took to MacCallum for stating in *The Monthly* that Sir Warwick Fairfax had 'belatedly' discovered Betty had conducted an affair with Menzies. MacCallum was described by *SIQ* as 'the-gossip-of-Byron-shire'.

SIQ asked Sally Warhaft, editor of *The Monthly*, if she had checked on the Menzies/Fairfax affair before publishing MacCallum's claim as a fact. She replied: 'I spoke to Mungo about this. When I first read it I said I felt very uneasy about it. He said he'd talked to a lot of people and it was common knowledge and he's published it before. I accepted Mungo's insistence that his sources were strong.'

SIQ then quoted A. W. Martin in Volume 1 of *Robert Menzies—A Life*, with Menzies writing to Betty in 1939, when he was overseas, saying he would have a drink with her on his return. *SIQ* made a fair point that it would be an unusual way to conduct an affair if Menzies wrote to Betty saying he would have a drink with her at the Warwick Fairfax household. Various authorities are quoted by *SIQ* debunking the suggestion of an affair although none—except Gavin Souter, author of the Fairfax histories *Company of Heralds* and *Heralds and Angels*— had worked in Parliament House when Menzies was in power.

SIQ asks: 'Why would Warwick Fairfax wait until the 1961 federal election to oppose Menzies for a deed which had allegedly occurred some two decades previous?' Why indeed. Looking at the McNicoll interview with Menzies, it seems to the author that the story could be about the wrong wife, Betty. If there indeed was an affair, it might have been with Hanne. MacCallum was correct in saying the Menzies affair was taken as fact by hundreds. One final point: *SIQ* says that journalist Gideon Haigh stated he had interviewed A. W. Martin, who said Ian Fitchett 'had debunked the rumour in a personal conversation with him [Martin]'. This is second-hand evidence. The author can report firsthand evidence from Fitchett, who told me in the mid-1960s of Menzies' affair 'with Warwick's wife'. In the author's discussion with people in the Sydney society set, I discovered it was taken as fact that Menzies had an affair with Betty, Fairfax's first wife. I have gone into what is now political folklore of the Menzies affair simply because it is an interesting aspect of the life of one of the giants of Australian politics.

The McNicoll interview revealed a lot about Menzies. He certainly did not realise it was to be published. Asked by McNicoll whether the Country Party should amalgamate with the Liberals, Menzies went further and said the Democratic Labor Party (DLP) should also be part of the amalgamated party. He went on to complain about the new Australian Party established by Gordon Barton:

Sir R: Of course this damned Australia Party.

McN: What a pack of bastards they are. You know—I think they're beyond the pale because as Malcolm Fraser pointed out to me on the phone the other day, a lot of their policies are on parallel with the Communist Party.

Sir R: Of course they are. Well I remember this little squirt (Gordon) Barton coming with two or three fellows when I was Prime Minister and all they wanted was that IPEC to be given the third interstate airline. Well I had gone to great pains to create the two airline policy and so I had to say to them,—'Well look I am sorry—nothing doing. The two-airline policy is right and I am not prepared to depart from it.' And when he left that day I had settled it. If I had said 'yes', he would today be the President of the Liberal Party. Because I had said 'no'—he hates the Liberal Party—determined to destroy it. And for a silly rabbit like Gorton to be trifling with this fellow—oh, it's outrageous.'

This did not say too much for competition and the market economy. (Gordon Barton was a brilliant businessman who founded the Australia Party, a precursor of the Australian Democrats, and built up IPEC, a major courier company. This was eventually taken over by the trucking company TNT run by Peter Abeles.) Menzies' comments suggest the adherence now of the Liberal Party to competition and the market was not a view supported by the party's founder. The anti-Catholic prejudice of the two men is shown when the following arose from a discussion about Whitlam:

> Sir R: Whitlam is pretty shrewd…in a parliamentary sense. I know when he is reading a speech, but I also know he knows how to read it. I hate him.

> McN: What do you think of this move last night? (Whitlam's inducing Senator Vince Gair to abandon the DLP by accepting the offer of appointment as Ambassador to Ireland and The Holy See.)

> Sir R: I knew Gair years ago—when he was Premier of Queensland. He was a pain in the neck every time we had a Premiers conference. Conceited little booby.

> McN: Bog-Irish booby.

> Sir R: Oh, bog-Irish booby. But this is the most blatant piece of bribery I've ever seen.

Yet it was to attract the Irish-Catholic vote that Menzies became the first prime minister to give 'state aid'—subsiding the interest paid by the Church for science blocks in private schools. And it was Gair and his DLP colleagues who kept Menzies in power after the Labor split. In a conversation I had with Whitlam, he pointed out that no Catholic was appointed to head a department or an instrumentality between 1952 and 1972 by Menzies, Holt, Gorton or McMahon. Gough Whitlam was unaware of Menzies' comments about him until I interviewed him soon after his ninety-first birthday. He was puzzled as to why Menzies (when eighty-three) would have told McNicoll that he 'hated' Whitlam. Menzies knew Whitlam's father, Fred, who was the Crown Solicitor (a connection strengthened by the fact Menzies' brother Frank was the Crown Solicitor for Victoria).

Fred was Deputy Crown Solicitor in the early 1920s and, when the Parliament moved from Melbourne to Canberra, Whitlam's father moved from Sydney to be Assistant Crown Solicitor. Whitlam said Menzies would have been aware of his father on several counts. Canberra was a small town then and, public servants overwhelmingly dominated professional and social activities in the national capital. The Whitlams even lived next door to a Menzies, Sir Robert's brother

Les, who was a public servant and returned soldier. Fred Whitlam became Commonwealth Crown Solicitor in the first Menzies Government. Whitlam said Menzies was aware of his father and of course, through him, he would have been aware of his son, Gough, before he entered Parliament. Whitlam thought what could have grated on Menzies was his lack of understanding of what was going on in the Labor Party. Former senior diplomat Richard Woolcott refers to this in a conversation with Menzies at the St Regis Hotel, New York, in 1965:

> He [Menzies] said he did not believe Arthur Calwell would ever become Prime Minister, but Jim Cairns would. It was 'inevitable' that the Labor Party would come into government in the future. Deep down, Menzies remarked, Cairns was an honest man, despite some of the foolish things he had said, and he had brains too. Members of Parliament did not really trust Whitlam but they did trust Cairns. 'He probably prays every night that my name will be struck from the book of life. I must have more time for him than he has for me', Menzies said. Whitlam, according to Menzies, was 'a bit precious'.[5]

Menzies' view of Cairns as superior to Whitlam was not the majority view of the Caucus. Cairns challenged Whitlam for the Labor leadership in 1968 and Whitlam won, 38 votes to 32. It was closer than Whitlam expected. According to Graham Freudenberg, this was partly due to the defection of two NSW right-wingers: Fred Daly, who had his own leadership ambitions, and Frank Stewart, who found Whitlam overbearing. Cairns, whom Menzies said was honest, ended his political career ignominiously—Whitlam sacking him because, as Treasurer, Cairns misled the house. Menzies sent Whitlam a message of condolence when his father died. Whitlam also remembers that when Menzies' second son, Ian, died, Menzies' daughter, Heather, and her husband were at the Australian Embassy in Manila. Whitlam, as Prime Minister, was in Manila at the time and gave her a lift back to Australia on the VIP aircraft. Menzies wrote a letter thanking him.

Whitlam believes he might have aroused Menzies' ire when the Liberal leader cast aspersions on Reg Pollard (a minister in the Chifley Government). Whitlam defended the Labor stalwart, comparing his record with that of Menzies. Pollard had been commissioned in the field as second lieutenant in World War I. He was wounded in France and invalided home in 1918. Earle Page had attacked Menzies for not serving in World War I . The author believes Menzies, who had absolutely dominated the Parliament after the death of Chifley, was uneasy at the prospect of Whitlam challenging him as the outstanding parliamentary performer of his day.

---

5   Woolcott, Richard 2003, *The Hot Seat: Reflections on diplomacy from Stalin's death to the Bali bombings*, Harper Collins, Sydney.

Because of ill health, Menzies almost missed the 1952 Commonwealth Economic Conference held in London. The main problem dealt with at the conference was one that had dogged the sterling bloc (which included Australia) since the end of World War II: convertibility of sterling into US dollars. In June 1949, the High Court ruled that petrol rationing was unconstitutional under the defence powers. Chifley introduced petrol rationing to show Australia was a responsible member of the sterling bloc, and this policy was much appreciated by Britain. The Chifley Government persuaded all the States to either give their powers to the Commonwealth or legislate to restore petrol rationing. The reimposition of rationing began on 15 November—25 days before the December 1949 election. As Martin says: 'The re-imposition of petrol rationing on the eve of the election gave the opposition, especially the Country Party, an unprecedented opportunity to lure electors with a promise of abolition.' Fadden had driven the petrol-rationing issue harder than Menzies throughout the campaign. This was yet another example of the electorate being lied to and those responsible for the lie being the beneficiaries at election time.

To make matters worse, Fadden proposed that to tide Australia over in the few months until the Menzies–Fadden Government could end rationing, the Government could draw on defence reserves of petrol. A commentator, N. L. Cowper, was furious: 'This was a discreditable suggestion which would have raised a storm of protest and accusations of treason if the roles had been reversed and it had been made by a Labor Leader.' So in 1952 the Americans, although refusing to budge on their highly protective tariff barriers, were pressing for multilateral trade. It was a good idea, but it would not work without convertibility of currencies. Would Menzies have had a twinge of conscience about this topic? There was a large element of hypocrisy about his victory over the Chifley Government in 1949. True, a major factor in the defeat of Labor was Chifley's stubborn insistence on proceeding with legislation to nationalise the private banks. Menzies rightly made this a major issue. Yet, as explained above, another issue was the refusal of the Chifley Government to abandon petrol rationing on the grounds that it would create such a demand for dollars as to weaken the sterling.

Menzies was a renowned Anglophile—'British to the bootstraps', as he once described himself—and the prime minister who fawned on the young Queen Elizabeth during the 1963 royal tour: 'I did but see her passing by; but I will love her till I die', said Menzies in the King's Hall reception (reciting an 'Old Bard'). The Queen was visibly embarrassed. Yet in 1949, in a grab for power, he was prepared, against the direct interests of Britain, to use petrol rationing to come to power. A. W. Martin summed it up nicely writing of the 1949 election campaign: 'And in what some saw as a rather unworthy bribe, especially to country voters, he undertook to "make it our business to get petrol in adequate supplies".'[6]

The Age, for one, thought 'there is a doubtful wisdom in raising hopes that if a Liberal–CP government took office, the need for petrol rationing would soon be over'. Though a lively debate on petrol rationing had been going on for some months, 'nothing has emerged to convince people trying to keep a detached view that rationing could be avoided or made unnecessary by a change of office-holders'. And later Martin explained that 'despite claims that petrol was available from sterling sources, the British government appealed to Australia to go with rationing'. In a footnote, Martin adds: 'On June 2 Fadden claimed in Parliament that the New Zealand Minister of Finance, Walter Nash, had told a deputation of motoring interests that "dollars were no longer the reason for the continuation of rations".' Subsequently, Nash denied that he had meaningfully made such a statement and asserted that rationing was retained 'at the request of the UK government, which had affirmed, under existing conditions, the savings of petrol saves dollars'.

Menzies was anything but an autocratic prime minister who insisted on getting his own way. He believed in letting ministers run their portfolios as they saw fit and would interfere only if he believed there was a chance of a serious administrative or political error. An excellent chair of Cabinet, he had the facility to sum up a Cabinet debate on a matter before moving on to the next item on the agenda. Cabinet was anything but a rubber stamp and, like all Coalition cabinets, in his, there was no formal voting. Menzies, on political matters, would consult widely with his ministerial colleagues whose advice he valued. He would, of course, have sought advice on military and strategic matters—the wars in Korea and Vietnam, for instance. Like Menzies, none his closest colleagues had experienced military service. But there were many who had on both sides of the Parliament.

---

6   Martin, *Robert Menzies*, vol. 2, p. 118.

5. Ming's Men

A feature of the return to power of Menzies in 1949 was the number of returned servicemen who came into the Parliament at that election on the Government side. Before 1949 there were quite a number of MPs who had served in both the Boer War and World War I. Among the 1949 contingent of ex-servicemen were some outstanding military figures. Charles Anderson, a lieutenant colonel who represented the seat of Hume in southern New South Wales for the Country Party, was awarded both the VC and an MC. He served in both wars and was a prisoner-of-war (POW) in Malaya. Then there was Bill Bostock, air vice marshall, who served in both wars and rose to the rank of chief of the air staff, who represented Indi (Vic.) for the Liberal Party. Alexander Downer senior—father of a future Foreign Affairs Minister—was a POW in Changi, Singapore, and represented the SA seat of Angas for the Liberals.

Henry Baynton Somer (Joe) Gullett, Military Cross, wounded twice, represented the seat of Henty (Vic.) for the Liberal Party; he had served in the Middle East, France and New Guinea. Reg Swartz, the Liberal member for the seat of Darling Downs (Qld), served in Burma and then spent 3.5 years as a POW of the Japanese, including some time on the notorious Burma–Thailand Railway. David Fairbairn, representing the seat of Farrer (NSW) for the Liberals, had served in the RAAF and was awarded the DFC. Gordon Freeth was also ex-air force and represented the Liberal seat of Forrest in Western Australia. John Gorton was a flight lieutenant in the RAAF and served in the United Kingdom, Singapore and at Milne Bay, where he was severely wounded; he rose to become Prime Minister.

Another with an outstanding war record was Sir Wilfred Kent Hughes, who represented the seat of Chisholm in Victoria for the Liberals and came into the Federal Parliament in 1949 after serving in the Victorian Parliament. Kent Hughes enlisted in the AIF in 1914, served with the Australian Light Horse Brigade and was awarded the Military Cross in 1916, mentioned in dispatches four times. He enlisted in the Second AIF in July 1940, rose to the rank of lieutenant colonel, served with the Eighth Division in Malaya and, following the fall of Singapore, was a POW. Charles William Davidson, who was elected for the Country Party to the Queensland seat of Capricornia in 1946, was wounded as a lieutenant in World War I and, in World War II, served in New Guinea and rose to the rank of lieutenant colonel. In 1958, he was Deputy Leader of the Country Party.

Menzies avoided appointing ex-servicemen as ministers of their former service, so Davidson became Minister for the Navy. Menzies believed an ex-army man would give undue deference to the Army brass. John Cramer, a real estate agent and an influential figure in the NSW Liberal Party, won the seat of Bennelong for the Liberals in 1949, and, although not an ex-serviceman, he was appointed Minister for the Army in 1956. In the official *Parliamentary Handbook*, it somewhat lamely states he 'inspected Australian troop installations and conditions of service in Malaya, June 1959'. The men who had distinguished themselves in active service were certainly not rushed into the ministry; Kent Hughes, Gorton, Fairbairn and Swartz did not make the ministry until 1958. Only four prime ministers had active service in either World War: Stanley Melbourne Bruce, Earle Christmas Page, John Grey Gorton and Edward Gough Whitlam. When Whitlam became Prime Minister in 1972, he told Eric Walsh the ranks of Labor politicians contained more veterans of the Boer War than of World War II.

This was one of Whitlam's exaggerations. In the mid-1950s only two in the Labor Caucus—Senator Don Cameron and George Lawson—had served in the Boer War. Many had served in World Wars I and II. Senator Stan Amour, Senator John Harris and Reg Pollard (the last rose to become a minister in the Chifley Government) were wounded in World War I. Others such as Whitlam had served in the RAAF during World War II, including Justin O'Byrne, President of the Senate in the Whitlam Government, who was shot down over France and spent 3.5 years as a German POW.

Lance Barnard, Whitlam's deputy leader, and Jim Cairns, who unsuccessfully challenged Whitlam for the ALP leadership, were among many who enlisted in the AIF, and most saw service in the Middle East and/or New Guinea. Robert Joshua (Ballarat, Vic.) entered Parliament as an ALP MHR, and in the great Labor split became Leader in the House of the ALP (anti-communist). He was a captain in the AIF in 1940, was promoted to lieutenant colonel and was wounded three times in action in the Middle East and New Guinea. Many on both sides of Parliament had high regard for Joshua and Labor MPs regretted losing him in the split.

Tom Uren, tall and rangy, with a face showing the effects of his brief career as a professional boxer, won the western Sydney seat of Reid for Labor at the 1958 election and was a political warrior of the left faction, which he led after Jim Cairns retired in disgrace in 1977. Uren was responsible for the Albury–Wodonga decentralisation project as Minister for Urban and Regional Development in the Whitlam Government. In the war against the Japanese, Uren was captured in Timor and, as a POW, suffered cruelly on the Burma–Thailand Railway construction. In Parliament, his great passions were proper recognition for ex-servicemen and women (particularly POWs) and advancing the cause of world peace (which in the eyes of many Liberals meant he was a communist). He also energetically derided the Liberals and their policies at every opportunity.

John Carrick, prior to entering the Senate in 1971, was General Secretary of the NSW Liberal Party and in that role he mentored John Howard, spotting him as having considerable political potential. Carrick, like Uren, was captured during fighting in Timor and spent his time as a POW in the notorious Changi Prison in Singapore. At one stage, the WA Labor Senator Peter Walsh, a senior minister in the Hawke and Keating Governments, said during a senate sitting that Carrick was 'the fattest man ever to leave Changi'. It is hard to imagine a more disgraceful and ill-deserved insult to a notable and decent Australian who had suffered so much in fighting for Australia.

When Tom Uren heard of this, he confronted Walsh and threatened to do considerable damage to his person if he ever vilified Carrick again. Uren was the enemy of the Liberal Party and therefore its representatives in Parliament, but the bond of mateship between Australian POWs could not be sundered by mere politics.

The Menzies' ministry, when I arrived in 1951, had some formidable performers apart from the Prime Minister himself. There were Artie Fadden, Eric Harrison, who was a renowned brawler on the floor of the Parliament, Phil McBride, Harold Holt, John McEwen, Percy Spender, Richard Casey, and the redoubtable Earle Page, one of the founders of the Country Party who was first elected to the seat of Cowper in 1919 and was not defeated until 1961. Treasurer, Arthur Fadden, an accountant, entered Parliament in 1937 and represented the Queensland seat of McPherson. After Menzies' wartime government collapsed in 1941, Fadden became Prime Minister from 29 August to 7 October 1941, his government collapsing when two independents withdrew their support and Labor under John Curtin came to power. In government, Menzies and Fadden formed a coalition after the defeat of Labor in 1949; Fadden was Deputy Prime Minister and Treasurer. He and Menzies were not at all close.

'Artie' Fadden was one of the most likeable characters in Parliament House. Despite suffering from time to time at the hands of the newspaper proprietors— particularly Frank Packer—he was on good terms with gallery journalists. Artie took the bad times on the chin and had an endearing quality—found rarely in current politicians: he never resorted to the cover-up of claiming that damaging statements, from his own mouth, were 'taken out of context'. Artie would say he had never been misquoted, but often wished he had not been quoted. During the Korean War wool boom, Fadden imposed a 'double tax' on wool in his 'horror' budget of 1951. Unsurprisingly, this was greeted with rage in the bush—the power base of the Country Party. Packer launched an all-out attack against Fadden in *The Daily Telegraph* but Fadden was not to be shifted.

He displayed much courage under tremendous pressure and was not sheltered at all by Menzies. When Menzies was overseas and Fadden was Acting Prime

Minister, should some unexpected disaster strike—either a flood or some other mishap—Artie would call a press conference to discuss how he intended to deal with the problem. These conferences were held in Menzies' office, with Fadden sitting in Menzies' chair behind Menzies' desk. On one occasion, he complained, half-joking, half-serious, about the work 'the big bastard' left him. He pulled open a desk drawer and it was stuffed, not with official papers, but poems Menzies had penned at his desk.

Some government MPs stayed at the Hotel Canberra—a convenient stroll from Parliament House. They included Fadden, Richard Casey and Liberal backbenchers such as Joe Gullett, Bill Falkinder and Bruce Graham. After the house rose for the night, there would be some serious drinking in the Hotel Canberra lounge and I occasionally joined in with Don Whitington, with whom I had then teamed up. Graham had a wooden leg as a result of a war injury and sometimes, when he had passed out, Gullett and co. unscrewed the leg to fill the top with bottle tops, creating a mysterious rattle when Graham walked. It was said (probably unkindly) that the popular manager of the hotel, Thornley Thorpe, received an Imperial Award for putting Artie to bed on many occasions.

Yet despite these late-night drinking bouts, Artie Fadden would turn up at Parliament House about 8 am, often puffing on a big cigar, as he climbed the stairs into King's Hall. A small group of afternoon-paper journalists, including E. H. (Harold) Cox of the Melbourne *Herald*, would gather at the top of the stairs to waylay Artie. The Treasurer often used these encounters near budget time to drop some hints about what might be in the budget, no doubt flying a kite to test public reaction to a proposal he had in mind. Sometimes it appeared that Fadden was giving a policy issue an airing to send a signal to Menzies of what he and the Country Party might expect from the Prime Minister down the track. Cox, being the senior journalist, would do most of the talking to Artie. One morning, Ian Fitchett from *The Age* unexpectedly appeared at this little gathering and joined in the conversation with Fadden. When Fadden had departed along the government lobby, Cox chided Fitchett for horning in on the talk with Fadden. Fitchett flared up: 'How dare you—standing there in your piss-stained trousers.' This hurt all the more because the man from the Melbourne *Herald* did indeed wear piss-stained trousers.

When Chifley died in mid-1951, leaving Evatt as leader, Labor tragically lost the services of John Dedman, the most obvious successor to Chifley and founder of the successful postwar reconstruction scheme. Dedman was defeated in his seat of Corio in 1949 by renowned champion cyclist Hubert Opperman, who later became a senior minister in Menzies governments.

Neil (later Sir Neil) O'Sullivan was regarded as the token Catholic in Menzies' 1949 Cabinet. Even though Labor rat and Catholic Joe Lyons led the non-Labor parties as Prime Minister from 1932 to 1939, since Federation, Catholics had been somewhat rare in the solidly Protestant non-Labor parties. Sectarianism was found in all facets of Australian society—in politics, the Public Service and business. It was believed that Country Party leader, Sir Earle Page, and Joe Lyons had come to an agreement regarding departments to be dominated by Protestants and Catholics. True or not, post war, Catholics were over-represented in the Tax Office and the group of departments dealing with trade, commerce, agriculture and customs.

Menzies emphasised from 1951 on at least the value of the Australia, New Zealand and United States alliance (ANZUS). Labor MPs during the Menzies' era and after correctly claimed Curtin was responsible for establishing the basis for this alliance when he turned to Roosevelt to save Australia from the Japanese. Curtin was asked by the Melbourne *Herald* to provide a New Year message for the Australian people and it was published on 27 December 1941. In the message, he made a historic declaration: 'Without any inhibitions of any kind, I make it quite clear that Australia looks to America, free of any pangs as to our traditional links, or kinship with the United Kingdom.'[1]

The Indonesian adventure in the 1960s of 'confrontation' with Malaysia raised the question of the value of the ANZUS alliance to Australia. Menzies decided Australia had to support Malaysia. Established on 16 September 1963, Malaysia was a union of the states of Malaya, Singapore (later kicked out) and the North Borneo states of Sabah and Sarawak. Indonesian President Sukarno saw this as an attempt to strengthen 'Nekolim' (neo-colonialism, colonialism and imperialism) to erode the Indonesian revolution against the Dutch (the prewar colonial rulers of the Dutch East Indies). Malaya's Western-aligned Prime Minister, Tenpaku Abdul Rahman, had agreed to allow permanent basing of British and Commonwealth forces in the country. Sukarno remembered that Malaya had given assistance to the rebels of the Revolutionary Government of the Indonesian Republic (PRRI) in 1958. In that year, when Sukarno was abroad, a group of Sumatran military officers and Masyumi politicians had proclaimed the PRRI, which Sukarno would return to only in the figurehead role of president. Soon after the proclamation of Malaysia, Sukarno announced Indonesia must 'gobble Malaysia raw'.

Menzies decided Australia would give Malaysia every assistance it required, military or otherwise, to turn back the challenge of Indonesia. Malaysia was pressing the United States to intervene, but neither President Kennedy nor Secretary of State, Dean Rusk, responded. Washington made clear that the problem was one entirely for Britain, Australia and interested members of

---

1   Day, David P. 1999, *John Curtin: A life*, Harper Collins, Sydney, p. 438.

the Commonwealth. Later, Kennedy agreed that if Malaysia were attacked the United States would come to its assistance with air and naval forces, but he ruled out ground troops.

In April 1964, RAAF engineers were sent to Borneo, in addition to minesweepers and helicopters already dispatched to aid Malaysia. Foreign Affairs Minister, Garfield Barwick, then declared that if Australian forces were attacked, the United States would come to our aid under ANZUS. He conveniently forgot about the declaration by Washington that no troops would be involved. Sukarno protested at Malaysia being elected as a non-permanent member of the UN Security Council by taking Indonesia out of the United Nations. All this came to an end in 1966 when confrontation ended, and Indonesia rejoined the United Nations in 1967—a good outcome for Menzies, Australia and the United Nations.

Another Menzies appearance on the world stage was not successful. On 26 July 1956, Gamel Abdul Nasser, President of Egypt and a hero of the Arab world, having headed a *coup d'état* to overthrow the corpulent and hated King Farouk in 1952, announced Egypt would nationalise the Suez Canal Company. The company built and owned the canal and, from 1869, had the right to operate it for 99 years. The company was headquartered in Paris and the British had acquired a major share in 1875. By an international convention, the canal was supposed to be open to ships of all nations. The British had troops stationed in Egypt essentially to guard the canal. Following anti-British pressure in Egypt, the British withdrew their troops from Egypt—the last departing in 1956. Soon after, Nasser announced nationalisation.

The British, French and Israelis were appalled and so was Menzies. The author reported the parliamentary debate about the Nasser nationalisation and recalls how passionate Menzies was about the danger to Australia's traditional trade with the mother country, which passed through the canal. (This was not all that distant from mid-1961 when the UK Macmillan Government attempted to join what was then called the European Common Market and to hell with trade ties with the Commonwealth.)

The US Secretary of State, John Foster Dulles, devised a plan, agreed to by most Western countries, for an international body, under the aegis of the United Nations, to run the canal. Yet Dulles would not lead the delegation to Cairo to put the proposition to Nasser, and Menzies, at the urging of Macmillan, agreed to lead it. Despite Menzies' best efforts, the talks broke down in early September 1956 and nothing was achieved. Unbeknown to Menzies and the United States, Britain, France and Israel had entered into a secret deal to take over the canal by force. Israel attacked Egypt on 29 October 1956, entered the Sinai and dropped paratroopers within 50 km of the canal. Then British and French forces entered the Canal Zone, it was claimed, to keep the warring parties of Egypt and Israel apart. US President, Dwight Eisenhower, would have none of this and pulled the rug from under the conspirators. Within a week, the British–French action had come to a halt in the face of pressure from Washington. A majority of the gallery believed Menzies' conceit had got the better of him and he was foolish to believe he could act as an honest broker between Britain, the Europeans and Nasser.

The Suez crisis was not a complete loss for Menzies as he managed to rid himself of a potential challenger: Richard Gardiner Casey, the Minister for External Affairs (and later Governor-General). Canberra writer John Nethercote,[2] on the fiftieth anniversary of the Anglo–French invasion of Egypt, recalled that Casey was opposed to the use of force in the canal. Casey warned that world opinion would be overwhelmingly against the United Kingdom if it used force and, inferentially, against Australia if it supported the use of force.

Casey had made an injudicious remark to a reporter—later used against UK Prime Minister, Sir Anthony Eden, in the Commons debate by the British Labour leader, Hugh Gaitskell. Menzies was in the Commons at the time, listening to the debate, and was furious—his anger being conveyed to Casey by departmental officials. On his return to Australia after the abortive Cairo visit, Menzies brought on a vote for the deputy leadership of the Liberal Party—a vacancy having occurred with the appointment of Eric Harrison as High Commissioner in London. Casey was eliminated on the first ballot and the final vote went to Harold Holt over the ponderous Senator Bill Spooner. (How things would have worked out had Spooner won puzzled the gallery at the time. The concept of the second-most important man in the Liberal Party sitting in the Senate was indeed novel.) Menzies' friend A. P. Herbert penned a piece of doggerel and sent it to Menzies. It reflected British colonial arrogance and overt racism:

> Expect no gratitude from any man
> From India, say, or Pakistan:
> Under the wing of Nasser and the Russ
> I hope they prosper as they did with us
> Though Allah knows why they suppose a pal
> The man who stole, and stoppered, the canal.
> Forget, forgive; but then a mighty hand
> To two who did not doubt the Motherland!
> In all the turbulence, the fools, the frenzies,
> One rock of sanity was Robert Menzies.

---

2   *The Canberra Times*, 4 November 2006.

As usual, Australia was there—New Zealand, too—God bless the faithful. A blot on the reputation of the Menzies Government (which could have brought it down had it not been for the Labor split) was its failure in trade. Despite wool prices soaring because of the Korean War, and having come to power by promising to disband petrol rationing, the Government faced a serious balance-of-payments crisis from the beginning of the 1950s.

Import licensing was introduced from March 1952 and was not lifted until 1960. In short, importers had to get a licence from the Government to import. To deal with the administrative burden, the Central Import Licensing Branch was established, operating from 52 William Street, Sydney. Laurie Stroud, a former senior official in the Trade Department, worked in the branch as a young man. In a conversation with the author, he explained the donkey work of processing applications was conducted by a hastily assembled group from all walks of life: returned servicemen with intermediate certificates, many carpenters, taxi drivers, but few graduates.

With so much power in the hands of bureaucrats—which often had serious impacts on many businesses—there were lots of complaints. Stroud remembers when an importer came to the inquiry counter and demanded to talk to someone about why he could not get a licence for an imported magazine:

> Nobody else was around and I was asked to talk to him, which I did and to the best of my ability and explained what the policy was. It didn't satisfy him. In the *Daily Mirror* next day *on the front page* was the story thundering that a callow youth was deciding what could be read by the Australian community.

It cost Stroud money. He was in a more senior job than one paid the base rate at that stage, and this meant that even though he was a junior, he was paid as an adult. He explains:

> When the Public Service inspector in Sydney saw this criticism of the bureaucracy in the media, he immediately contacted the head of the import licensing branch and said: 'What's all this about' and it came out that I was acting in a more senior job. The Public Service inspector delivered an ultimatum: either that guy's acting in a job that is not worth the classification, or he's not doing the full duties of the job, so I was summarily dropped back to the base grade.

The more influential businesspeople did not turn up at the front counter in William Street; they went to Canberra to see the Minister for Agriculture and Commerce, McEwen. What they did not know was that McEwen would have made up his mind in advance of seeing any delegation whether he could revise a licensing decision or not. If he could help and if those seeking his assistance were important to him and the Government, he would see a visiting delegation. If not, the task of breaking the bad news fell to his undersecretary, Reginald Swartz. A rotund, pleasant man, quite bald with a round face and a neat moustache (he was known throughout Parliament as 'Curley'), Swartz had a polite manner that belied his heroic background.

He enlisted in the AIF in November 1940 with the rank of captain, served with the 2/26 Infantry Battalion in the Malaysian campaign and spent 3.5 years as a POW, some of it on the ghastly Burma–Thailand Railway. He won the Queensland seat of Darling Downs in 1949 for the Liberals. Swartz would see the delegations pleading for an import licence, hear them attentively and then say 'no'. In the gallery and among importers, he became known as the 'Abominable "No" Man'. Swartz went on to become a senior and successful Cabinet minister.

Nothing the Fairfax press had done to Menzies could be compared with the attempt by Warwick Fairfax to engineer the defeat of the Coalition at the 1961 election. Graham Freudenberg[3] was Arthur Calwell's press secretary and speechwriter in the lead-up to the 1961 election and had an insider's knowledge of what Fairfax was up to. For Fairfax to work for the election of a Labor government shook the Sydney establishment to its foundations. Yet we must go back a few steps to understand the background to the 1961 drama.

Despite Menzies' claim to be a master of economic management, as explained previously, a balance-of-payments crisis led to the imposition of import licensing in 1952. In 1960, Treasury persuaded the Treasurer, Harold Holt, to press Cabinet for the abolition of import licensing. Jack McEwen resisted, warning this could cause a rush of imports and again threaten the balance of payments. Many believed McEwen's attitude was motivated partly by the protection it gave to Australian manufacturers. In any case, McEwen proved to be right and imports flooded in, leading to Holt slamming the brakes on the economy, with a credit squeeze through the Reserve Bank. Interest rates went up and heavy sales taxes were applied. This in particular hurt the car industry and led to lay-offs. When unemployment reached 2.7 per cent, this was widely regarded as a scandal. In later years governments were immensely proud if unemployment dropped below 5 per cent. About this time a Tasmanian economist, Professor Torleiv Hytten, stated the economy would be much healthier if there was a 'pool' of 5 per cent unemployed. This led Labor wit Les Haylen to observe that '[t]hings are mighty cool in Professor Hytten's pool'.

In 1957, Maxwell Newton, a former Treasury official, was appointed political correspondent for the *Sydney Morning Herald*. He had a considerable impact on political journalism and played a major role in events that almost led to the

---

3   Freudenberg, *A Figure of Speech*.

shortening of Menzies' reign. Many in the gallery regarded him as a blow-in, not even a journalist. Most of his early writings for the *Sydney Morning Herald* were confined to economic matters and the business of political writing was left to the more experienced bureau head, George Kerr. Max soon won most of us over. Raucous, witty, gap-toothed and a heavy drinker, Max was a dynamic personality, hugely talented and a first-class economist.

Later, as editor, Newton was responsible for the *Australian Financial Review* going from a weekly to an outstanding daily paper. The *Australian Financial Review* was originally designed as a paper to appeal to those interested in the stock exchange and equity investments. It still is, yet Newton realised that to broaden its appeal the paper needed to get more into broad economics and the connection between politics, government and economics. He left the stock-exchange side to specialists and dismissed this area of the paper as 'the Chinese section'—inscrutable except to keen investors. Newton was largely responsible for the gallery coming to grips with economics. The strength of the *Australian Financial Review* was, and is, its Canberra staff, with such talents as David Love (no relation to Les), Max Walsh, Robert Haupt and Brian Toohey. Newton got Rupert Murdoch's *The Australian* off the ground when it first began publishing in Canberra.

The 1961 election was late in the year (9 December). In the run-up to the election, the credit squeeze began to bite hard, hurting many businesses, including John Fairfax's river of gold: its domination of the classified ads in Sydney. Long a critic of Menzies, the Fairfax press took the unprecedented step of supporting the election of a Labor government. Unbeknown to the gallery, Calwell had given R. A. G. (Rags) Henderson, Managing Director of Fairfax, an undertaking not to have any form of nationalisation in the first term of a Labor government. This alone illustrated the desperation of Calwell—an old-fashioned socialist all his life—for victory.

Yet it was a meaningless promise. The High Court had made it clear that virtually any form of nationalisation breached Section 92 of the Constitution. Graham Freudenberg, then Calwell's press secretary/speechwriter, knew of the deal and explains[4] how Newton, at the direction of Fairfax management, supplied speech notes for Calwell. Newton was able to work on the solid economic material given to Calwell by two Australian National University economists, Dr Horrie Brown and Professor Alan Hall—both Labor supporters. Newton devised a Keynesian economic policy for Calwell—summed up in a sentence: 'To restore full employment, a Labor government will budget for a deficit of £100 million' (then 3 per cent of the budget). A lot more was to be heard about Newton in

---

4 Ibid.

later years. Menzies went into the election supremely confident and came out shaken to his core. Had it not been for Jim Killen's narrow victory in Moreton, Menzies would have lacked a majority.

A highlight of the year in the 1950s was the winter meeting in Canberra of the Premiers' Conference and Loan Council—the six States and the Commonwealth. Officials had already carried out most of the bargaining and the meetings rarely went for more than a day. What each State got by way of taxation reimbursements was in accord with a strict formula presided over by the Commonwealth Grants Commission. In the broad, the two wealthy and more populous States of New South Wales and Victoria would have some of the taxation raised from their State passed over to the other four States—described officially as the 'mendicant States'. The premiers used the meetings mainly to complain bitterly about the stinginess of the Menzies Government in providing essential (they were always 'essential') funds over and above what they were entitled to under the Grants Commission formula.

Before they arrived in Canberra, they all pumped out propaganda about how they were determined to stand up to Menzies this time around. The premiers and their entourages usually stayed at the Hotel Canberra on the night before the premiers' meeting and would caucus there (Liberal and Labor) on tactics for the coming meeting. Although they did not necessarily come from the same side of politics, there was an affinity between the premiers of New South Wales and Victoria. They complained (and to this day still do) that the two biggest States were unfairly treated and too much of the taxes paid by their citizens was being directed to the other four States. The Parliament did not meet normally in the middle of winter and the Premiers' Conference and Loan Council meetings were held in the House of Representatives chamber, with the Premiers' Conference the first event. This meeting decided what each State should get by way of direct-purpose grants over and above the taxation reimbursements.

The gallery reporters were allowed into the opening session of the Premiers' Conference when each premier, in order of seniority (New South Wales first, Tasmania last), would deliver a generalised speech pleading for the maximum benefit for his State. The Federal Treasurer would follow, with a summing up by Menzies. The press would then depart and the bargaining began. Menzies and the Treasurer, Artie Fadden (and when Fadden retired, Harold Holt), were up against some tough nuts, including the redoubtable Victorian Liberal Premier, Henry Bolte, NSW Labor Premier, Joe Cahill, and the wily SA Liberal Tom Playford, who was Premier, Treasurer and Minister for Immigration for that State from 1938 to 1965.

The most fervent and dogged critic was undoubtedly Bolte, who attacked Menzies before, during and after the conference. Bolte often demanded a return to income-taxing rights for the States, but never pushed it to the point where it might become a reality. Like all the premiers, he was happy to have the Commonwealth collecting tax for him. They took no responsibility for the level of tax, yet had the agreeable task of handing out the money to their citizens in various forms.

The Loan Council met in private to discuss the borrowing requirements of each State. State political correspondents, whom the premiers knew well, accompanied the State ministers and officials to Canberra. This neat arrangement ensured that after the meetings newspapers throughout Australia would invariably be dominated by premiers warning of the setback to their State because of the mean treatment handed out by Menzies and Fadden. Until the era of instant TV communications across the nation, the comments of premiers about the outcome of the conference could not be transmitted to the various capitals for replay on TV news that evening. Hence, TV crews from local stations met the premiers on their arrival back at the airport of their city.

Ken Begg[5] recalled an incident after one conference involving one of the gallery's notable characters, Les Love. Les, when sober (as he was on this occasion), was polite, correct and deferential to those in authority. He was then in the ABC bureau in the gallery and as he left for the bar someone said to him if he ran into the Victorian Premier, Sir Henry Bolte, ask him what flight he was on for the trip back to Melbourne. ABC Melbourne wanted a crew at Tullamarine Airport to meet the Premier. As Love walked down a flight of stairs from the gallery into the opposition lobby, he encountered Bolte and the Deputy Premier, (Sir) Arthur Rylah. According to Begg, Les said: 'Excuse me, Sir Henry, could you tell me what flight you're on, please?' Bolte responded: 'Ah, get fucked.' Les instantly returned fire: 'Get fucked yourself.'

The gallery was treated well by Menzies on these occasions. The premiers and officials had drinks in the government party room during the lunch break and at the end of the meetings. The gallery joined in these two sessions, making contact at a social level with the most senior politicians in the land outside Canberra. The senior journalists in the gallery were mindful of the need to keep up with current political developments in the States as they were reminded of it almost every day in phone conferences with their news editors. Later, Prime Minister, John Gorton, aroused great anger in the gallery by barring journalists from these drinks sessions.

Menzies had a high regard for the Public Service and, unlike recent prime ministers, he did not seek advice from his own staff on matters of government policy. He had his own suite of policy principles, of course, known to his public

5 Interview with former members of the gallery and the author, Old Parliament House, Canberra, 18 December 2004.

service advisers. He greatly valued the advice of people such as Allen Brown (Secretary of the Prime Minister's department), Roland Wilson (Secretary of Treasury), Fred Wheeler (Chair of the Public Service Board) and H. C. 'Nugget' Coombs (Governor of the Reserve Bank, who had been an influential adviser to Labor governments).

Unlike John Howard, who got rid of many departmental heads on coming to power in 1996, Menzies firmly believed in the integrity and independence of the departments of state and did not question whether they would serve his government loyally, as they had served Labor governments. If a minister brought a novel or risky submission to Cabinet, Menzies wanted to know what the minister's department thought about the submission. New policies of considerable importance were normally scrutinised by an interdepartmental committee of representatives of departments with interest, or expertise, in the policy.

Menzies, like many prime ministers before and after him, saw himself as a world statesman. In fact, Menzies' foreign policy excursions were, for the most part, badly judged and based on prewar conceptions of the way the world should be. His eyes were on the northern hemisphere and the great powers, rather than on our region. It is not generally recognised his achievements were more in the field of domestic rather than foreign policy.

First and foremost, he benefited from the solid economic foundations left him by the Chifley Government. When Curtin came to power in 1941, after the collapse of the Fadden Government, Chifley was both Treasurer and Minister for Post-War Reconstruction. Labor was already planning for peace. In that government, the capable John Dedman was Minister for War Organisation of Industry and Minister in Charge of the Council for Scientific and Industrial Research (the forerunner of the CSIRO). Dedman, in the 1945 Chifley Government, was Minister for Post-War Reconstruction and gave the drive to the remarkably successful postwar reconstruction policies he largely conceived. With the economy spinning along nicely, Menzies realised it was best left alone.

Today the byword of every government is 'reform'. Few institutions or policies these days are seen to not require reform. Menzies was of the 'if it ain't broke, don't fix it' school of thought. His simple policy towards industrial relations was based on the Commonwealth Conciliation and Arbitration Commission (CCAC). If there was a serious strike running, or threatened, his answer was to tell the combatants to go to the CCAC—the independent umpire—and obey its decisions (which the unions often ignored). His abiding gifts to Australia can be seen in universities and in the national capital. Menzies appointed a committee headed by Sir Keith Murray, a noted scholar and Chair of the British University Grants Commission, to recommend measures to deal with the increasingly parlous state of Australian universities. On 28 November 1957, Menzies tabled Murray's report and announced acceptance of its recommendations, involving very large expenditures. This was to have profound long-term consequences for tertiary education, with the Commonwealth, rather than the States, looked to to solve the ever-recurring problem of university funding.

A similar policy initiative—state aid to private schools—was seen at the time, rightly, as a piece of populist politics designed to get a desperate prime minister over the line. Menzies had almost lost the 1961 election, but was saved by Jim Killen's narrow win in the electorate of Morton—a win resulting from the distribution of communist preferences to one of the Parliament's most theatrical bangers of the anti-communist drum. The communist vote actually came about from the 'donkey' vote—a term applied to uninterested voters who simply number their ballot paper in order from the top down. Menzies had given some aid to Catholic schools in the Australian Capital Territory (for which the Commonwealth had responsibility). He took the approach that a wider application of such aid was a matter for the States. Yet in his policy speech for the 1963 election he promised state aid to private and public schools for construction of buildings and facilities for the teaching of science and was returned with a comfortable majority.

The gallery believed that it was Neil O'Sullivan who gave Menzies the idea of offering state aid. DLP senators Jack Kane and Vince Gair told gallery journalist Eric Walsh that Tasmanian Senator George Cole had sold the idea of state aid to Menzies. Cole was elected as a Labor Senator in 1950 and left the party in the great Labor split. As a DLP Senator, it is more than likely Cole was acting on behalf of Bob Santamaria. Fiercely anti-communist, Santamaria founded a new organisation, the National Civic Council (NCC), and edited its newspaper, *News Weekly*, for many years. His followers, known as 'Groupers', continued to control a number of important unions.

Those expelled from the Labor Party formed a new party, the Democratic Labor Party (DLP), which was dedicated to opposing both communism and the Labor Party, which they said was controlled by communist sympathisers. Santamaria never joined the DLP but was one of its uniting influences. Maybe Cole put the idea to Menzies and the Prime Minister then tried it out on O'Sullivan, who would certainly have advised for it. Whatever the source of the idea, this was an inspired piece of opportunism by Menzies. He skewered Arthur Calwell, who was prevented from matching Menzies by the Labor Party platform prohibiting aid to private schools.

The nation can also thank Menzies for turning Canberra—still a country town in the 1950s—into a world-class national capital. Following the Depression and World War II, little had been done to provide infrastructure for the national capital. Thousands of federal public servants and the whole of the Defence Department and the three services were comfortably ensconced in Melbourne, secure in the knowledge that they would never be called to Canberra. Menzies changed all that. For example, the central lake had been a key feature of Walter Burley Griffin's winning design for the national capital. Menzies declared this should be achieved with the necessary damming of the Molonglo River. Around Australia a cry went up that it was all a waste of money and many schools or hospitals could be erected for the cost of the dam. Menzies was undaunted and, in 1957, he announced the decision to move the Defence Department to Canberra by 1959.

The top brass at Victoria Barracks in Melbourne was aghast at the prospect of leaving their comfortable life in Melbourne—far removed from the national government. Similar plans were made for moving major departments such as Civil Aviation, Transport, and Labor and National Service to Canberra. Hundreds, if not thousands, of public servants refused to make the switch and resigned. Menzies pushed ahead, quite content to live and work in the bush capital with his family. In his farewell press conference, Menzies was asked whether Canberra was one of his 'blunders'. Menzies responded with feeling: 'Canberra is my pride and joy. It is indeed.' Menzies, more than most prime ministers, enjoyed living in Canberra. He would turn up at Manuka Oval to see a local game of Aussie Rules or cricket and was content at the Lodge. He must have done some grave spinning on hearing that John Howard refused to live at the Lodge and instead installed his family in Kirribilli House, which Menzies, many years before, had restored as a guesthouse for foreign VIP guests of the Government.

While his decision to step down undefeated was widely lauded, Menzies' failure to leave the Liberal Party with a good choice of talented ministers to take over his leadership was widely criticised. The founder of the Liberal Party had let go, or removed, plenty of talent: Tommy White, Dick Casey, Percy Spender and Garfield Barwick. Again, firmly in charge after his near-death experience at the 1961 election, Menzies assumed Harold Holt would take over. Non-Labor parties—at least at the federal level—have a poor record on fostering potential leaders. The Nationalists had to rely on Labor rat Billy Hughes as Prime Minister from 1915 to 1923, and another Labor rat, Joe Lyons, from 1932 to 1939. Menzies' first prime ministership had lasted only from April 1939 to August 1941 before his party ditched him. Now everything was on Harold Holt's shoulders.

Holt was regarded as a worthy successor to Menzies, but the point was the Liberal Party room saw no alternative when Menzies retired. McEwen was privately critical of Menzies' failure to leave the Liberals with talented leadership. On the other hand, 'Black Jack' McEwen had fostered the trio of Doug Anthony, Ian Sinclair and Peter Nixon. Such was the dearth of talent in the Liberal ranks in the House of Representatives that, with Holt's disappearance, the Liberals took the unprecedented step of turning to a Senator, John Gorton, for leadership (he turned out to be a disaster). Menzies was directly responsible for this. Admittedly, Paul Hasluck could have been given a chance at the leadership, but he was politically inept. He was so aloof that although he wanted to succeed Holt, he did not lobby hard for the job. Hasluck, from his lofty heights, believed that his colleagues would surely see his superiority over Gorton. If they could not, he was not going to beg for party-room votes.

A feature of the daily business of the House of Representatives was the adjournment debate—late in the evening, when the question was put 'the house do now adjourn'. The members were then entitled to speak on any subject. This was when the more outrageous and scandalous stories often broke, and journalists drinking in the non-members' bar would await the cry 'they're on the adjournment' before dashing up to the gallery to check. The favoured time for major speeches by ministers or leading opposition figures in the house was 8 pm, when the parliamentary broadcast was coming from that chamber. Normally, the parliamentary sitting week covered Tuesdays, Wednesdays and Thursdays. Broadcasts from the house were on Tuesdays and Thursdays and from the Senate on Wednesdays.

The broadcasting of Parliament began on 10 July 1946 amid some controversy. The ABC, a government instrumentality, was ordered to undertake the broadcasting of what was widely believed to be the most turgid and boring radio broadcasts ever put to air since the appearance of Marconi's wonderful invention. Initially, the ABC metropolitan stations broadcast the proceedings almost in their entirety. Apart from denying programs for ABC radio listeners in the cities, many citizens in rural areas had no access to the broadcast. To overcome this, the ABC agreed reluctantly to switch the broadcasts to its Radio National network, which then had, and still has, some of the best programs to be found in any form of broadcasting. Later, a spare bearer was used for broadcasts of Parliament and the ABC's News Radio network resulted.

Ulrich Ellis was a prominent staffer to Country Party ministers in the 1950s and 1960s. Balding, short and bespectacled, he appeared on first meeting as a most ordinary man. Fortunately, he was ordinary enough to turn up in the non-members' bar. He was a gifted journalist and historian and was an intellectual driving force of the New England new-State movement, which in the 1840s, six decades before Federation, saw the emergence of separatist agitation in the region. I remember him as staffer for Sir Earle Page. Despite Page's savage 1939 attack on Menzies' failure to enlist in World War I, Page was Health Minister in Menzies' Cabinet after 1949 (see Chapter 4). The old adage held true: there are no friendships in politics, only convenient alliances.

Ulrich Ellis was keen to educate gallery members on the benefits he envisaged flowing from the creation of more States. The founding fathers provided for the creation of new States in the Constitution. Sections 121–4 give the Commonwealth Parliament power to create new States and decide on their representation in Parliament. Any proposal to form a new State from part of one or more of the original States (the six States) requires the agreement of the State Parliaments involved. Additionally, the agreement of electors of the original State or States is sought in another referendum. There is not the remotest possibility of the Parliament in any State giving up sovereignty to any part of its land. The best hope is the likelihood of the Northern Territory being given statehood by the Commonwealth Parliament, without a referendum.

Gough Whitlam enhanced his leadership aspirations as a backbench member of the Parliamentary Joint Committee on Constitutional Review, which was formed to conduct a wide-ranging review of the Constitution. The media devoted considerable space to the 1959 report of the committee. It recommended facilitating the creation of new States by dropping the power of States to veto the creation of a new State within their boundaries, or shared boundaries with other States. It recommended referendums of all the voters of a State and of the area to constitute a new State. If both referendums recorded a majority in favour of a new State then the Commonwealth Parliament would exercise its existing power to form a new State or States.

All the work of the committee came to nought and the Menzies Government did not take up any of its recommendations involving constitutional change. In his 1965 pamphlet *Labor and the Constitution*,[6] Whitlam made quite clear he was a centralist (apart from local issues) and was prepared to compose his policies accordingly. He argued there were few functions State parliaments performed that could not be better performed by the Australian Parliament or by regional councils. The States, he argued, were too large to deal with local matters and too small and weak to deal with national ones. Although spending more than half a century in the press gallery of the Federal Parliament, the author does not favour a centralist approach. A continent, at least in a democracy, cannot be ruled with the greatest efficiency by a single federal government. A hospital in Kalgoorlie would surely not be run as well by bureaucrats in Canberra as by bureaucrats in Perth.

In my early years in politics, State rights did not loom large as an issue. Day-to-day politics—scandals and power plays—were the jungle in which politicians and gallery journalists prowled. And in the next chapter, there are examples of what was found in this political jungle.

---

6   Whitlam, E. G. 1965, *Labor and the Constitution*, Victorian Fabian Society, Melbourne.

6. Parliament Disgraced by its Members

One of the more sensational events involving parliamentary privilege occurred after I arrived in the gallery in 1951. The Treasurer, Arthur Fadden, was to deliver his budget speech in August of that year. On budget day, the lock-up for the gallery began in the afternoon. At the dinner adjournment of the house, Fadden briefed the government MPs on the contents of the budget at a special meeting of the party room. Having been briefed that excise rates were to go up on a range of items—whisky and other spirits and cigarettes—a number of government MPs rushed to the members' bar to order these items before the price rose. 'Insider trading' was an unknown term in those days, but it fitted the situation perfectly. In a savage piece designed to arouse voter fury, Alan Reid reported this grossly opportunistic behaviour in the Sydney *Sun*. Reid also charged MPs with running Parliament as a club solely for their own benefit. At that time beer was in short supply and publicans rationed sales of bottled beer to a weekly quota for their regular customers. Reid's point was that the non-members' bar rationed these hard-to-get items (including cigarettes), while there were no restrictions on sales to MPs from the members' bar. Reid reported that one Sydney-bound MP's car was so loaded with beer that a rear spring broke.

In the gallery there was great concern. While it was widely anticipated that the Sydney *Sun* staff might be kicked out of the Parliament, we feared the non-members' bar and dining room might be closed to all gallery members. This was in the minds of members of the house when they ordered an inquiry by the Privileges Committee—one of the terms of reference asking it to examine 'the wisdom or otherwise of continuing the extension of privileges to other than members of Parliament'.

Fortunately, wisdom prevailed and privileges for gallery members (including Reid) remained. The special meeting of the gallery carried a resolution strongly supporting Reid and declaring 'that the facts contained in it [Reid's article] are correct'. The Privileges Committee conceded that the article was not 'wholly untrue' but was grossly exaggerated and, among other things, conveyed a false impression about the conduct of parliamentarians. It ruled there was a breach of privilege but considered 'the house would best serve its own dignity by taking no further action in the matter'. No doubt all MPs were aware of the danger of a long-running fight with the gallery and, ultimately, the newspaper proprietors by attempting a lockout of the gallery from Parliament.

In 1955 Reid recruited me for his small *Sun* bureau and I was both flattered and excited. Reid was one of the best journalists in the gallery and courageous, as he had shown in his exposure of the greed of MPs raiding the members' bar before excise went up on spirits. Reid's number two, Bill Bissell, was quiet, middle-aged and an experienced journalist. Don Whitington told me that when Reid was young he was an alcoholic. Like others with an alcohol problem, such as Curtin and Bob Hawke, Reid had the grit to turn teetotaller. He was, however, a chain-smoker of 'roll-your-owns'. Towards the end of his life, he lost a lung to cancer, yet he still did not entirely give up the smokes. Reid authored a widely read weekly column and was influential on both sides of the Parliament. He was the first press gallery journalist to 'discover' B. A. Santamaria, the leading figure in the split that tore apart the Labor Party in the 1950s.

In 1957 Don Whitington, a former head of bureau of *The Daily Telegraph*, invited me to join his one-man band: Australian Press Services. For the next 22 years, my life in the gallery revolved around Don and our business. He was a complex character, and I owe him a lot, both as a friend and as an educator on matters of journalism and politics. Educated at Friends High School in Tasmania, he completed a wool-classing course, and worked as a jackeroo, assistant bookkeeper and chauffeur for H. R. Munro at Keera Station in New South Wales, and broke into journalism through contributing articles to various papers. Don and Eric White in 1944 were members of a government-sponsored press delegation to study the war effort in Canada and the United States of America. White, a former journalist, had been at the second Albury conference in 1944 when Menzies was uniting non-Labor parties into the Liberal Party. White became the Liberal Party's first public relations officer. In Washington, they discovered two areas of journalism almost unknown in Australia: political newsletters and public relations operators.

They came back to Australia and Don established, with Eric White, *Inside Canberra* and other newsletters and the Eric White Associates public relations business. They also founded the *Northern Territory News* and the *Mount Isa Mail*, where the well-known journalist Alan Ramsey gained early experience. Don was not at all taken with the 'spin' in public relations work and he and Eric parted company on a sour note. Eric White Associates was a great success and was the first and most prominent company in this business after the war. It recruited mainly journalists on the basis that much of its work consisted of trying to insert 'puff' paragraphs into newspapers, or in some other way get a friendly media mention for a client company. Later, public relations companies developed far greater expertise in the field of commerce and economics and their business consultancy work, in the end, was far more important than press relations.

In many ways, Don was conservative. He regarded the wearing of sunglasses or coloured shirts an affectation and although he was well to the left in politics, most of his best mates, particularly Bill Snedden, were on the Liberal side. Snedden was quite a ladies' man, and, when Immigration Minister in the Holt Government, he made a trip to Europe to inspect Australia's immigration offices. His inspection task in Germany led him to invite a local woman (one of the immigration office staff) to spend some days with him in various parts of Germany. During the course of this affair, he gave the woman a family signet ring. On his return to Australia, he was in a panic about getting the ring back and prevailed upon the Australian staff in Germany to persuade the woman to return it. She did, only after persuading the Australian Immigration Office to provide her with a rent-free flat.

I owe it to Don Whitington for, among other things, acquiring some knowledge of good food and wine (in retrospect, something I could have done without). Don and I toiled away on a number of newsletters as well as the flagship, *Inside Canberra*—still edited weekly by the author. The newsletter business was hard work but the writing was the easy part; far harder was selling subscriptions. We also wrote a weekly political column for newspapers in rural and provincial Australia, *Behind the Headlines*, dispatched by telex to some 60 papers in an era when many were owned and operated by family companies. Some of the small weekly papers received our column for the magnificent sum of 10 s. a week. This source of revenue gradually dried up as papers closed down or sold out to city newspaper interests.

Don Whitington and I also represented United Press International (UPI), a major American wire service, and we believed it was because of this connection that the Chinese refused us visas to travel with Gough Whitlam on his historic visit to China as Leader of the Opposition in 1971. UPI subeditors in the United States had difficulties understanding the intricacies of Australian politics and the Westminster system. The dismissal of Whitlam in 1975 was an example. UPI could not understand why 'this guy Kerr', appointed by the Queen, dismissed Whitlam. To explain to someone in America whose whole experience of politics was in the context of the US Congressional system was beyond me. UPI could not grasp the concept Kerr was acting in accordance with the unwritten 'reserve power' of the Governor-General, having nothing to do with the Queen. 'But, goddam it', said UPI, 'he's appointed by the Queen'. Even more difficult was explaining that if Whitlam had been able to phone the Queen before the dismissal came into effect, he could have had Kerr removed.

For some years, we also provided a political commentary service for Sydney radio station 2CH. Don was afflicted with a nervous stutter. He hardly stuttered at all in conversations with his close friends, but under a little pressure, he could stutter badly. So it fell to me to do the daily commentary for 2CH—a valuable experience. It occupied up to 90 seconds, and a lot could be said in that time. It was also different from the short commentary—not much more than 30 seconds—I had done as the Ten Network correspondent in Canberra. We also represented a number of rural papers and even though Don had considerable experience of matters rural, and me none, I therefore kept in touch with trade and agricultural issues—often complex and controversial.

Don's main interest was people and he preferred writing politics, mainly party politics and particularly the players in it. He was good at it, so I turned my attention to the fields of business and trade—a vast area of activity I knew little about, and the more I learned from a variety of business and government sources, the more it interested me. Don, possibly because of his break with Eric White, had little time for lobbyists and public relations people. In contrast, I have found them a great source of material. Of course, lobbyists are pushing the interests of their clients at every opportunity, but they need to earn the trust of journalists. They will not earn this trust by pushing false and biased material. I have a good working relationship with many of them and find the skilled lobbyist can provide valuable insights into the attitudes of the Government or political parties towards various issues. Many of the best lobbyists have had considerable experience either in the Public Service or as ministerial staffers.

Only two significant buildings housed government departments when the Parliament moved from Melbourne in 1927: East Block and West Block—both within easy walking distance of Parliament House. East Block accommodated the Prime Minister's Department. The Canberra Post Office and Treasury, among others, occupied West Block. The back bar at the nearby Hotel Canberra was one of the favourite watering holes for senior Treasury people. The Royal Canberra Golf Club's original 18-hole course—built by the Government for the residents of Canberra and for many years maintained by the Parks and Gardens branch of the Department of the Interior—was an important social centre from 1927 on. The clubhouse, a rambling weatherboard building, was to the rear of the Albert Hall—a landmark on Commonwealth Avenue.

The clubhouse bar was patronised by many senior public servants, including the Secretary of the Treasury, Roland Wilson, and other senior Treasury officers such as Jack Garrett, Colin Conron, John Lloyd and John Stokes. Despite its rather grand name, the Royal Canberra Golf Club was by no means an exclusive establishment and democracy ruled. Anyone could join for a reasonable annual subscription and members included public servants—from departmental heads all the way down to Commonwealth car drivers. In the 1950s, one of the members was Jim Moroney, a colourful character, Secretary of the Department of Agriculture and a dab hand with a billiard cue. When he later moved to Melbourne as General Manager of the Australian Wheat Board, I saw him defeat the Victorian commercial travellers' champion in a snooker challenge. Jim liked a drink and a yarn. One night in the Royal Canberra bar, Moroney got into quite an argument with another member, a Commonwealth car driver. Punches were thrown and the committee had to decide what to do about it. Moroney's status as one of the exclusive band of public servants at the top—a department head—did not save him. He was given a suspended sentence of about three months—accepted by Jim without demure—and he returned to the club after his period of banishment.

From the 1920s to the 1970s, the Hotel Wellington, opposite York Park on National Circuit, was the late-afternoon drinking venue for most of the press gallery when Parliament was not sitting and the non-members' bar closed at 4 pm. Friday night at the Wello was party night, especially after the introduction of 10 pm closing. In 1976 Prime Minister, Malcolm Fraser, opened the National Press Club on National Circuit. There was a mass exodus from the old pub to the Press Club, which was closer to Parliament than the Wello. Friday nights became even more popular for press people and senior public servants. John Stone, the controversial head of Treasury, was one who enjoyed mixing with the press and frequently breasted the Press Club bar. His utterances were generally blunt and candid and followed closely by journalists. Not that he gave any Cabinet secrets away, but at least, talking to Stone, one could get the drift of what the Secretary of the Treasury thought about many economic and political issues.

When the Molonglo River was dammed to create Lake Burley Griffin, it flooded the old Royal Canberra Golf Course. Amid considerably controversy, in 1962, Royal Canberra moved to the magnificent Westbourne Woods site at Yarralumla with Government House as its neighbour. Westbourne Woods had been developed in the early twentieth century as an arboretum for the Forestry School at Yarralumla. The argument from the environmentalists was that golfers would damage the arboretum. This did not stand up, particularly considering that as early as 1945 the Forestry and Timber Bureau had recommended Westbourne Woods be closed to further public access because of the likelihood of damage to trees and 'because the arboretum would flourish better if it was developed as a golf course'.[1]

Despite heavy clay soil on the site, a top-class course was developed, and it became one of the notable courses in Australia. The clubhouse was adequate but not outstanding and the essential egalitarian nature of the club persisted. Gordon Freeth, the Liberal member for the WA seat of Forrest and a senior minister in the Menzies, Holt and Gorton Governments, was a keen golfer at Royal Canberra. For a time, his government car driver was Rex Day, the champion of Royal Canberra. Frequently, Day would chauffeur Freeth in the

---

1   Royal Canberra Golf Club 1977, *Royal Canberra Golf Club Jubilee History 1926–1976*, The Club, Canberra, p. 37.

minister's Commonwealth car to the course, bets were laid and, after they played 18 holes, Rex Day usually took the money. Then there would be a few beers in the clubhouse and Day would don his driver's uniform and chauffeur the minister back to his office in Parliament House. With the possible exception of New Zealand, could one imagine this sort of relationship in any government of the Western world?

In the early years of Royal Canberra, prime ministers had a connection to the club. Just seven months after the Duke of York, in May 1927, opened the provisional Parliament House, Prime Minister, Stanley Bruce, drove the first ball to officially open the 18-hole course. George V granted use of the prefix 'Royal'. The privilege was never in doubt, with the application for royal title coming from the Prime Minister, Joe Lyons, President of the club in 1938 and 1939. Royal Canberra has been regarded by other clubs in the district as rather snooty about the royal prefix ever since. Billy Hughes was a keen golfer—described in the official history of the club as a 'golfer whose eccentricities on the golf course were as noticeable as others he displayed in the Prime Ministership and in other cabinet posts'.

The Royal Canberra's history also tells us that Hughes gained a reputation as an indefatigable searcher for a lost ball. Frank McKenna, former Deputy Secretary of the Prime Minister's Department, had a story of how one of Hughes' partners, tired of waiting and searching with him and having first one and then another group pass through them, dropped an almost new ball into a tussock and shouted: 'Here you are, Mr Hughes, here it is.' Billy examined the ball carefully, then replied: 'No, that's not it, brother.' He pocketed the ball and continued searching. I chaired a committee of members tasked with writing the history of Royal Canberra to mark its centenary in 1976. For a book written and designed by a committee, it turned out to be a worthwhile and handsome publication when published in 1977.

Jack Fingleton, a prominent journalist in the gallery, was a friend of my father's; the two had written for the long since defunct Sydney sporting paper *The Referee*, part of the Joynton Smith newspaper group, notably including *Smith's Weekly*. Jack opened the batting for Australia in the 1930s and worked as a journalist on the Sydney *Sun* and the *Sydney Morning Herald* from 1928 to 1942. In the gallery, he was correspondent for English, Indian and South African newspapers and the author of outstanding cricket books, including *Cricket* and *Brightly Fades the Don*. I met his closest friend, Bill (Tiger) O'Reilly, one of Australia's greatest bowlers and for many years a cricket correspondent for the *Sydney Morning Herald*, when Tiger occasionally came to Canberra to spend time with Jack. Covering test cricket for a number of papers was one of Jack's principal sources of revenue. As a consequence, he was frequently away from the gallery covering these matches.

I acted as backstop for him when he was away for the English-language Argus newspaper group in South Africa. Jack instructed me that the main stories of interest from Australia for the group were anything to do with sharks or Aborigines. Jack, like many Australians of his generation, would today be described as a racist and, like Menzies, he believed white rule must continue for many years in South Africa. Menzies cultivated Jack and wrote forewords for a number of his books. Menzies would frequently invite him for a drink and then ask technical questions about cricket, such as why such and such a batsman was frequently caught in the covers. Jack would give an explanation, later put by Menzies as his own expertise when discussing cricket with the great and famous or in the commentary box. Menzies was the first prime minister to put himself before voters as a keen follower of sports—something later followed by Bob Hawke, John Howard and Kevin Rudd. Only Hawke possessed any sporting prowess.

A letter Fingleton wrote to my father on his first trip to South Africa in 1931 with the Australian test team says a lot about the attitude of young men at the time. On the letterhead of the Royal Hotel Durban, dated 25 November, he wrote:

Dear Robert,

Come to Africa lad! A man of your genius would knock these niggers cold. What a country! What girls! Stand back there! Believe me, I have never seen such glorious looks & figures—& are we popular. At the moment I'm afraid I will have to send to Aussie for some men to help me through. Rushing like hell, son. All the best. Will write later. Drop me a line.

Yours Jack F.

When I arrived in the gallery, Jack was friendly to me, although he rarely asked after my father—nor did Bobby ask after his friend. I suspect the two might have fallen out over racism. My father had changed and was appalled by racism. He was a strong supporter of the campaign to end apartheid in South Africa and Jack was certainly not. I suspect they might have had a disagreement over this issue. As the letter makes clear, Jack as a young man was keen on girls, yet, following his marriage to Philippa, daughter of Laurence Street (later Sir Laurence, Chief Justice of New South Wales) and noted feminist and social worker, Jessie Street, he adopted a strict Catholic approach to his children. Young men attracted to his lovely daughter, Belinda, were rigorously vetted. Jack was very much opposed to communism and worried about its possible progress in South Africa. His social and political views were very much at odds with the decidedly leftish outlook of his mother-in-law, Jessie Street. She visited Moscow before the war and expressed pleasure that women in the Soviet Union had equality of work with men.

At the golf club, Jack objected when the 'f' word was sprayed around. Jack was by no means a wowser, but had what many would regard as an old-fashioned view of what constituted acceptable behaviour. He once told me that in reporting a major cricket match (I think at the Sydney Cricket Ground), he was shocked to see star batsman Doug Walters smoking as he came to the players' gate, pausing before going onto the ground to stamp out his cigarette. Jack was a splendid fielder and on one occasion a brown snake put his skills to the test at the Royal Canberra Golf Course. I was playing a round with Jack and we found a large brown snake sunning itself in the middle of the sixth green—conveniently, for the snake, close to the waters of Lake Burley Griffin. From about the distance of a cricket pitch, Jack began hurling clubs at the offender. He was way wide of the mark, but finally this attracted the attention of the snake and it departed.

Menzies began the tradition of a Prime Minister's XI playing a one-day cricket game against touring international teams at Manuka Oval. Menzies being filmed in the press box at Wimbledon or at a cricket test match discussing the game with commentators reinforced his reputation as a sports enthusiast, but he was not an achiever. Evatt, on the other hand, although not an outstanding athlete at the University of Sydney, was a keen team player—secretary of the university cricket club and chairman of inter-faculty football. In recognition of his services to sport, he was elected a Life Member of the University of Sydney Sports Union.[2] Yet unlike Menzies, Evatt hardly ever mentioned sport in his political career.

A much less grand ball than the King's Hall variety was the annual gallery ball at the Albert Hall, next door to the Hotel Canberra in Commonwealth Avenue. The ball was held in mid-winter, and the old hands knew the trick of putting newspapers on their windscreens, held on by the wipers, to keep the frost off. One of the annual balls in the early 1950s was a lively affair and finished with some drama. Ray Maley (*The Argus*, later Menzies' press secretary) and his number-two, Fred Coleman, got into an argument with the constabulary outside the Albert Hall. Fred was trying to calm it all down, yet could not shut Maley up. Ray asked a constable, 'Don't you know who I am?' They finished up in the police lock-up in Civic.

Unaware of these goings on, I got back from the ball to my room at the Hotel Civic, which was directly opposite the police station in Northbourne Avenue. In the middle of the night, I was woken, I think by John O'Hara, who was doing

---

2 Buckley, Ken, Dale, Barbara and Reynolds, Wayne 1994, *Doc Evatt: Patriot, internationalist, fighter and scholar*, Longman Cheshire, Melbourne.

a whip-around to raise the bail for Ray and Fred. Next morning, they fronted the magistrate, who happened to be none other than Frank Green, Clerk of the House, who filled in as a judge when necessary. Green was a great mate to the gallery and, whilst not reflecting on his magisterial independence, the gallery believed he must have decided that Ray and Fred's run-in with the coppers had already cost them several hours in the lock-up and they were let off with a severe lecture from the Bench.

Menzies' arrogance was on display in 1955 following the dramatic events arising from a claim by Charles Morgan, a Labor backbencher representing the seat of Reid (NSW), including Bankstown, of breach of privilege of Parliament. Morgan had been engaged in an ongoing dispute with Raymond Edward Fitzpatrick, a wealthy businessman, who, among other things, owned *The Bankstown Observer*, a small suburban paper. Morgan had been launching attacks on Fitzpatrick under parliamentary privilege and, to counter this advantage, Fitzpatrick hired Frank Courtney Browne, a Sydney freelance journalist who ran a somewhat scurrilous newsletter, *Things I Hear* (known in the gallery as *Things I Smear*). I had a passing acquaintance with Browne in the 1950s. He was a drinking mate of Don Whitington, and I joined them at times when in Sydney at the Newcastle Hotel, in George Street, close to Circular Quay—then a haunt for an arty Sydney crowd.

There was nothing arty about Browne. He was a boots-and-all style of journalist and just the man to do what Fitzpatrick admitted he wanted done: 'stop' Morgan's mouth. *Things I Hear* cast its net widely for material, often insulting and frequently amusing. Sir Francis Chichester made the first single-handed yachting voyage around the world, following the clipper route and, on arrival in Sydney—his only stop—he spent several weeks relaxing and repairing his yacht, *Gipsy Moth IV*. His wife flew out from England to join him during his stay. Browne reported that anyone who had met Lady Chichester 'could well understand Sir Francis's predilection for long, solitary ocean voyages'. Browne was not a member of the Australian Journalists' Association and therefore was not bound by its ethics code. Apart from Don and I, Browne had few friends in the gallery, and he had made many enemies on both sides of the Parliament. Clem Lloyd said of Browne, '[a]lthough his writings were often scabrous, Browne was a formidable pamphleteer, able to transfix an unfortunate victim with venom and invective'.[3] This made Browne the ideal victim for an unbridled and unjustified use of parliamentary power never before attempted at the federal level.

So vigorous was the Browne onslaught in *The Bankstown Observer* that Morgan claimed privilege in the house in 1955, claiming an attempt was being made to

3   Lloyd, C. J. 1988, *Parliament and the Press: The Federal Parliament Press Gallery 1901–88*, Melbourne University Press, Melbourne.

intimidate and silence him. The house referred his complaint to the Privileges Committee. In a star-chamber procedure, the committee met in private, denied legal representation to Fitzpatrick and Browne and submitted them to cross-examination. Fitzpatrick freely admitted the aim was to stop the attacks by Morgan in the Parliament. The committee found both guilty of a breach of privilege, yet advised the house to 'best consult its dignity' and let the matter drop. The house accepted the finding of the committee and the two were brought before the bar of the house to explain themselves.

I was in the house to witness and report on one of the most dramatic moments ever in the Australian Parliament. First Fitzpatrick and then Browne were called to the bar of the house on Friday, 10 June 1955. They came through the main door of the house from King's Hall accompanied by the Serjeant-at-Arms. At the entrance to the chamber itself there was a horizontal metal bar, placed across the end of the passageway, and they each in turn stood at this bar, directly facing the Speaker, Archie Cameron. The house was packed for this historic injustice. It is worth turning to Hansard to understand what happened:

Friday, 10 June, 1955

Mr. Speaker (Hon. Archie Cameron) took chair at 10 am. and read prayers.

NEWSPAPER ARTICLES.

Report of the Committee of Privileges.

Pursuant to the resolution passed by the House on the 9th June—That Raymond E. Fitzpatrick and Frank C. Browne be notified that at 10 a.m. tomorrow the House will hear them at the bar before proceeding to decide what action it will take in respect of their breaches of privilege.

The Serjeant-at-Arms having informed Mr. Speaker that Raymond Edward Fitzpatrick and Frank Courtney Browne were in attendance on the House.

Mr. Speaker: Inform Raymond Edward Fitzpatrick that the House will now hear him.

Mr. Raymond Edward Fitzpatrick having appeared at the bar of the House.

Mr. Speaker: Raymond Edward Fitzpatrick, the House has adjudged you guilty of a serious breach of privilege by publishing articles intended to influence and intimidate a member, the honorable member for Reid (Mr. Morgan), in his conduct in the House and in deliberately attempting to impute corrupt conduct as a member against the honorable member for

Reid for the express purpose of discrediting and silencing him. Have you anything to say in extenuation of your offence before the House determines what action it will take? You may now speak.

Mr. Fitzpatrick: I would like to apply for permission for Mr. Mason, my counsel, to act on my behalf.

Mr. Speaker: The resolution of the House entitles you to speak personally, not your counsel.

Dr. Evatt: Mr. Speaker...

Mr. Fitzpatrick: I would like to apologize to the House for what I did. When the article was published in the newspaper I had no idea that it was against parliamentary privilege. I humbly apologise.

Mr. Speaker: Have you anything further to say?

Mr. Fitzpatrick: No.

Mr. Speaker: Raymond Edward Fitzpatrick, you will withdraw from the chamber while the House deliberates.

Mr. Fitzpatrick having withdrawn.

Mr. Menzies: I suggest we hear the other person charged.

Mr. Speaker: Serjeant-at-Arms, inform Frank Courtney Browne that the House will now hear him.

Mr. Frank Courtney Browne having appeared at the bar of the House.

Mr. Speaker: Frank Courtney Browne, the House has adjudged you guilty of a serious breach of privilege by publishing articles intended to influence and intimidate a member, the honorable member for Reid, in his conduct in the House and in deliberately attempting to impute corrupt conduct as a member against the honorable member for Reid for the express purpose of discrediting and silencing him. Have you anything to say in extenuation of your offence before the House determines what action it will take? You may now speak.

Mr. Browne: Mr. Speaker and honorable members, I have something to say in extenuation and mitigation of my offences, but it must remain a slightly impersonal plea, because I have been convicted of an offence which, according to Australian justice, has not been fully proved. I base that on this: It is considered right...

Mr. Speaker: You will take your hands off the bar. [In his emotion, Browne had been gripping the bar. At this point and not recorded in Hansard, he took a step back, clicked his heels and gave the Nazi salute to Cameron. The Speaker was powerless to do anything about this calculated insult, other than visibly fume. Browne continued with even greater passion.]

Mr. Browne: It is considered the right of every Australian citizen charged with an offence that he, first, must be charged; and secondly, he must have legal representation. That is denied to me even here. He must have the case against him proved, and he need not answer incriminating questions. Then there is the fact that he must have the right to cross-examine his accuser. And lastly, he must have the right to appeal. There is also another inherent right, which is observed in every court in this Commonwealth, and every court where there is any reasonable conception of justice—that he shall present his case in an atmosphere which shall not have had the effect of prejudging him before he comes in.

Now, Mr. Speaker, let me ask you how what has happened to me this week squares up with that. First, I have been convicted and never charged. Secondly, at no time have I had legal representation. Thirdly, the case against me has not been properly proved. Fourthly, I have never had the right to cross-examine my accuser. And fifthly, I have no right to appeal. As far as the last is concerned, it is the inherent right for a man to have his case taken in an atmosphere that does not allow him to enter the court-room with the hatred, not only of spectators but of practically everyone in the court-room, including the jury, stirred up against him to a point where, if this was a community of another type, I doubt very much whether he would get into the court at all; he would be lynched on the way in.

I come to that last point. Last night, the right honorable the Prime Minister, the greatest orator in the history of this country—and you can put Alfred Deakin in, too—and, I suggest, one of the most vindictive men in the history of this country, rose and, in the way that only he can do, poured scorn on me. It has been done before; I know that, but never quite under these circumstances. In effect, last night he acted as a stage manager, and the purpose of his stage management was one thing and one thing only—'Bring Browne in here to grovel for mercy, and if he does not grovel for mercy, put him in for life'.

Sir, I am not asking for any rights for myself. I know very well that I have made personal enemies of members on both sides of this House in the course of doing what I believe to be right, no matter what other people think about it. There is no question about the attitude of the right honorable the Prime Minister, sir, towards me—none whatever. There is no question about the attitude of my erst-while great and good friend, the Right Honourable the Treasurer [Fadden], towards me. There is no question, sir, about the attitude of some of the members on the Opposition side of the House. I have been facetious at least about some of them; I have been more than facetious about some of them. But that is by the by.

I am not asking merely for myself. I am not standing here as Frank Browne. What happens to Frank Browne in this assembly does not matter very much. He is an obscure and inconspicuous figure in the community—not a newspaper Barron [sic], sir, not a man who can command a might[y] organ with which really to intimidate a member if he tried. No, I cannot do that. I produce an obscure suburban newspaper of four sheets of foolscap a week, so I am not a very big figure. You might say that I am a worker—a phrase that is frequently bandied about which I think I can be classed as. So that I am asking not for myself, sir, but for those who may follow me, that this House does not seek to impose very strict punishment, but that it will delegate my trial to a body, a legal tribunal, in which I will have my rights, and if I am then shown to be guilty—well, the hardest gaol in the land is too good for me. And there would be no appeal. I would not plead mitigation. I am prepared to take my chance under those circumstances. All I ask for is that the general public be shown, sir, that you do not bring people here to Canberra to deprive them of their rights, that the law-makers do not set themselves above the law, and do not place their good name better than that of the constituents they represent. Surely that is not too much to ask, sir.

I say that, if this Parliament establishes a precedent and takes the right of punishment into its own hands, the rights that have been fought for since 1215, and even before, are seriously endangered. You talk about intimidation, sir. You visit exemplary punishment—or, for that matter, the degree of punishment does not matter to me—and what happens? There will not be a journalist in the land, not a newspaper proprietor in the land, who will feel free, because once you establish a precedent you might say, 'Oh, yes, Browne did an awful thing.' But you will not wait for someone else to do an awful thing. You will get a border-line case and inevitably in a border-line case you get somebody who says, 'Throw him to the lions; crucify him,' and they crucify him. That has been the lesson of tyranny in every country. There is not a thing that Hitler did that he could not justify—not a thing. Read *Mein Kampf* and you will wonder how he ever went to war and, when he did go to war, how we could ever reconcile it with our consciences to fight.

The law of this country has ample provision for any punishment that I have earned. I ask that this House will not take a final step of inflicting punishment, because with any move in that direction, however tempered—if it consists of an apology—the principle has bone. Sir, it establishes the fact that here is not only a court, but a court which absolves itself of every idea that we have had inculcated into us on the score of natural justice when a person is charged with an offence—in fact, a court that is prepared to convict him without charging him. Even the Star Chamber, that body which is bandied around every time somebody wants to justify himself as a true blue democrat, did not go that far. I say this, and I say it quite sincerely—that what you do to me is of no moment, perhaps, in a physical sense to anybody but me—no moment whatever.

But you are exporting locomotives and other things to those countries that are struggling towards democracy in South-East Asia. If you export the locomotives and you neglect to export some of the elemental principles of justice which they know nothing about, well, it will all be in vain. Your Colombo plan will be nullified. Everything you give them they will misuse, including the rights of legislative bodies. Now, sir, I do appeal to you. It is not a question of the merits of the case, and it is not a question of the rights of the case. I know that you have unlimited rights. If I were tried for murder and convicted after due trial, I suppose I would look forward to being out in about fifteen years, if I were good. But, sir, I do not know what I can look forward to here. You may say, in effect, 'Put him away and shut him up', and what welcome news that would be to some of the members present!

Sir, if you fall back on your rights—and your rights are 300-year old rights—to deal with me here, you will have forfeited any right—not you personally, but every member here—to stand at next election time on the stump and sing hymns about liberty, equality and fraternity.

Mr. Speaker: Have you concluded?

Mr. Browne: Yes.

Mr. Speaker: Frank Courtney Browne, you will withdraw from the chamber while the House deliberates.

Mr. Browne having withdrawn.

Mr. Menzies: Mr Speaker, I propose that, these addresses having been made to us, you suspend the sitting for half an hour so that we may take them into account.

Sitting suspended from 10.19 to 11.10 a.m.

When the sitting resumed, Menzies told the house that Browne had shown unparalleled arrogance in his appearance before the bar and exhibited his contempt for the Parliament. Menzies, instead of following the advice of the Privileges Committee that the house should 'consult its own dignity', insisted on severe punishment and moved the motion for a three-month jail term.

Evatt, as Opposition Leader, was put in a difficult position. Browne and Fitzpatrick were in deep trouble because of the actions of a Labor MP. Caucus decided on a free vote for Labor MPs. Evatt moved, unsuccessfully, that instead of a jail sentence the offenders should be fined. It was decided the Parliament did not have power to do this, only to impose a jail term.

Evatt told the house the procedure was improper, the offenders did not face any specific charge, they had no right of appeal and their guilt had become an accomplished fact in their absence. All this after Frank Green, Clerk of the House, had told Menzies there was no breach of privilege. Menzies would have none of this and insisted on the severe punishment of jail. Evatt had no sympathy for the miscreants but, in his judicial way, regretted the Parliament had not drawn up its own procedures for dealing with privilege and instead had simply accepted the House of Commons process. Evatt said the house had to refer to the 'musty precedents of another country'.

The house voted overwhelmingly for Menzies' motion—55 to 12 in the case of Fitzpatrick and 55 to 11 in the case of Browne. Many Labor and Liberal voters abstained from the vote. Whitlam surprised the gallery by voting for imprisonment—a forgotten piece in the history of the former Labor Prime Minister. Of the three men steeped in the law and regard for British common law, it was Evatt who shone through while Menzies and Whitlam voted for injustice. Morgan, whose complaint led to this travesty of justice, was the last speaker against the Menzies motion and suggested Browne and Fitzpatrick not be imprisoned, but released on payment of money and meeting certain conditions. He abstained from voting when the question was put.

Lawyers immediately applied to the ACT Supreme Court for *habeas corpus* to allow the two to be freed from custody from the police lock-up in Civic, but as so often happens with cases involving the behaviour and proceedings of Parliament, the court refused to tell the Parliament what to do and the appeals of the lawyers were turned down. Media and public reaction to the jailing of Browne and Fitzpatrick were mixed. *The Age*, then owned by the Syme family, published a grovelling editorial.

As the Prime Minister has pointed out, it was not simply a question of whether a Member of Parliament had been defamed. Attacks had been made on a member in an attempt to prevent him from carrying out his duty to his constituents. The Government had acted promptly to safeguard its institutions and its principles. On the other hand, the *Sydney Morning Herald*, in an angry comment, said:

> Two men were ordered to be imprisoned for three months in Canberra yesterday. They were convicted and sentenced without trial, in the ordinary sense of the word, without being allowed representation by counsel and finally, so far as the House of Representatives was concerned, without the right of appeal…And it has risked a strong public feeling that no citizens, of this free country, whatever their misdemeanours, should be gaoled except by due process of the law and the Courts.

Eric Baume, dashing journalist and broadcaster and my first editor on the *Mirror*, did not wait to pick up the public mood on the Browne–Fitzpatrick case. The day after their sentencing, in his *This I Believe* commentary for radio 2GB Sydney, Baume ripped into the Parliament, in language itself risking a charge of breach of privilege. Baume was an independent and gutsy character. Well-known journalist Valerie Lawson, in her entry on Baume in *The Australian Dictionary of Biography*, records that in 1938 Baume, in a 2GB commentary, was critical of Nazi Germany. This led to a complaint from the German Consul-General and the disgraceful removal of Baume from the air.

It is almost unbelievable a parliament would have the audacity to jail a journalist for attacking a politician. In the aftermath, Menzies agreed to bring at least a sense of fair play to citizens required to front the Committee of Privilege by, for example, allowing anyone accused to have the right to a lawyer to defend them. Nothing ever came of this. No such outrage has occurred since and it is unlikely (but not impossible) to be repeated in the future, and the powers of the Parliament to mistreatment of citizens remain untouched.

Richard Woolcott was appointed in 1964 by one of Canberra's top mandarins, head of the then Department of External Affairs, Sir Arthur Tange, as the department's first public information officer. Woolcott was personable, above average height, dark and handsome. Dick, as everyone knew him, was an authority in the field of foreign policy, a lucid and able communicator; he soon became a valuable source for the gallery. Prior to his appointment, less senior officers were cautiously allowed to give some basic background about issues to gallery journalists. Woolcott, however, was given a remarkably free hand to 'background' the gallery on issues. 'Background', in journalistic parlance, means material that can be used in a story, but not attributed; 'off the record' is material not be used at all; and 'on the record' is material that can be directly attributed to an informer. Journalists should generally shun accepting 'off the record' material. If they later come by the material from another source or research, the original provider might claim a breech of journalistic ethics. The aim is to get usable material.

There was, however, plenty of even more interesting material in Parliament House relating to indiscretions by prominent parliamentarians—affairs, drunken escapades and the like—some of which was usable and much that was not.

7. Booze, Sex and God

Booze, sex and power suffused the old parliamentary building and they could be sensed particularly in the non-members' bar. The entrace to the non-members' bar was on the ground floor at the rear of the building, on one side of the two large courtyards, each dominated by a huge poplar tree dating back to the 1920s, planted during construction of the building. The non-members' bar was the social centre for all who worked in the place, including the parliamentarians. They had their own bar, but often preferred the company available—particularly female—in the non-members' bar. When the Parliament was sitting, the non-members' bar was a busy meeting spot in the evening, right up to one hour after the house or the Senate rose—generally about 10.30 or 11 pm.

When the bar closed, drinkers drifted off to various offices and drinking spots around the building. Like most licensed establishments throughout Australia at the time, here, ladies did not enter the bar. Off the non-members' bar, a small room for ladies was served via a hatch from the bar. Here there were at least as many male drinkers as there were females. Some years later, the ladies' 'brown room', as it was called, was shut and ladies came into the bar. The extra space was used to expand the non-members' bar, which, although still crowded, was a little more comfortable. It was a place for gossip, tips and assignations, as well as for excessive drinking. The gallery, until the old building was vacated, was a very boozy establishment.

Excessive drinking made one of the annual gallery dinners, addressed by the Governor-General, Sir William Slim, a lively affair. The great British general of World War II and hero of the Burma campaign was the guest of the gallery at the Hotel Canberra. He succeeded at Yarralumla Sir William McKell, a former NSW Labor premier, appointed by Chifley. The dinner was in a private room and Slim sat at the head table with the gallery office-holders, including the treasurer, Les (Lapper) Love.

Despite his aversion to Tooheys beer (the brew served in the hotel), Les managed to sink a fair quantity of it in the pre-dinner drinks session and, by the time Slim spoke, Les was asleep. Slim's address was gripping, as he outlined the horrors of the Burma campaign, with the Allied forces up to their armpits in 'Japs', snakes and mosquito-infested swamps. Les suddenly awoke and declared to the dinner his trade mark 'LAPPY DAYS'. Whereupon a bristling Slim turned to him and, through gritted teeth, said in measured tones: 'You wouldn't have thought it happy days if you had been there [pause] *son.*' Quite properly, the diners refrained from roaring with laughter. Les was too far gone to be embarrassed. Slim soon got over the incident and we all had a wonderful night.

Before we left the private dining room for another room for the post-dinner drinks (the serious part of the evening), Les had passed out again. Someone had draped him over one of the hotel's antique couches when we left. After an hour or so, I thought it best to check on Les and returned to the dining room. He was still passed out on the couch, but must have revived at some stage and lit a cigarette. Passing out again, his lighted cigarette had fallen from his hand, burning a large hole in the couch. I carefully placed a serviette over the hole, moved Les onto another couch and, rather to my shame, left him.

The shine was somewhat taken off the luminous career of Sir William in 2007 when David Hill, a former general manager of the ABC, authored *The Forgotten Children*,[1] based on his experiences as a Fairbridge kid transported to Australia. He raised allegations against Slim in a newspaper interview about his book. Later, Robert Stephens, a former orphan committed to the Fairbridge Farm School at Molong, in an interview with *The Australian*, made specific allegations against Slim. In brief, he claimed that when Slim paid a visit to the school Stephens was required to sit on Slim's lap in the back seat of the official car. The British war hero, Stephens said, slid his hand up the inside of his shorts and fondled his bottom. The Fairbridge Foundation Council Chairman, John Kennedy, said the council would consider whether Fairbridge should accept responsibility for sexual abuse of the boys, but nothing more was heard of it. When Sir William's term as Governor-General ended in 1959, he returned to Britain, elevated to the peerage as a viscount and appointed Chairman of the London Fairbridge Society.

There were few teetotallers in the Old Parliament House. Menzies certainly enjoyed a drink and could carry his liquor well, but on one occasion in the house, he appeared affected by alcohol. Menzies had generated much heat in 1951 proposing legislation to ban the Communist Party of Australia, and initially the Labor Party blocked it in the Senate. The legislation gave the Government power to 'declare' a person, or an organisation, 'communist' and a person so declared was barred from any employment by the Commonwealth, or with a trade union. In the house in that year, Menzies had a heated run-in with the colourful Labor MP from Sydney Eddie Ward. Menzies was speaking of a measure to amend the double-dissolution provisions of the Constitution, particularly when the Senate could have equal numbers on either side, and Menzies asked rhetorically, 'What would happen then?' Then came the following exchange:

> Ward: 'The right honourable gentleman could declare a couple of the Labor Senators.'

> Menzies: 'I am obliged to the Honourable Member for the suggestion, I could think of at least one Labor Senator whom it would be easy to declare.'

---

1   Hill, David 2007, *The Forgotten Children*, Random House, Sydney.

Ward: 'The fuehrer has spoken.'

Menzies: 'I can think of one member of this House [obviously Ward] who might escape only by the skin of his teeth.'

Chifley (Leader of the Opposition): 'The Right Honourable Member [Menzies] is on dangerous ground.'

Menzies: 'I agree, on dangerous ground. I suggest to the Right Honourable gentlemen that he might restrain his interjectors; that of course, the problem does not arise because—'

Chifley (cutting in): 'I suggest that the Right Honourable gentleman should not make threats.'

Menzies: 'I never make a threat that I do not carry out.'

Ward: 'The Right Honourable gentleman is drunk with power.'

This exchange greatly upset Chifley, who later said that Menzies had shown what was in his mind before he had time to put a 'curb on his tongue'. A. W. Martin, Menzies' biographer, said that the journalist Ian Fitchett, who was in the press gallery that evening, believed Menzies was slightly affected in his behaviour by drink—an occurrence Fitchett had never seen before.

One of the more spectacular drunken performances of the 1960s was in the Senate chamber, when Labor Senator from Western Australia Harry Cant found himself seriously drunk and trapped by a division. The doors were locked and the division required Labor senators to cross to the other side of the chamber, sitting in the places of the government senators for the count, while the government senator moved to the opposition benches. Cant was overcome by an urgent need to vomit. Looking around desperately, he came to a decision. Opening the desk drawer of the government senator's desk where he was seated, he was violently and noisily sick into it.

When the division was over and the senators resumed their normal places, the government senator in whose place Harry had sat was understandably disgusted. The stench created by this extraordinary happening filled the chamber. He did not draw the President of the Senate's attention to the outrage or make a fuss. Urgent action was required. All this had taken place in the full view of the journalists in the Senate press gallery and those in the public gallery. News of the outrage was soon all over Parliament House and journalists rushed to get the story. Medical practitioner Dr Felix Dittmer, a Queensland Labor Senator, had the answer. He denied Cant was drunk and ordered that an ambulance be urgently called to take Cant to the Royal Canberra Hospital, just across Commonwealth Avenue Bridge in Acton. Dittmer stated that Cant was suffering from an acute case of 'renal colic'.

The ambulance arrived and a Labor colleague suggested to Dittmer that it would be discreet for Harry, now prone on a stretcher, to be taken through the back exit of Parliament via the kitchen. Labor Deputy Senate Leader, Pat Kennelly, rejected this. So the little procession of the two ambulance officers carrying the stretcher with Cant prone, and Dittmer leading, made its way through the Senate opposition lobby, across King's Hall where visitors gaped, and down the front steps to the waiting ambulance. In hospital, Cant made a speedy recovery and was discharged the next day. From then on, if an MP entered either the house or the Senate looking a little confused, the interjection would go out: 'Renal colic.'

Gough Whitlam was involved in a lively incident on the floor of the house after one dinner break. Whitlam was sitting in the Opposition Leader's chair when Jim Forbes, a Cabinet minister, came into the house apparently the worse for wear. After some disparaging remarks from the opposition side, someone on the government side suggested Forbes was suffering from 'a bad back'. Whitlam responded, 'It's what he's put in his guts that's rooted him.' After this incident, if someone came into the chamber looking somewhat tired and emotional, there was a new interjection to add to 'renal colic': 'bad back.' The 'bad back' incident did not damage Forbes' reputation and, in later years, he was elected Federal President of the Liberal Party. A graduate of the Royal Military College at Duntroon, Forbes served with the 2nd Australian Mountain Battery in Bougainville, and was awarded the Military Cross in 1945.

Because so many MPs could be vulnerable, both sides of politics avoided attempting to make political capital from the boozing habits of MPs. If, however, alcohol is seen as affecting someone's public life, they are open to attack. Given the pressures of parliamentary life and the entertainment offered MPs (particularly since the move to the permanent Parliament House), the behaviour of parliamentarians is generally commendable. No doubt many do get drunk, but they do not make a spectacle of themselves within the Parliament.

On matters of sex, the Australian Parliament has always been broad minded, as has the Australian population, certainly post war. Sexual encounters and adulterous affairs have been well known and common in the Parliament; it is said that powerful men have strong sexual urges and many women like powerful men.

At the 1961 election, Calwell went within one seat of winning government and Menzies was saved only when Jim Killen scraped by in the Brisbane seat of

Moreton, courtesy of the donkey vote that directed communist preferences to him. Killen, a great practical joker, invented the story that Menzies had telegrammed him, declaring, 'Killen, you are magnificent'. No such telegram existed and Menzies issued no denials. Despite his magnificence, Killen had to wait until 1969 to enter the ministry, when Gorton made him Navy Minister. Killen was one of the most-liked characters in the Parliament and had many mates in the gallery, including my partner, Don Whitington, who took every opportunity to boost him in *Inside Canberra*. Killen was at his very core a parliamentarian. Immaculately dressed at all times, with a neat RAAF moustache (like his great friend Gough Whitlam, he served in the Air Force during the war) and invariably with a red-carnation boutonniere.

A ferocious anti-communist, Killen paraded himself as a hard-right politician. For example, he defended apartheid, but Killen gave me the impression this was all a bit of an act. It was the popular thing to do in the Menzies era so Jim did it. His greatest mates were both on the Labor side: Gough Whitlam and Fred Daly. In advance of the 1972 election, noted English commentator and TV star David Frost came to Australia and interviewed, separately, Whitlam and Prime Minister, William McMahon. Frost's standard entry to an interview was to put a quick, unexpected first question. He asked Whitlam what did he consider was McMahon's best attribute. Without hesitation, Whitlam replied, truthfully, 'his persistence'. Frost asked McMahon had he ever told a lie. McMahon replied, in that strange quavery voice: 'I have never, ever told a lie'—an answer arousing mirth around Parliament House.

Killen frequently passed notes, via an attendant, to Whitlam in the house. The note passing aroused great suspicion with McMahon, who had dumped Killen from the ministry when he replaced Gorton. When Parliament next met after Frost's interview with McMahon, Killen, in the chamber, sent a note over to Whitlam, reading: 'Evensong will be at 6 pm to celebrate the end of Diogenes' search.' (Diogenes was the ancient Greek whom legend says wandered around Greece in daylight carrying a lantern and searching for an honest man.)

In the 1970 half-senate election, Syd Negus, an independent, was elected to represent Western Australia. He was an example of the occasional quirks of the Senate voting system and there was no reason he should have been elected. He campaigned for election on the basis of opposition to death duties, yet while the States had death duties, the Commonwealth did not. Negus devoted his maiden speech in the Senate to this issue. Killen phoned Negus to tell him what a great speech he had made and suggested it was so worthwhile he should also deliver it in the House of Representatives. Asked how this could be done, Killen said if he contacted the Government Whip in the House and slipped him a fiver it could be done. Negus thought this a great idea and off he went.

The reaction of the Whip is unknown. Gil Duthie held the Tasmanian seat of Wilmot for Labor from 1946 to 1975. Smallish and likeable, Duthie was a natty dresser. Killen phoned him, adopting a fruity English voice and introduced himself as the editor of the English magazine *The Tailor and Cutter*. He explained he would be visiting Australia and was anxious to interview Duthie because of the Tasmanian's reputation for stylish clothes. Gil was most flattered, appointments were made, but somehow, despite many apologies for missed appointments from the editor of *The Tailor and Cutter*, the interview failed to take place.

Killen made it to Cabinet rank as Minister for Defence in the Fraser Government where he adopted a very stiff-upper-lip, Westminster style of administration of the portfolio—quite out of keeping with his real character. When senate estimates committees sought to interview senior people in the military and the Defence Department, Killen instructed them not to attend. He told the committee he was minister and he was responsible to Parliament, which was true. The members of the armed forces and the bureaucrats in the department, according to Killen, were responsible to him as minister, not to the Parliament. His position was untenable and looked like a cover-up. Ministers in the House of Representatives simply did not go before senate committees to be questioned and since he could not go before estimates committees he finally had to agree that members of the military and the department could.

In 1976 Killen ran into serious trouble and, although I was not in any way involved in the hurt he suffered, I was under deep suspicion. *Nation Review*, a leftish, highly entertaining publication based in Melbourne, described itself as 'nosy like a ferret'. The 22–28 October issue featured a front-page bold headline: 'The Romantic Ministers.' Inside, Mungo MacCallum's story began:

> Before Tuesday there had been exactly three veiled references to what has been the most publicly discussed association in Canberra this year: that between the Defence Minister, Jim Killen, and the Social Security Minister, Margaret Guilfoyle. The first was a line which appeared in the Brisbane *Courier-Mail*, the day after Guilfoyle was elevated from the outer ministry to the Cabinet and quoted by Monty Molonglo the following week: it said that Guilfoyle would assume the 12th position in Cabinet, directly under Killen. The second reference came in the newsletter *Inside Canberra,* which stated that people were talking about 'the regular juxtaposition of bedrooms occupied by leading members of the government parties' at a Canberra hotel. The hotel at that stage was the Canberra Rex.

MacCallum, noting the third reference, in *The National Times*, claimed the Prime Minister, Malcolm Fraser, was concerned about the personal behaviour of members of his party, and that a minister had been asking members of the press gallery about the likelihood of stories getting into print. Soon after, Killen cut me in the government lobby. I had been on friendly terms with him because of my association with one of his best friends, Don Whitington. Then the penny dropped; he thought I was responsible for the reference in *Inside Canberra*. Killen would assume it could not have been written by Don, yet it was. Whitington, like most of us in the gallery, was addicted to gossip and he liked to spice up *Inside Canberra* whenever he could. To my great sadness and that of his second wife, Helen, and his many friends, Don passed away the next year. I decided then to clear the air with Killen. It could not hurt Don now. I sought him out and told him if he blamed me as being the author of the hurtful *Inside Canberra* item, he was wrong; Don wrote it. He accepted this and our good relations resumed.

The alleged association between Killen and Guilfoyle strained relations between Killen and his good friend Gough Whitlam. As MacCallum reported, Bert James, Labor's muck-thrower, asked Fraser a question in the house as to whether the Prime Minister was concerned about the 'personal behaviour of certain ministers' that could impair national security. Fraser dismissed it in a sentence: 'I think the honorable gentleman has deserved his own condemnation.' As MacCallum said, visibly shaken, Killen sent a note across the chamber to Whitlam, saying it was the roughest thing he had ever heard in Parliament. Whitlam sent a note back saying it had nothing to do with him and it was Bert James's exercise, not Labor's. Killen accepted this and remained until his death in 2007 a close friend of Whitlam's.

James's question was not considered very remarkable in the gallery, or around Parliament House. Backbenchers could, within limits, ask what they liked. It would be inconceivable today, however, for any backbencher of the major parties to ask such a question without clearance from his party leader. I do not believe Don or anyone else should have raised the Killen–Guilfoyle affair. In Australian journalism, the general rule is that the sexual affairs of politicians and public figures are not raised, unless it can be claimed this impinges on the duty and responsibility of someone in public office. There was nothing in the affair between two ministers endangering the national interest. The other practical point is that both sides of the Parliament know among their numbers there are, or could be, MPs engaged in affairs. An open slanging match would help neither side nor the national interest.

The media and the Labor Party focused on Prime Minister Gorton's encounter with a young woman, Geraldine Willesee, because it could have involved the national interest. There was a covert suggestion of a sexual element when Gorton impulsively took her to a late-night meeting at the American Embassy. Sex was not the point of the attack on him—coming as it did from both the Labor Party and his own side of politics, particularly from Edward St John QC, a brilliant Sydney barrister. Rather it was Gorton's lack of judgment.

The bombshell sex story of the Whitlam Government was the affair involving the Deputy Prime Minister, Dr Jim Cairns, and Junie Morosi. It led to questions in the Parliament only when Cairns appointed Morosi chief of staff in his office. Again, it could have involved questions of the national interest.

Don Chipp was elected to the Victorian seat of Higginbotham in 1960, then moved to Hotham and retired from the house in 1977. Having founded the Australian Democrats in that year, he then entered the Senate in 1978 as leader of that party and retired in 1986. Chipp was not always the middle-of-the-road, fair-minded politician he liked to portray himself as. As Navy Minister, he took a very tough line against the Liberals in the party room, including St John, who pushed for, and got, a second royal commission into the *Voyager* disaster. St John's maiden speech was devoted to the case for a second royal commission. Chipp joined with Prime Minister, Harold Holt, in interjecting during the speech—a serious departure from accepted behaviour in a maiden speech.

Minister for Customs and Excise in the Gorton ministry after the 1969 election, Chipp presented himself as the small-'l' liberal who believed in loosening up strict rules relating to the behaviour and rights of citizens. He made a name for himself by removing the ban on the sale of various books, such as *Portnoy's Complaint*. Yet, to show that he was a man of family values who would not tolerate pornography, he ordered customs to crack down on imported porn. Further, to emphasise his relentless pursuit of porn, he had pornographic books and magazines seized by customs available in his office so that MPs could see for themselves what a grand job he was doing. Male MPs from both sides of politics visited his office regularly to view the porn, particularly the graphic pictorial material—of course just to be informed of the great job the minister was doing.

His private secretary at the time was a young customs officer, Trevor Wright, a friend of mine. The seized porn, sent across to Chipp's office from customs, was the responsibility of Trevor and, if an MP desired to view the disgusting material, it was produced from Trevor's desk drawer. He noted that many MPs, some of whom portrayed themselves as high-minded adherents of the Christian faith, appeared regularly seeking to view the latest porn. Chipp also arranged showings of pornographic films seized by customs in its tireless efforts to save the population from exposure to lewd and degrading material. These films were shown over the dinner adjournments at the theatrette of the National Library— close to Parliament House. The showings were free—naturally attracting many with a close interest in the work of customs.

'God bless America' has long been invoked at the conclusion of important speeches in the United States. In recent decades, with the rise of the Christian right, there is much call on the Almighty to go further to assist in the defeat of enemies of the United States. US President George W. Bush, who gave up the bottle and found God, regularly asked for divine intervention to assist in the contest against Muslims in Iraq. In the Federal Parliament, each day's sittings begin with a prayer by the Speaker and Senate President to the Lord 'to direct and prosper our deliberations for the true welfare of the people of Australia'. The Lord's Prayer is then read.

In October 2008, media reports suggested the Labor Speaker, Harry Jenkins, advocated scrapping this practice. Issuing a 'clarification' statement, Jenkins said his comments were in relation to an interview of procedure and he mentioned he received a wide range of opinions about the prayer, including the appropriateness of using the 1901 Church of England version of the prayer and whether it should be updated 'to the relevance of the prayer in modern Australia'. Predictably, Kevin Rudd and Malcolm Turnbull immediately declared they opposed scrapping the prayer.

Yet many people would believe no prayer is needed, from whatever faith. When the Federal Parliament first met after Federation, no prayer was offered. This led to a storm of protest from various Christian evangelical organisations, the Parliament gave way to the pressure and the prayer became part of proceedings. Gregor McGregor, leader of the Labor Party in the first Senate, protested that the prayer was a breach of the Constitution. He had a good argument. Section 116 of the Constitution states: 'The Commonwealth shall not make any law for establishing any religion, or for imposing any religious observance, or for prohibiting the free exercise of any religion and no religious test has to be required as a qualification for any office or public trust under the Commonwealth.'

The Constitution does make concessions to the Almighty. The Preamble refers to the parties to the Constitution, having agreed to unite, 'humbly relying on the blessing of Almighty God'. The oath of office requires those coming to office to swear to be 'faithful and bear true allegiance to Her/His Majesty...[insert name of current monarch], Her/His heirs and successors according to law. So help me God.' The Constitution sets out an alternative affirmation—a concession to atheists and others—asking for those swearing an oath to be loyal to the monarch and so on, but deleting 'So help me God'.

Devout Catholic Brian Harradine, the former independent senator, objected in the Senate to other senators reciting the prayer when it was being read by the President of the Senate. 'We are not in church,' he noted. Harradine protested that the Senate's Standing Orders stated the President and nobody else would say the prayer. When the President began reading the prayer, in a clear protest, Senator Peter Baume would don his *yarmulke* (a skullcap) and recite a Jewish prayer.

Apart from that, Australian politicians are not given much to calling on the Lord to assist. In postwar Australia, voters have been quite happy to install prime ministers who were not at all religious, or at least were not seen to be enthusiastic Christians to the point of regular attendance at church. Ben Chifley was a lapsed Catholic, Bob Hawke an agnostic and Whitlam an unashamed atheist. Unlike Kevin Rudd, Menzies, Holt, Gorton, McMahon, Fraser and Howard were not at church every Sunday.

8. Evatt, Splits and Garters

I had a lot of contact with Herbert Vere Evatt when he was elected Labor Party leader after the death of Ben Chifley in 1951. Evatt was by no means a close friend of Chifley. Among other things, Evatt, when he stood down from the High Court, had attempted to take over Chifley's seat of Macquarie in 1940, but in the end he had to settle for the Sydney seat of Barton, in the south-western suburbs. David Day, in his *Chifley—The biography of J. B. Chifley*, said that Evatt, after appearing unsuccessfully before the High Court to fight off challenges to Chifley's legislation to privatise the banks, said that the legislation was so bad that it was indefensible. A mythology has arisen that Evatt was some sort of bumbling, half-silly figure, probably arising from his premature senility towards the end of his career. Nevertheless, he was an outstanding Australian, possessed of a powerful intellect, an outstanding lawyer, High Court judge, Attorney-General and Minister for External Affairs. As leader of the Australian delegation to the founding meeting of the United Nations, in San Francisco in 1945, he became the champion of small powers. Partly because of Evatt's work, after three months of political struggle, the Charter of the United Nations became a more humane document and larger in scope, containing provisions for the poor, the weak and the oppressed.[1]

In 1948, Evatt was elected President of the General Assembly of the United Nations. With his wife, Mary Alice, 'the Doc' was a notable patron of the arts, and gave encouragement to struggling young Australian artists including Russell Drysdale and Sidney Nolan. The Evatts purchased many artists' paintings and drawings and donated them to art galleries and local councils around Australia.[2] Despite his powerful intellect, Evatt lacked the experience, political cunning and ability to bend to handle the disaster of the Labor split in the 1950s.

Reporting Evatt's speeches in the house was difficult. His years at the Bar and on the Bench had left him with a habit of failing to finish each sentence. Lawyers often get halfway through a sentence to make some point and then (as if in parentheses) mention a precedent they assume the judges will know. (For example, 'My Lords, the defendant does not have to, at this point prove his identity—*Williams v the Crown 1921*'). This approach did not work well in a political speech. It was not a great problem for Hansard because Evatt (or his staff) would make clear what he meant when they corrected the Hansard Green, the transcript of what Hansard had recorded. It is called the Green because of its colour (green in the House, pink in the Senate), and was sent to MPs for correction some half-hour or so after they had finished speaking. They could

---

1   The Evatt Foundation, University of Sydney, NSW.
2   Ibid.

not, however, change the sense of what Hansard had recorded. For example, if an MP said he knew something of such and such, he could not use the Green to say he knew nothing of such and such. Over the years, there have been some hectic debates about MPs attempting to doctor Hansard in various ways.

Menzies dramatically announced to the house the defection of Vladimir Petrov, an officer of the Russian Ministry of Internal Affairs (or MVD) from the Soviet Embassy on 13 April 1954. Evatt was absent at an old boys' dinner of his school, Fort Street High, in Sydney. This was on the eve of an election and ended any chance of Evatt being elected Prime Minister. The fact Evatt was not informed in advance of Menzies' proposed announcement that night became a major political issue in the weeks that followed. Worse still, Fergan O'Sullivan, then Evatt's press secretary, confessed to the Labor leader five days after the 1954 election that he was the author of a document, 'H', written to inform Russian journalists and agents about the personalities, foibles and political leanings of gallery journalists. In the gallery, we were staggered by this news. O'Sullivan was a popular figure and nobody could have conceived that he could be so naive as to have so endangered his reputation.

Much worse was to come for Evatt. When he debated the Petrov Royal Commission's report in the House of Representatives, Evatt said that he had written to the Foreign Minister of the Soviet Union, Viacheslav Molotov, to ascertain whether certain Russian-language documents in Petrov's possession were genuine or forgeries, and Molotov replied that they were forgeries—'[f]abricated on the instructions of persons interested in the deterioration of the Soviet–Australian relations and discrediting their political opponents'. Evatt declared: 'I attach great importance to this letter.' The members of Caucus could hardly believe this astounding misjudgment by Evatt of relying on the word of the Soviet Foreign Minister. I was in the house that night reporting his speech and, when Evatt made this assertion, the faces of those sitting behind him spoke volumes of the disaster that had overtaken the Opposition and the Labor leader.

In the early hours of 21 November 1954, on the adjournment debate, an extraordinary event occurred in the house. It illustrated the depth of the split in the ALP. Labor MPs from Victoria, who were later to form the Democratic Labor Party (DLP), were still sitting on the opposition benches. The drama involved Victorian Jack Mullens, a fierce anti-communist, a brilliant speaker and Labor veteran, and frontbencher Reg Pollard, a minister in the Curtin and Chifley Governments. On the stroke of midnight, Mullens rose to deliver a withering attack on Australian journalists Wilfred Burchett and Frank Hardy. Hardy was later to write the classic *Power Without Glory*, about the infamous John Wren, who built a fortune on an illegal 'tote' in Melbourne by bribing the police and politicians. The following edited extract from Hansard illustrates the depth of bitterness engendered by the split:

Mr. Mullens (Gellibrand) (12 midnight): At question time today I endeavoured to direct attention to the activities of two Australian 'Haw Haws' who, in my view, are traitors to our people and to the policies that we should uphold. I refer to Wilfred Burchett, who is correspondent in Korea for the Melbourne *Guardian* and ostensibly correspondent for the Paris newspaper *Le Soir*. He exceeds the bounds of liberty in his radio propaganda in which he directs his shafts persistently and tenaciously, but I hope ineffectively, against our Australian boys and our American allies who are fighting in Korea. The second man to whom I refer is the famous, or infamous, Frank J. Hardy, who is now stationed in Moscow. He is a salacious slanderer and smear merchant who is now in an environment that befits him. He is the Moscow correspondent of *The New Times*. I shall give some typical examples of the propaganda that is disseminated by these gentlemen. Burchett has written in a despatch from Korea—'If the people of the world strongly enough demand it, U.S. war-mongers can be forced to agree to an armistice...The war-mongers' dream of an easy victory in Korea have [sic] been finally shattered.'

Hardy contributed the following passage to *The New Times*:

'Before the beginning of this century, our people were fighting the dead hand of British Imperialism. Just when victory seemed to be within their grasp along came decadent, bloodthirsty American Imperialism.'

And later, Mullens said:

I am amazed at the colossal unawareness of the Government and its almost complete indifference to the propaganda which, while it is not always as obvious as is that which is disseminated by these buccaneers, is nevertheless, tenacious and designed subtly to condition the Australian community to a breaking of its morale in order to pave the way for the entry of these self-styled commissars. It is time that the Government did something about such propaganda. There is a tone abroad in this community that is derogatory to our ally, the United States of America. It emanates from the likes of these leeches upon the body politic who were most anxious that American boys should defend Australia. Now, the smear campaign is called for. In their eyes, every beauty lies in Russian imperialism and the United States of America is the home of warmongers. By implication, Australians, too, are warmongers. Today, these gentlemen are pro-Russian, pro-Egyptian, pro-Persian and pro-everything but pro-Australian. It is the duty of an enlightened government to do something about this matter. We have our own destiny to forge. I declare emphatically that I stand for the God of my fathers and the destiny of my children. Come rack or ruin, I shall never bend my head to any storm of this nature. I invite the Government to say unequivocally whether it intends to keep these traitors out of Australia; and, if not, whether it intends to deal with them effectively when they return to this country. No specious plea of liberty on the part of the Government will satisfy me in this matter. It is the bounden duty of the Australian community to defend itself if not in our own interests, at least in the interests of generations to come. I do not hesitate to make this plea as a good Labor man.

Mr. Pollard (Lalor) (12.26 a.m.): I do not claim to be as good as, or a better Laborite than, the honorable member for Footscray.

Mr. Speaker: Order! There is no member for such an electorate in this House.

Mr. Pollard: I meant the honorable member for Gellibrand Mr. Mullens. I take this opportunity to dissociate myself from what appears to have been a request to the Government and to this Parliament—

Mr. Mullens: The honorable member is defending the 'Coms'.

Mr. Pollard: I am not.

Mr. Speaker: Order! I ask the honorable member for Lalor to address me.

Mr. Mullens: They are two 'Coms', and the honorable member defends them.

Mr. Pollard: Obviously the honorable member for Gellibrand is just as competent at making false accusations—

Mr. Speaker: Order!

Mr. Pollard: Against a member of this Parliament, in the House, as he is to take advantage of parliamentary privilege to attack men who are outside it.

Mr. Mullens: Oh, get out! They are a couple of 'Coms', and the honorable member is defending them.

Mr. Pollard: I am defending the right of free speech.

Mr. Mullens: Free speech for Hardy!

Mr. Speaker: Order! I ask the honorable member for Gellibrand to refrain from interjecting.

Mr. Pollard: I am defending what the great Churchill and the great Roosevelt were prepared to advocate. They stood for the Four Freedoms, and the Allies fought for those Four Freedoms, which were: Freedom from fear, freedom from want, freedom of speech, and freedom of worship. I do not want to do the honorable member for Gellibrand an injustice, but it appears to me that he asked the Government to take some action to prevent two men, who are now in foreign lands, from continuing to write and express their opinions about the international situation.

Mr. Mullens: That is plain rubbish, and the honorable member knows it.

Mr. Speaker: Order!

Mr. Pollard: The honorable member for Gellibrand wants to keep out of the country two Australians, and because I say that they should be allowed to re-enter this country and tell the people about what they say, and what they think—

Mr. Speaker: Order! Will the honorable member face the chair, and address me. [Pollard had his back to the Speaker, directly facing and berating Mullens.]

Mr. Pollard: The honorable member for Gellibrand and I, if he is so disposed, could meet those two men in public debate, and deal with their arguments. After all the British Empire was built up on the struggle for the right of men to express their opinions, however unpalatable those opinions were. For the honorable member for Gellibrand to say that I am defending Communists, as such, is a perversion of the truth, and an unfair attack upon me, and I brand him for what he is—a narrow-minded skunk.

Mr. Speaker: Order!

Mr. Mullens leaving his seat, and advancing towards the table.

This brief Hansard reference hardly caught the drama I saw from my seat in the press gallery. Mullens was on his feet trying to climb over the desks in front of him, in an obvious attempt to join in physical combat with Pollard on the floor of the Parliament. Sitting alongside Mullens, Pat Galvin, an SA backbencher, tried to restrain him but got a Mullens' elbow in his ribs for his trouble. Finally, Mullens was restrained from getting to Pollard. The Speaker, Archie Cameron, made no serious attempt to warn Mullens and prevent the scene of two Labor men at one another's throats, but simply let the Labor Party tear itself apart on the floor of the house. Hansard takes up the action:

Mr. Pollard: [still with his back to the Speaker, addressing Mullens as he attempted to climb over the desks in front of him] He is a man who is prepared to do violence.

Mr. Speaker: Order! The honorable member for Gellibrand will resume his seat.

Mr. Mullens: Is not the honorable member for Lalor required to withdraw his remark that I am a narrow-minded skunk?

Mr. Speaker: That remark was entirely unparliamentary, and I ask the honorable member for Lalor to withdraw it.

Mr. Pollard: I withdraw the words to which objection has been taken, but I expect the honorable member for Gellibrand to withdraw the statement that I have defended the Communists.

Mr. Speaker: I think that those words also should be withdrawn. Any quarrels may be settled outside the chamber.

Mr. Pollard: The honorable member for Gellibrand has not withdrawn the words to which I have objected.

Mr. Speaker: Order! I ask the honorable member to withdraw the statement to which exception has been taken.

Mr. Pollard: I have withdrawn the words that I addressed to the honorable member for Gellibrand.

Mr. Speaker: Yes, and I request the honorable member for Gellibrand to do likewise.

Mr. Mullens: What is the statement that I am asked to withdraw?

Mr. Speaker: The statement that the honorable member for Lalor was a defender of the Communists.

Mr. Mullens: I accept his statement that he is not a defender of the Communists, and I withdraw the words to which objection has been taken.

Mr. Speaker: Very well. The incident is closed inside the chamber.

Pollard wound up his speech and Eric Harrison wound up the adjournment debate with standard assurances that matters raised in the adjournment debate would be referred to the responsible minister. Finally, the Speaker, Archie Cameron, had his say on the extraordinary event that he had presided over:

Mr. Speaker, in view of what has just occurred, I direct the attention
of honourable members to Standing Order 80, which reads as follows—

'The House will interfere to prevent the prosecution of a quarrel
between Members arising out of debates or proceedings of the House
or of any committee thereof. If any attempt is made to prosecute quarrel
within the four walls of this building, I had asked the House to enforce
the standing order. What honorable members do outside the building is
their own affair.'

This seemed a clear enough suggestion from the Speaker that Mullens and
Pollard slug it out in the parliamentary rose garden. In 1955, the split became
official at the federal conference of the ALP in Hobart. A number of Victorian
State Labor MPs left the ALP, as did seven federal Victorian MPs: Mullen,
Keon, Bryson, Joshua, Cremean, Andrews and Bourke. They formed the DLP
in April 1956 and none was re-elected. But eventually they had the balance of
power in the Senate, with the DLP represented by former Queensland Labor
Premier Vince Gair, Frank McManus (Vic.) and George Cole (Tas.). By directing
their preferences to the Government, the DLP undoubtedly played a key role
in Menzies' success at elections from then on. It was not until the Whitlam
Government came to power that the DLP was finally ousted from the Senate.

The 'Movement'—or to give it its full title, the Catholic Social Studies
Movement—was the brainchild of B. A. Santamaria and could trace its origins
back to 1939. The Movement was a secretive organisation dedicated to defeating
communist influence in the unions. So powerful was the Movement that it
eventually gained control of the Victorian Labor Party. Evatt denounced the
Movement, and Labor became embroiled in an all-consuming internal struggle,
eventually leading to the formation of the DLP.

As well as the issue of the influence of communists within the Labor Party
and the unions, the split had deep sectarian roots. This did not mean that all
Catholic MPs in the ALP were to join the DLP, nor were all DLP MPs Catholics,
but the dispute was sectarian based to a large degree. The split even damaged
friendships in the press gallery. Kevin Power, the head of bureau for the Sydney
Daily Mirror, was a Catholic and an overt supporter of the DLP side of politics.
His friend Ian Fitchett was not, and I recall one stormy scene in the gallery
when Fitchett said to Power: 'You're a fucking Grouper, Power.' There was no
denial from Power and his angry reply was, 'Shut up, Fitchett.'

Like other pubs in Canberra, the Kingston Hotel in Canberra Avenue was home
to a number of journalists and was well known to me. Directly opposite the
'Kingo' was the Soviet Embassy—a few hundred metres east of Manuka. From
a first-floor window in the pub, Australian Security Intelligence Organisation

(ASIO) agents kept a watchful eye on who came and went through the embassy's front gate. The Kingo was the venue for one of the most important conferences ever held in Canberra: the 22 March 1963 Special Federal Conference of the ALP. There were 36 delegates, six from each State—a form of federalism similarly embodied in the Australian Senate, which has an equal number of senators from each State. The conference was asked to consider whether the federal parliamentary Labor Party should support Menzies' legislation authorising the construction by the United States of a naval communications station on North-West Cape in Western Australia.

The External Affairs Minister, Garfield Barwick, described it as 'a wireless station, nothing more nor less'. This was a cover-up. A wireless station, indeed! It was far more important than was portrayed by the Government. Together with other stations around the world, North-West Cape was a vital part of the US nuclear weapons program. These stations had the capacity to communicate with US Polaris nuclear-powered submarines capable of launching a nuclear missile strike against any target in the world and were at the very tip of US capability to deter nuclear attacks. The station at North-West Cape thus helped keep the Cold War cold, not hot. Within the Labor Party, it raised a question of national sovereignty over Australian soil.

At the Kingston Hotel, the delegates debated the base legislation after Calwell had addressed it and then withdrew. Under ALP rules, the leader and deputy leader were not delegates and did not have a vote, yet they were required to carry out the decision of the conference. The conference was still debating well into the night and Calwell, impatient and accompanied by Whitlam and Freudenberg, left Parliament House to go to the hotel and join journalists waiting for an outcome. As Freudenberg recalls, on the stroke of midnight, the vote was taken narrowly accepting Menzies' legislation, conditional on the base being jointly controlled and Australian sovereignty guaranteed.

The Daily Telegraph published a bombshell picture of Calwell and Whitlam waiting in the dead of night outside the hotel for the vote. Menzies leapt on this to point out that Liberal MPs were not directed by anyone as to how they should vote. Labor MPs on the other hand were instructed by '36 faceless men'—a devastating term he coined. They were not to know it then, but Menzies, *The Daily Telegraph* and the 36 faceless men were to change the face of politics and lead to the election of the Whitlam Government. This humiliation strengthened Whitlam's determination to end the absurdity of the Labor machine's unelected apparatchiks instructing the parliamentary wing how to vote in Parliament. He succeeded magnificently.

Another brutal exercise of power by ALP officials followed, when the Treasurer, Jack Renshaw, brought down the annual budget for the NSW Labor Government, which had been in power for 23 years. It provided special grants to Catholic and other non-government schools for building science laboratories. Arthur Calwell had assured the Premier, Bob Heffron, that this did not contravene ALP policy. Calwell had not reckoned on intervention by the WA ALP Secretary, Joe Chamberlain. Chamberlain was deeply antagonistic to the Catholic Church and the role of its bishops in the Labor split. The Federal Executive met in Adelaide in October and Chamberlain put forward a successful resolution ordering the NSW Government's grants for science laboratories to be cancelled. Cyril Wyndham, the first full-time ALP National Secretary, was sent to Sydney to ensure the instruction was followed. A week later, Menzies announced the 30 November election—a year early. He had seen his opportunity on state aid and a feature of his campaign was to promise almost exactly the proposal Renshaw had vainly put up.

Shortly before the 1963 election, the Queen made Menzies a Knight of the Order of the Thistle, a Scottish honour entirely within her gift to award. In the gallery at the time, there was much discussion that this would have disappointed Ming. He would have been ambitious for the supreme honour: the Order of the Garter, founded in 1344 by Edward III—also solely within the gift of the Queen. Winston Churchill, who resisted any honour throughout most of his long political career, finally consented to take a Garter knighthood. In the house, replying to Menzies' announcement of the early election, Calwell showed his scholarship and flair for off-the-cuff remarks:

> My distinguished friend, the Prime Minister, is now, one might say, a Scottish nobleman. He is a member of the most distinguished, the most ancient and most noble Order of the Thistle. If I, as an ordinary Australian bloke, may address my noble Scottish friends, I would say to him in the words of Macbeth:
>
> Lay on, Macduff,
>
> And damn'd be him that first cries, 'hold, enough'.

Calwell was later to be made a Knight of the Order of St Gregory the Great by Pope Paul VI. Freudenberg recalls a brilliant cartoon by Rigby of Calwell in full armour, lance at the ready, charging into the house, declaring to a cowering Menzies, 'Have at thee, Sir Thistle! Equal terms at last.'

US President John Kennedy was assassinated on 23 November 1963, one week out from the election at which Labor suffered a heavy defeat. The assumption, which I share, is that voters were alarmed by the Kennedy assassination in the Dallas motorcade, seeing it as a signal of the heating up of the Cold War. Many decided it was no time to risk a Labor government. Although he might not have won, Calwell would have made a much closer race of it but for the Kennedy shock.

Freudenberg resigned as Calwell's press secretary/speechwriter following another Chamberlain attack on state aid. Freudenberg had been press secretary/ speechwriter to Calwell since July 1961, and had come to believe—despite his personal regard for the old stager—that Calwell was standing in the way of success for the Labor Party by his determination to hang on to the leadership. Freudenberg was right, and this was the general view of the gallery and a majority of rank-and-file ALP members.

Calwell's two great personal tragedies were the death of his only son, at eleven years of age—a victim of leukaemia. Calwell wore a black tie every day of his life from that point on. The other tragedy was the rupture of his relations with the Catholic Archbishop of Melbourne, Daniel Mannix. Calwell's wife, Elizabeth, was a staunch supporter of Sinn Fein, the political wing of the Irish Republican Army (IRA). Freudenberg remembers that at lunches he attended with Calwell and his wife, Elizabeth would rail against Bob Santamaria and the Catholic establishment. Shunned at their parish church in North Melbourne, the Calwells sought refuge in the Christian charity of the St Francis Church in the city.

Elizabeth was particularly bitter following her sacking as social writer for the Melbourne Catholic paper, the *Catholic Advocate*. She blamed the Melbourne Catholic establishment for this, believing it to be an act of spite against her husband.[3] In *A Figure of Speech*, Freudenberg (not a Catholic) tells how he broke with Calwell after the then Opposition Leader had received a powerful letter from Bishop James Carroll, Auxiliary to Cardinal Gilroy. Carroll came from a staunch Labor family and played an important role in resisting Bob Santamaria's National Civic Council penetrating New South Wales. Carroll's letter complained that despite traditional Catholic support for Labor, the ALP turned its face against any form of assistance for private schools.

Although shut out of the Melbourne Catholic establishment, Calwell held to his belief in state aid for Catholic schools, as did his deputy, Whitlam, who saw the writing on the wall in the 1963 election campaign when Menzies offered aid to private schools. Calwell was so impressed by the Carroll letter that he proposed to have it typed up and presented to the 8 February 1966 meeting of the ALP Federal Executive. Events at the Federal Executive changed his mind. Joe Chamberlain believed state aid breached Section 116 of the Constitution: 'The Commonwealth shall not make any law for establishing any religion...'

---

3   Conversation with Freudenberg.

He decided on an all-out attack on state aid. Before Calwell could produce the Carroll letter at the Federal Executive, Chamberlain successfully moved for the party to challenge in the High Court the state aid given by the States and the aid to science laboratories legislation of the Menzies Government. The ALP's legal and constitutional committee was instructed to draw up the appeal. As the leading member of this committee, Whitlam furiously attacked the Chamberlain motion as reckless, vindictive and electoral suicidal. He warned that if the resolution was adopted he would not serve on the committee—a promise he kept after the resolution was adopted. Calwell was silent throughout the drama, but inwardly delighted his challenger, Whitlam, was getting himself into a mess.

The Carroll letter did not surface. Freudenberg, after the meeting, asked Calwell what had happened to the letter and received the reply: 'The opportunity didn't arise.' Calwell asked Freudenberg to prepare a radio broadcast script for 3KZ, a Labor station in Melbourne, justifying the Federal Executive's action. He refused and Calwell gave the job to extreme left-winger Bill Hartley, a protégé of Chamberlain's and Secretary of the Victorian ALP. When Freudenberg realised the Hartley radio script directly attacked Whitlam, he resigned. His letter of resignation stated he could 'no longer give him [Calwell] the loyalty to which the leader of the Labor Party is entitled'.

Calwell was one of the most complex and interesting personalities in the Parliament. Above all an Australian nationalist, he was fervent in his opposition to the tradition of British governors-general occupying Yarralumla. Nor was he a monarchist. At a time of speculation about who Menzies would have as the next Governor-General, he appointed the Hon. William Philip (Viscount De L'Isle), the last British representative to occupy the office. Philip bumped into Calwell in King's Hall and asked him who he thought might get the next job. He remarked: 'There is only one Governor-General better than an Australian and that is a member of the royal family. They know how to do the job.' And this was long before Kerr's outrageous sacking of Whitlam.

Calwell was right. Whitlam retained the confidence of the Lower House, yet he was sacked. No member of the royal family, in these circumstances, would ignore the advice of the Prime Minister. Whitlam was immediately on the attack against Hartley, declaring to the media, 'this extremist group [controlling the Federal Executive] has deliberately humiliated the parliamentary party…it will and must be repudiated.' In a TV interview, he commented on the state aid decision: 'I can only say we've just got rid of the 36 faceless men stigma to be faced with the 12 witless men' (the Federal Executive).

The Federal Executive met hastily to deal with the Whitlam challenge. Chamberlain failed to have Whitlam expelled from the party due to an extraordinary stroke of luck for the deputy Labor leader. Rex Patterson, a former deputy director of the Bureau of Agricultural Economics, in 1966 won the Queensland federal seat of Dawson in a by-election. He visited Canberra to thank those members of the ALP who had assisted him in his campaign. He was visiting Allan Fraser, the member for Eden-Monaro (NSW), when Fraser took a call from Calwell. An excited Calwell exclaimed, 'We have got the big bastard [Whitlam], he will be gone by lunchtime.' Overhearing this, Patterson immediately alerted Whitlam's office and contact was made with Jack Egerton, State ALP President. Egerton urgently telephoned the two Queensland delegates to say, 'If you vote to expel Gough Whitlam, I'll have your balls'. That was the beginning of the end for Calwell. (Egerton was later in disgrace with the ALP and lost all his positions when, in defiance of his party's platform, he accepted a knighthood from the corrupt Queensland Nationals Premier Joh Bjelke-Petersen. Egerton was brought down by his arrogance.)

Following his resignation, Freudenberg went back to his bolthole of Melbourne's *TheSun News Pictorial*, and when Whitlam attained the leadership, became his press secretary. They had for years had an unspoken understanding that Freudenberg would join Whitlam when he became leader.

Ministers cultivate gallery journalists, and some, such as Peter Howson, were assiduous in working on journalistic contacts. Howson, like Gorton, was a fighter pilot, and, when flying a Royal Navy Fleet Air Arm Albacore over Malta, in company with four Hurricanes, he took on some 70 German planes. Howson was shot down and had a deep and long scar on his face to show for it.[4]

Howson was Liberal MP for the Melbourne seats of Fawkner and later Casey. Slight and handsome, with a clipped English accent, he was an old-school conservative, a friend of Harold Holt, but an enemy in Victorian politics of John Gorton. Howson's diary (*The Life of Politics*) is one of the most informative and interesting books on Australian postwar politics ever published, recording his various attempts to widen his contacts with gallery journalists. Yet his tactics initially were puzzling. He records (19 September 1963): 'I had to get the Serjeant-at-Arms to carpet (Ian) Fitchett (*Sydney Morning Herald*) for entering our party room. We will get a blast from him in his weekly article next Tuesday. But it will be a salutary lesson for the press gallery.'

Just what offence Fitchett had committed is unclear. He certainly would not have attempted to enter the party room during its regular weekly meeting. Although journalists had to pass the doors of both the Coalition and the Labor party rooms in the government and opposition lobbies, they were not permitted to even 'linger' in the corridors while a party room meeting was in progress. At other times, journalists often were in the party room to see if an MP they wished

---

4   Reid, Alan 1971, *The Gorton Experiment*, Shakespeare Head Press, Sydney, p. 35.

to interview was inside. During Premiers' Conferences, gallery members were welcome in the government party room—a venue for government-provided drinks. At that time, Howson held the junior position of Deputy Government Whip. He was either brave or foolhardy in taking on Fitchett, although it was unlikely the Serjeant-at-Arms would have revealed to Fitchett who had dobbed him in.

The late George Kerr, when he was political correspondent for the *Sydney Morning Herald*, told the author of a colourful incident involving a leak from the government party room. Treasurer, Arthur Fadden, was to brief the government party room during the dinner adjournment on the legislation he would introduce that night to make major changes to the banking system, including splitting the Reserve Bank away from the government-owned Commonwealth Bank. This had been the subject of controversy in the party room, with some of the younger backbench Liberals pressing Fadden to go further than he proposed by putting the private banks on the same footing as the Commonwealth Bank. Fitchett, then political correspondent for *The Age*, and Kerr were keen to get any snippet from the party room on the Fadden briefing.

They arranged that Kerr would patrol the bottom government lobby, one floor down from the party room, and collar anyone he could after the meeting broke up. Fitchett positioned himself in King's Hall, which was crowded with members of the public waiting to get into the public galleries for the resumption of the sittings in the house at 8 pm. Kerr got very little from those MPs he intercepted and hurried to King's Hall to confer with Fitchett. Just as he arrived, he saw Bill Wentworth hurrying away from Fitchett. At this point, Fitchett, both hands cupped around his mouth to form a megaphone, roared at the retreating Wentworth: 'Wentworth, you're a coward and a c**t.' Obviously, the Member for Mackellar had given nothing away. The next day, Fitchett was seated in the tiny *Age* office on a commodious old leather lounge chair, when Wentworth sheepishly appeared at the door to mend his fences with *The Age* correspondent. 'Fuck off, Wentworth,' barked Fitchett. From that point on, Wentworth was Fitchett's best party-room leaker.

Every bureau head had his leaker—from both the government and the opposition party rooms. Menzies was angered by such leaks because they could be seen as a demonstration that he was not completely in charge and many of the leaks amounted to criticisms of him and his government. Labor leaders, and particularly Evatt, were angered and often wounded by leaks. During the Labor split of the 1950s, the gallery was focused far more on the Labor Caucus than on the Coalition party room. During one tumultuous Caucus meeting, the Groupers (later to form the DLP) criticised Evatt, prompting the Labor leader to leap onto a table, shouting to the Labor Whip, Fred Daly: 'Take their names, Daly.'

Allan Fraser, the Labor member for the NSW federal seat of Eden-Monaro, was Kevin Power's prized Caucus leak. Before entering Parliament, Fraser was the political correspondent for the *Mirror*. Soon after each Caucus meeting, the phone would ring in Power's small office. Sometimes, when neither Power nor Les Love was in the office, I would take the call. A familiar voice would say: 'Have you a pencil?' Then he would dictate a complete story, starting something along the lines: 'Canberra Tuesday, Federal Labor Caucus was in uproar today when Opposition Leader, H. V. Evatt, attacked members of the Catholic Group movement and threatened to have them expelled stop quote I will not put up with this disloyalty unquote Evatt said stop.' And Fraser would go on to dictate a complete story, needing no rewriting and suitable for immediate submission to the *Mirror*.

Important party-room leaks in the Menzies era were less frequent, mainly because government activity was, by today's standards, subdued and the level of legislation much lower. Very occasionally Evatt, and later Calwell, would stand in the opposition lobby and give a hasty briefing of Caucus meetings to journalists. As Opposition Leader, Whitlam would often hold a briefing in his office to give journalists details. Later, the present system of briefings was formalised by both parties, with MPs, not senior figures, from each party room appointed to brief journalists. They are not to be quoted directly and they play down any party-room trouble. Nevertheless, these briefings provide a good basis for journalists to then seek out from their own contacts just what happened. Those appointed to do the briefings are often on the way up the slippery pole of politics.

Whether Labor is in or out of power, Caucus (the parliamentary Labor Party) is of greater interest to the media than the Liberal (or Coalition) party room. Caucus is all-powerful; the Liberal party room is powerless. All three of the major parties—the ALP, the Liberals and the Nationals—are, like Australia, based on a federation. There are autonomous State divisions, or branches, affiliated with the national ALP. The National Conference—the supreme policymaking body—is responsible for the party's platform. The National Executive, with the National Secretary as the chief administrative officer, administers the party. The role of Caucus is to implement the platform of the party, and it is free to set its own timetable for achieving this.

A Labor government cannot defy the platform, hence the National Conference was called to allow Labor to support Menzies' legislation to establish a US naval communications base at North-West Cape, even though the platform declared the whole of the southern hemisphere should be nuclear free. The conference also was required to approve the sale of the government-owned assets of the Commonwealth Bank and Qantas. Caucus elects the leader and deputy leader of the party and leader and deputy leader in the Senate and all ministers or shadow ministers. The capacity to make these appointments extends right down to which Labor MPs will get a perk trip abroad on a parliamentary delegation. Kevin Rudd, having won the 2007 election, asserted he alone would appoint the members of the Labor ministry, meaning Caucus nominally gave up its power to elect ministers.

Oddly enough though, the ministry Rudd selected accorded exactly with the list the factional Labor chiefs had agreed to. Peter Hartcher's book on the downfall of Howard, *To the Bitter End*, confirms that Rudd did not select the ministry alone. He writes that on the weekend of the Labor election victory in 2007, Rudd and Julia Gillard (of Martin Ferguson's Left faction) crafted a 30-member ministry, 16 from the Left, 12 from the Right, one from the Centre and one unaligned. The Right was under-represented by two and Right powerbroker Robert Ray kicked up a fuss, warning Rudd that what he was doing was akin to fighting a war on the western and eastern fronts at the same time. When the ministry 'selected' by Rudd was announced, Ray had got his way, with the Left losing two and the Right gaining two.

Menzies, in forming the Liberal Party, ensured that the parliamentary leader would have total control. Rank-and-file Liberal Party members could discuss policy at their various State and federal meetings, but this policy could not be imposed on the parliamentary Liberal Party. The only real power of the Liberal party room is to elect its leader and deputy, or to dump them. The Liberal party room may not direct the Cabinet, or reject a Cabinet decision. The Liberal leader decides who will be ministers and what portfolios they will hold.

The selection of Country Party (later National Party) ministers and their portfolios, if the two non-Labor parties are in coalition, is a different matter. National Party portfolios are negotiated between the two party leaders. The basis of the proportion of Liberal ministers against Nationals ministers depends on the share of House of Representatives seats each party holds after an election. The Nationals party room elects its share of ministers or shadow ministers. The Nationals leader is free to choose his portfolio and is additionally Deputy Prime Minister/Deputy Leader of the Opposition.

Menzies believed that, as backbenchers had no power in the legislative process, they had a perfect right to cross the floor and vote against the Government. (Crossing the floor against the Liberal leader is not, however, a good career move.) Liberal and Nationals ministers are bound to support Cabinet decisions, even though they might have disagreed with a decision in Cabinet. This rule did not apply to Labor, and efforts by Whitlam as Prime Minister to change the situation were resisted. Finally, Bob Hawke succeeded in adopting the principle whereby members of the ministry should always support decisions of Cabinet (but he allowed Stewart West to disagree).

The ambitious Peter Howson in his diaries[5] revealed his anxiety for promotion above his then position as Minister for Air: 'I must still try to get closer to some of the Liberal backbenchers. And I don't think I am much closer to the press gallery.' Closer or not to the press gallery, he displayed no knowledge of how it operated with his entry for 15 May 1967:

> Later in the evening I got John Bennetts of *The Age*—also chairman of the press gallery—to come down to see if I could manage to keep the press gallery quiet on the move of the Mirage squadron from Williamtown (near Newcastle) to Butterworth in Malaya. Unfortunately there were reports of their movements on the ABC tonight. Luckily all has gone well, after the first announcement we've heard nothing more and it looks as if we can keep the news quiet until the Mirages get to Butterworth later on this week.

Bennetts was not the chairman of the press gallery, he was the President. Further, Bennetts would not dream of going around the gallery telling journalists not to write about anything. If he had been so foolish, it would have guaranteed that every bureau would have reported the story Howson wanted to be kept quiet. It is surprising that Howson failed to understand that the gallery is not like a cabinet or a government department, a company or a troop of boy scouts.

Each bureau is answerable only to the media organisation it represents. The misconception persists even today with commentators (not in the press gallery) referring to the 'gallery rat pack' and suggesting they are led by one or other senior gallery journalist to take a particular line on some political development. It is true that when a big story breaks every bureau is after the story. Often they adopt the same slant or pin the blame or credit on the same politician. This is mostly the case when it is obvious which politician should bear the blame or receive the praise. There is no rat pack.

For some years there was an informal grouping of bureaus in the gallery, known as 'the Club', which in effect syndicated stories. Yet this was not a 'gallery rat pack' in the sense critics mean of attributing an unfair collective decision by the gallery as a whole to pursue some objective. The Club operated in the 1950s and 1960s and finally withered away with the arrival of new gallery members with a competitive spirit who spurned it. The Club flourished in the 1950s and mainly involved the swapping of carbon copies of news stories among papers at first confined to the Melbourne Herald group: Brisbane's *Courier-Mail*, the *Herald*, *The Sun News Pictorial* (both Melbourne) and *The Advertiser* (Adelaide). At

---

5 Howson, Peter 1984, *The Howson Diaries. The life of politics*, Don Aitkin (ed.), Viking Press, Ringwood, Vic.

various times, outsiders were also included in the 'Club': the Sydney papers the *Daily Mirror*, the *Sun*, *The Daily Telegraph* and the *Sydney Morning Herald*; plus *The Telegraph* (Brisbane) and *The News* (Adelaide).

Clem Lloyd[6] points out that on occasions when a paper was outside the Club, its bureau head, such as Alan Reid (the Sydney *Sun* and later *The Daily Telegraph*) and Ian Fitchett (*The Age*), could break stories that the much wider resources of the Club had failed to get. When Fitchett (who despised the Club) moved from *The Age* to the *Sydney Morning Herald*, he inherited Club membership. With the agreement of his editor, John Pringle, Fitchett terminated association with the Club. Lloyd observed:

> In many ways the 'Club' enshrined mediocrity. The fruits of the most skilled were delivered to the less efficient; in return, the better journalists had their flanks guarded and could rely on a cover for routine news. An area of political journalism which required individual skills and not the copy of others, I was to soon appreciate, was being on the road with political leaders in an election campaign.

---

6   Lloyd, *Parliament and the Press*.

9. Out on the Hustings: Getting in the votes

A Senate election on 9 May 1953 was the first election campaign I covered for the *Daily Mirror* and it was a tepid affair. The election was required by the Constitution. Normally a federal election is for the House of Representatives and half the Senate. Menzies, by calling a double-dissolution election on 28 April 1951, had the two houses out of step because after a double-dissolution the term of the Senate is backdated to the previous 1 July. In turn, this means half the Senate had to be elected three years later, hence the May half-Senate election.

Serious reporting came with the election of the House of Representatives only—called for 29 May 1954. Unlike the half-Senate election of the previous year, this was the first election in which Evatt, as Opposition Leader, was in a contest to decide the fate of the Government. The formal policy speech of the leader was and is regarded as the highlight of the election campaign. It was the moment—generally only three or four weeks out from voting day—when the political leaders would state with varying degrees of precision what they intended to do for the nation and, more particularly, the hip pocket. It was also obligatory to devote some high-flown rhetoric to the philosophical base of the leader's party and to explain how immeasurably superior it was to the opponent's party. These days, the Canberra press gallery relentlessly pursues opposition leaders, expecting them to state their detailed policies long before the election. Further, it is now customary to have separate launches in the election campaign for various aspects of policy. The formal policy speech then summarises these and invariably drops in something new just to keep the voters interested.

Travelling with Evatt in the 1954 campaign was an intense and testing experience. The accompanying journalists would have no idea in advance of what Evatt would say at his next meeting and had to get to grips with the often-complex points of his speech as he went along. He would promise a pension increase or some other social service benefit with little or no explanation of how it would be paid for. Menzies would promise nothing but a continuation of good Menzies governance—a policy he abandoned after his close shave at the 1961 election. He would also endlessly demand of Evatt that he explain how he was going to pay for his promises.

Unimpressive though Evatt's election speeches were, they were well grounded in economic expertise, provided mainly by Dr Ron Hieser, an Australian National University (ANU) lecturer and later a great mate of Bob Hawke when he came to the ANU. Hieser was a member of an informal academic group at the ANU of Labor supporters and was influential with the Doc. Hieser lived in the ANU-owned flats at Barton that provided accommodation for academic staff. Some distinguished academics resided there, including historian Russell Ward. The Sydney *Sun* rented one of the flats for staff, and, with my first wife, Lesley, I lived in the same block as Ron, directly behind the Hotel Wellington. Our first child, Susan, was born at that time.

Evatt was friendly and approachable on tour, although he could be cantankerous if he did not like a particular report about the campaign and would not hesitate to ring an editor to complain. A source of constant irritation for him were the press estimates of the size of the audience he was addressing, particularly the evening meeting—regarded as the most important event of the day and invariably held in a public hall. The size of the audience was seen as a measure of the popularity of the leader. In fact, it was no such thing, although it was a measure of the efficiency and advertising ability of the party branches in various electorates in getting a good roll up. On most days, Evatt and Menzies would hold two meetings a day: one at lunchtime so that workers could attend, and another at night.

Evatt had the accompanying journalists browbeaten over the issue of audience size. Estimating the size of an audience is not easy if the meeting is in a park or a football ground. It is easier in a hall with a known capacity. With the Doc ever on the warpath about crowd sizes, journalists would generally come to an agreement on the true size of an audience and then add to it by a quarter or so. More often than not, the Doc would still not be satisfied and would be whingeing to our editors about poor reporting of crowd size. Outside the cities, the local paper would report honestly on the crowd size but by then Evatt and his entourage would have left town.

Covering Evatt meetings was not easy. Generally, a press table would be provided and placed at the front of the hall. Outdoor meetings were difficult to report; having to stand and take notes did not improve my shorthand outlines or their legibility. The handy little voice recorders—now standard equipment for reporters—were unknown, as were the marvels of mobile phones, emails, faxes and photocopiers. Graham Freudenberg tells of how, travelling with Calwell in the 1961 campaign, he and a secretary would have to produce Arthur Calwell's press releases on manual typewriters with carbon copies. The press travelling with Evatt would generally be given sketchy notes of his speech at a meeting, always at the last minute and sometimes after Evatt had actually begun his speech. In any case, the notes generally had little relevance to what he would say to his audience. These meetings were open to all comers and there was no attempt to confine it to supporters, although they did get most of the seats at the front of the hall, mainly by turning up early. There would be lots of clapping, and almost invariably hostile interjections.

Menzies—a far more skilled public speaker on these occasions—thrived on interjections and could get his crowd clapping and laughing with his barbed and witty replies to interjections. The Doc was the opposite and would often try to deliver a serious debating point to an interjector, generally going right over the heads of his audience. Interjectors would not be ejected unless they seriously disrupted a meeting. Local party members often did the manhandling involved in ousting interjectors, rather than involving the police.

Reporting a lunchtime meeting was also difficult for afternoon-newspaper reporters. Often the Doc or Menzies would depart for the airport to get a flight to the venue for the evening meeting. Menzies and Evatt travelled mainly by TAA or Ansett, and the press party had to make their own arrangements to get the right flight and book hotels. Credit cards were unknown and it was a struggle to get money in advance from the office to pay these expenses. If I ran out of money, I had to beg for more to be dispatched, urgently, by telegram to a nearby post office. Afternoon-paper reps would leave meetings the instant the speech ended, rush to a phone and dictate a story to the office, hoping the Doc's or Menzies' press secretary would hold the plane for them. When we were flying to Perth with Evatt in the 1954 campaign, strong headwinds meant we had to land at Kalgoorlie in the early evening for refuelling. Several of the journalists went for a quick reconnoitre of the famous brothels in Hay Street where the girls, clad in minimum attire, stood in front of their individual brothels, which looked exactly like stables. It must be added we did not avail ourselves of their services, nor did we tell the Doc of this pornographic exercise.

I recall standing out the front of Lennons, then Brisbane's top hotel, with the Evatt party, other journalists and Clyde Cameron, the aggressive Labor MP (Hindmarsh, SA); a gorgeous young woman in a tight-fitting dress walked towards us and entered the hotel. She was a knockout and looked like someone from show business. Cameron made some licentious comment about her to our little gathering. Evatt immediately rounded on Cameron, saying something like, 'How dare you speak about that young women like that.' I never forgot this aspect of Evatt's character. He was a feminist long before we heard about it from Germaine Greer.

The *Daily Mirror*'s political correspondent and head of its Canberra bureau, Kevin Power, travelled with Menzies on this election campaign. Other newspaper representatives would swap over: the bureau head with Menzies for a week and his number-two travelling with Evatt, and vice versa the following week. Power would not, and covered Menzies exclusively. Les Love was Power's bureau offsider and would have been entitled to travel with Evatt, but Les insisted on travelling with the Country Party leader, Artie Fadden. This was not to advance himself as a journalist. Fadden made considerably fewer column inches than the Prime Minister or the Leader of the Opposition. Artie was much more fun to be with and was regarded by all as a great bloke. Wherever he travelled in the bush, Artie and his party were well received; the entertainment and hospitality were endless. With the Country Women's Association (CWA) a social force in every town, vast quantities of lamingtons, sandwiches and baked dinners were consumed, not to forget the oceans of beer provided. Travel was mainly by car, often on dusty, bumpy roads for five or six hours a day. Artie would speak in town halls in the evenings, but during the day he would spruik from the back of a truck with an audience of two if necessary.

The 1961 election, when Menzies was almost beaten, was the last in which television played only a minor role. That election campaign was fought in exactly the same manner as the political leaders at the beginning of Federation conducted their campaigns. They were fought at public meetings, but this changed with the development of TV as the pre-eminent form of media. For the 1972 campaign, Whitlam opted for opening in a big hall: Blacktown Civic Centre, way out in the western suburbs of Sydney. It was also designed as a spectacular TV event. McMahon on the other hand decided an opening in a big public hall was too risky and instead prerecorded his policy speech in a studio and made it available to all TV stations.

For McMahon, speech making was a challenge, partly because of his unusual quavering voice and partly because of a total lack of eloquence. Laurie Oakes and David Solomon devote a whole chapter of their book, *The Making of An Australian Prime Minister*, to the agony McMahon went through to get this speech right. Instead of attempting to tape a half-hour speech in one take, the producer broke it into short segments. This had the advantage of not having to do a complete new taping of the speech if McMahon made a mistake. Even then McMahon had to do some segments many times before getting it right. Even with an autocue at his desk, he found it difficult.

In 1974 Whitlam returned to Blacktown—the scene of his 1972 election launch. Opposition Leader, Bill Snedden, had blocked in the Senate a number of key legislative packages, particularly the Medicare legislation. Whitlam dealt with this, he claimed, by calling a double-dissolution election. The real reason was far more practical: Treasury had warned in 1974 that the economy was sliding and unemployment was certain to increase. Whitlam decided to get to the polls. Snedden had his campaign opening at an invitation-only function on Sydney's North Shore with the ladies of the blue-rinse set. Since Bob Hawke's 1983 election, campaigns have become super slick affairs, heavily managed by minders with the TV and radio media as extras in the drama. Press secretaries, also known as media advisers (and now called, somewhat contemptuously, spin doctors), played a central role in managing campaigns. In the United States, they are more accurately labelled 'publicists'.

10. Press Secretaries: Before spin doctors

None of Menzies' press secretaries could be described as a spin doctor, and they saw their role as providers of information (except Hugh Dash, who had no information to provide), rather than propagandists. They answered housekeeping questions from the gallery: when was the Prime Minister going overseas, or when would the Government say something about whatever; they issued press releases and notified the gallery of press conferences and important statements to be made in Parliament. They stayed away from attempting to sell policy, leaving that to their political masters. Television hit the political scene in full force in 1988 when the move was made from Old Parliament House to the permanent Parliament House. Press secretaries came to be seen as more in the mould of the American publicist. They did not hesitate to come up to the gallery to sell a line, or, just as often, complain about a report reflecting badly on their bosses.

Many of the press secretaries played favourites and fed material to journalists regarded as politically friendly. A good press secretary working for a humble backbencher will attempt to persuade the local press in the home electorate that a popular decision by the MP's side of politics—be it government or opposition—can be spun for the benefit of their boss. The MP might not have had the slightest influence on how the good news arrived. It does not matter; a press release can claim the boss has been 'tirelessly working' for such an outcome for years. It is easier if their MP master is from a rural or regional electorate. The local member outside the cities is a 'somebody' and well known, meaning local media report on their activities. The majority of city voters, however, have no idea who represents them, unless the MP is prominent in politics—maybe a minister or a senior opposition figure. Mort Nash, who for some years was press secretary to Curley Swartz, a minister in the Menzies, Holt and Gorton Governments, would seize a press statement favourable to the Government by another minister, cross out the minister's name, replace it with Swartz's name and wire it off to newspapers in Swartz's Queensland electorate of Darling Downs.

Prime ministers' press secretaries are a different breed and their task is difficult. For good or bad, the Prime Minister will get a lot of newspaper space and exposure in the electronic media. The media expects prime ministers to deal with, or comment on, virtually any major news item on a daily basis. John Howard and Kevin Rudd, even outside election campaigns, frequently gave one or two press conferences a day, plus a number of electronic media interviews, and perhaps a picture opportunity in a shopping mall or hospital. In Menzies' day it was a lot easier; all that mattered were the newspapers. At one of his occasional press conferences, if asked a question not directly related to his own portfolio, Menzies would simply advise the questioner to ask the relevant minister.

Menzies was acutely aware of the importance of a first-class press secretary. Before he returned to power in 1949, he was keen to have a press secretary of the calibre of Curtin's (and then Chifley's) legendary press secretary Don Rogers. Menzies wrote that 'Rogers has built up his chief in a really remarkable way; he knows exactly what the public want to read, and he has a really burning enthusiasm for Labor's cause…I simply can't think of one man who is anywhere near his class'.[1]

Menzies' press secretaries were (sequentially) Stewart Cockburn, Hugh Dash, Ray Maley and Tony Eggleton. I describe their qualities below.

King-Hitter: Stewart Cockburn

When I arrived in Canberra, Stewart Cockburn, an Adelaide man, was Menzies' press secretary. He tried to join the Navy at the beginning of the war, but an X-ray revealed a TB scar on his lung and he was rejected. He spent most of the war on Adelaide's *The Advertiser*—part of The Herald and Weekly Times newspaper empire—and, from 1947 to 1950, he was in London as correspondent for the Melbourne *Herald*. Cockburn saw quite a bit of Menzies in those years on the Liberal Party leader's visits to London. Back in Adelaide, Reg Leonard, later to become managing editor of *The Courier-Mail* and knighted, was Cockburn's chief of staff. Leonard, so Cockburn believed, was a talent spotter for Menzies.

Yet he was surprised to be asked by Leonard whether he would like to be Menzies' press secretary, succeeding Charles Meeking. Cockburn agreed to be interviewed by Menzies in Canberra. On meeting the Prime Minister, Cockburn told him he had to understand that until 1949 he had not voted for any party but the Labor Party. Menzies was unmoved. He said he did not care who Cockburn voted for as long as he thought he could 'do the job and be loyal'. (This is almost exactly what Menzies said when appointing Tony Eggleton some years later.)

As Menzies' press secretary, Cockburn was efficient but certainly not in the spin-doctor class of later practitioners. In the gallery, he was respected and seen as a straight shooter. The spectacle of a drunken Glenn Milne, a prominent News Limited columnist, rushing onto the stage to attack award presenter Stephen Mayne in December 2006 during the Walkley Award ceremony reminded me of

---

1   Martin, *Robert Menzies*, vol. 2, p. 2.

a much earlier event, involving Cockburn. During the 1951 election campaign, Cockburn was standing just to one side on the stage of the Adelaide Town Hall. Menzies was about to make his entrance and Cockburn, a bit edgy, was to give a signal to the ABC sound technician in the hall preparing to broadcast the event.

The hall was well filled when Ian Fitchett came to Cockburn and demanded to know there and then details of the trip the press party was to take with Menzies to the Woomera rocket range the next day. Cockburn was saying things such as 'in a minute, Fitch' and 'can't you see I'm busy'. With this, Fitchett, who could be a spiteful bastard, said: 'You're a fucking Murdoch stooge [a reference to Sir Keith Murdoch, Rupert's father and at the time running the Melbourne *Herald*]; 'you're holding it back for the *Herald*.' Cockburn's temper flared and he punched Fitchett in the face. Fitchett staggered back and then replied with a punch right on Cockburn's chin, almost knocking him out, but Cockburn responded and landed a punch into Fitchett's ample stomach.

A police inspector and Alan Reid (Sydney *Sun*) broke up the scuffle. Cockburn remembers an outraged Fitchett declaring: 'He king-hit me.' This he repeated many times the next day in Woomera and for some days after that. Cockburn said that although most journalists and people in the packed hall awaiting Menzies' arrival witnessed the incident, surprisingly there was absolutely no report in the media. In his conversation with the author, Cockburn said Fitchett reported to his editor that he had been involved in a scuffle and that was the end of the affair. In stark contrast, the unfortunate Milne's indiscretion was extensively reported in all the media. TV news (which lives off action pictures) gave it a prominent airing. He also retained his job.

Menzies, most unusually, decided to stage a 'picture opportunity' (although not for TV, which had yet to arrive), by returning to his hometown of Jeparit, Victoria. A test match was under way in Australia and Menzies, like Howard, portrayed himself as a 'cricket tragic' who was a devoted follower of the game but a hopeless player. With a small press party, Menzies arrived at Jeparit in a RAAF VIP DC3. The media gathered around him on landing and Menzies asked Cockburn, 'What's the score?' Ever efficient, Cockburn began reciting the itinerary: 'We go to the Town Hall where the Mayor——.' Through gritted teeth, Menzies snapped: 'Not that score, the cricket score.' Cockburn could not help.

Cockburn accompanied Menzies to London for the coronation of the young Queen Elizabeth, visiting Cape Town on the way home, where Menzies was guest of Daniel Malan, who headed the first South African government to lay the foundations of apartheid. Menzies was anxious to keep South Africa in the Commonwealth and he decided to break the journey back to Australia for talks with Malan. The Commonwealth was under heavy pressure at the time from the non-Anglo members for sanctions to be imposed on South Africa, or for it to be kicked out of the Commonwealth. Menzies had stated at press conferences the author attended that apartheid should be seen as a matter of domestic concern to the Malan Government and there should be no action against South Africa. On his return to Canberra, Cockburn was exhausted and, soon after, his annual X-ray revealed a scar on his lung. He was ordered to bed and stayed there for weeks.

'The Dasher': Hugh Dash

Menzies' next press secretary, Hugh ('the Dasher') Dash, was the antithesis of Cockburn. Nor was he anything like Don Rogers, whom Menzies so much admired. The Dasher knew nothing about spin and never tried it. He was a rugby league writer for *The Daily Telegraph* before coming to Canberra and was definitely not from the Sydney establishment, but was up with a lot of what was going on in Sydney society. He had been press secretary to Sir Wilfred Kent Hughes, then the Minister for the Interior, whose major task was running Canberra. Then with the departure of Cockburn, Dash turned up as Menzies' press secretary. The Dasher was a heavy drinker, downing a bottle of beer for breakfast, while for morning tea he would visit his good mate Jack Murphy, manager of the members' bar, for a bracing double gin. On the stroke of noon, when the bar opened, he would be first through the door of the non-members'. Like most heavy drinkers, he ate like a sparrow: four middies was lunch, and so the day would go on. He was never under the weather.

As far as the gallery was concerned, Dash—although much liked as a companion—was of no help and seemed without any knowledge of what the Government was doing. Perhaps he knew a lot, but in any case he suited Menzies. Dash would often say something that was quite odd—for example, that Menzies was not interested in what was in the papers. Yet Menzies was more than interested in what was in the papers, particularly the Fairfax press, as A. W. Martin makes clear. Dash once said to me, in the non-members' bar, 'That Disney crowd are a funny lot. They rang me to get a comment from the Old Man on some anniversary of Mickey Mouse; he's never heard of Mickey Mouse.'

A. W. Martin quotes Sir William Heseltine—the Prime Minister's private secretary from 1955 to 1959—on Menzies' liking for a wind-down drink at the end of the day. In the absence of his parliamentary colleagues, Hugh Dash and Heseltine were summoned for a whisky and chat before the Prime Minister went home. Dash, a particularly colourful character, had a notable sense of humour and a great fund of stories, many of them with a bluish tinge. Menzies, who himself never swore or told risqué jokes, was greatly attached to and entertained by Dash. An often-unrecognised element in Menzies was his liking for larrikins and other down-to-earth Australianisms. Two ministers who were particular favourites, Athol Townley and Senator Shane Paltridge, fell somewhat into this category. (Townley, representing the Tasmanian seat of Denison, and Paltridge, from Western Australia, were also well liked in the gallery.)

Menzies—unlike Fraser and later Howard—did not have a residence in his home city of Melbourne to spend time away from Canberra when Parliament was in recess. From the time he was elected in 1949, the Lodge was the only residence for him and his wife, Pattie (later Dame). Menzies had no close group of friends in Canberra and on Sunday mornings at the Lodge, time dragged. By mid-morning, Pattie would be busy preparing the Sunday roast (presumably it was the cook's day off). Often the phone would ring and Dash would be at the other end, whereupon Menzies would say in a loud voice (no doubt for the benefit of Pattie) something like, 'What, not another cable from London? Should I come in?' Pause. 'Oh, all right then.' The driver would be called, and from then until close to lunch, Menzies, Dash and the driver proceeded to spend a convivial time in the Cabinet anteroom over Sunday drinks.

Bernard Freedman had an experience belying the view of many outsiders that Menzies was a stiff and aloof figure.[2] Freedman, bureau head of the now defunct Melbourne daily *The Argus*, a pro-Labor paper, had often authored reports critical of Menzies. He was leaving the gallery in the 1950s to join the Public Service and was in Dash's office to say goodbye. Menzies' head popped around the door and Dash told the Prime Minister Freedman was leaving. 'Well', said Menzies, 'you'd better come and have a drink'. So the Prime Minister and the journalist moved to the cabinet anteroom. 'For the whole afternoon, we sat and Menzies served me whiskies and spent his time addressing me as if he was at a public meeting,' Freedman recalls.

'Good Shot': Ray Maley

When I came to the gallery, Ray Maley, who succeeded Hugh Dash, had been bureau head of *The Argus*. Ray was a tall, handsome man, with the classic film-star dimple in the chin, well dressed with an easy, likeable manner. We were both members of the Royal Canberra Golf Club. Bill McLaren, Secretary of the Department of the Interior (responsible for the administration of Canberra), was also a golf club member and was a target for Maley's ambitions. For some unknown reason, this department, which essentially was concerned with domestic administration within Australia, was responsible for the Australian News and Information Bureau (ANIB).

---

2   Oral history interview, Old Parliament House, 8 December 2004.

With the aim of attracting both migrants and investment from abroad, the ANIB was responsible for publicising the attractions of Australia abroad. Ray would drink with McLaren at the club and was always keen to play a round of golf with the senior bureaucrat in the Saturday club competition. Should McLaren hit a reasonable shot, Ray would enthuse: 'Oh, good shot, Bill.' Ray's cultivating did the trick and in 1955 he was posted to New York as the ANIB man. Maley told me it was as good as winning the lottery. Ray's posting ended in 1961 and soon after he was appointed Menzies' press secretary. Hugh Dash had been struggling with health problems for several years and Menzies was often without a press secretary and others on the Prime Minister's staff did their best to fill in. Menzies' regard for Dash was such that he was loath to replace him, but finally his health had so deteriorated that a replacement simply had to be found. Ray knew the gallery well and was an excellent choice.

He was only fifty-one when he died tragically, on 29 September 1964, during a ball in Parliament House in honour of visiting royal Princess Marina. There was dancing in King's Hall and at the beginning of the evening I was talking to Ray and his wife, Jean. Ray, in his dinner suit, looked a picture of glowing good health. He had been having heart troubles and was telling me how he had played golf the previous weekend and how delighted he was that his heart was stronger. They turned from me to pose for a photographer when suddenly Ray staggered backwards and fell, hitting the back of his head on the parquet flooring. Bystanders rushed to help and comfort Jean. Labor Senator Dr Felix Dittmer was called and pronounced Ray dead. He was probably dead before he hit the floor.

Tony Eggleton: The great survivor

Menzies was in no hurry to find a replacement following the death of Ray Maley, finally settling on Tony Eggleton, a professional press secretary, not a partisan propagandist. Not for him the spin and the bullying tactics of more recent practitioners. He was a first-class journalist. In 1950 Eggleton left England for 12 months' experience on the *Bendigo Advertiser*, not knowing he was to be captured by Australia. Next he worked in Melbourne and helped put the first ABC televised news to air in 1956, before applying for a new position: Director of Naval Public Relations.

The then Navy Minister, John Gorton, sought someone who had worked in all three media—radio, TV and print—and there were not too many journos about at that time with those qualifications. Eggleton, in his first year on the *Bendigo Advertiser*, interviewed Gorton, then a new senator from northern Victoria.

Gorton (even then noted for his I'll-do-it-my-way approach) interviewed Eggleton for the job, overruling the Secretary of the Navy Department, who believed Eggleton was too young.

With Eggleton's appointment, the Navy had a PR division of one person—not much compared with today's battalions of PR staff in the Defence Department and the three services. On the night of 10 February 1964, off the NSW coast near Jervis Bay, the aircraft carrier *HMAS Melbourne* collided with the destroyer *HMAS Voyager*, cutting it in two, with a loss of 82 sailors' lives. Eggleton, still with the Navy and not on Menzies staff at that time, discovered Menzies was furious, having not been told immediately of the disaster and learning about it the next day on the morning news.

The Chief of the Navy Staff, Hastings Harrington (known in the Navy as 'Buggery Grips' because of the hair he grew on both cheeks), instructed Eggleton not to inform the media of the disaster. Eggleton told the author:

> I didn't think that was very sensible and as the night went on, I told the Chief of the Navy Staff that it was an impossible situation and we had to make a statement. Finally we did make a statement. Menzies was impressed by the fact that at least someone in [the] Navy was trying to do something that night in the public interest. As a result of all that, the top naval people sent me over to Parliament House to try to cope with the Prime Minister and help with his news conference.

In the 1964 Senate election campaign, Eggleton worked with Senator Shane Paltridge, the Defence Minister, learning later that this was at the instigation of Menzies. Eggleton returned to naval headquarters in Canberra after the election and was later recruited as Menzies' press secretary. Eggleton told the author of his first discussion with Menzies in his new job:

> I met the PM and I still remember him saying to me 'Look, laddie (he never called me anything else other than 'laddie' for the whole time I was with him), I have a fair command of the English language, so you won't have to write my speeches, but I would like some help with the media. I don't care what your politics are, as long as you feel you can work with me and for me—for my government…Look, laddie, you will come up with all sorts of things you want to do and I will just say 'no', but if you come back the next day, I may say 'yes'. I normally say 'no', but you shouldn't feel that you can't come back.'

Eggleton accepted this advice and often came back for another go after Menzies had refused something. Eggleton became press secretary about the time the Prime Minister became Lord Warden of the Cinque Ports. Menzies rang Eggleton one evening and said:

> Look, I've just been rude to a pressman. I was walking to my car from the back entrance [of Parliament House] and Jack Allsop [AUP] tried to stop me and I was quite short with him. I have been thinking about it over dinner and I was much ruder to him than I should have been. What shall I do?

Eggleton advised him to invite Allsop in for a cup of coffee and a chat. He assured Menzies he did not need to get involved in questions he did not want to answer. Eggleton told me that Jack Allsop thought it was Christmas and that Menzies was so pleased he remarked, 'I might be rude more often and get opportunities like that.'

Menzies' long career came to an end on 20 January 1966 when he told the joint government party meeting of his decision to retire. In his place, the Liberals elected Harold Holt. Menzies went to Government House and told his old foe, the Governor-General, Richard Casey (by then Baron Casey), he intended to retire. The following day, Australia's longest-serving Prime Minister held a much-anticipated press conference at Parliament House, with radio and TV hook-ups reaching across the nation. It lasted 50 minutes and there were 40 questions. The room was packed and in addition to virtually every gallery journalist, other journalists and broadcasters came to Canberra for the event.

In his opening statement before taking questions, Menzies said: 'This is something that doesn't happen very frequently—for a man to go out of office under his own steam. I've gone out of office before today under somebody else's steam, but this time under my own.' He explained that at the due date of the next election, he would be seventy-two:

> I couldn't see myself at seventy-two after, by that time 17 years of prime ministership and six years leading the opposition and a lot of history behind that, couldn't see myself saying to the people of Australia, 'I want you to give me another term.' I don't think it would be fair to them and I don't think it would be fair to me, for that matter.

Menzies said the job had taken its toll. 'One becomes tired, not quite 100 per cent efficient. And I have an old-fashioned belief that the Prime Minister of this country ought to be 100 per cent efficient at all times.'

He spoke of his great affection for his wife, Dame Pattie, and, by chance, in interviews earlier in the day, Harold Holt and Bill McMahon had spoken of their wives. This probably prompted a strange question: 'How do you feel about retiring at the very moment when the first woman Prime Minister [Indira Gandhi] in the world is appointed? Is this a trend?' Menzies answered:

Well, I'll convey to Mrs Gandhi your ideas on this matter. I know her. She's an extraordinarily able woman and I wish her well. But she's not my wife. I have one of my own. Harold has one of his and Bill McMahon, God be praised, has one of his [laughter]. We are not answerable for our wives. They, poor dears, are answerable for us. [Ceylon in 1960 boasted the world's first woman prime minister, Sirimavo Bandaranaike, widow of Ceylon's assassinated Prime Minister, Solomon Bandaranaike.]

The first question, to everyone's surprise, came from a brash junior *Daily Mirror* reporter, Alex Mitchell, who beat the old hands for Menzies' attention: 'Sir Robert, you've talked about all the achievements of your time in government, but what about the failures?' Menzies gave the questioner a withering stare and replied: 'There weren't any.'

John Bennetts of *The Age* followed up: 'What about the Communist Dissolution Bill—wasn't that a failure?' (He was referring to Menzies' defeat in the 1951 referendum to ban the Communist Party.) Menzies deadpanned again: 'The Bill wasn't but the vote was.' In cricketing terms, the Prime Minister was playing with a dead bat.

The feature of the conference was the out-of-character performance by Jon Gaul, the political correspondent for *The Canberra Times*. A reserved young man, Gaul had been hyped up by his editor to put some searching questions to Menzies. Given his instructions, Gaul decided to mull over his tactics in advance in the non-members' bar—a lengthy process. By the time he made it to the conference room, Gaul was rearing to go. He shot question after question at Menzies, who patiently answered each of them. Gaul asked whether the buoyant Australian economy was due to Menzies' management, or to the Prime Minister's good fortune. He asked whether it was true that Menzies 'rode the wave' of the Australian economy. Menzies replied, 'I can assure you I'm no surfie.'

Finally, other journalists forced Gaul to give way. Les Love got the call and was so excited he lost his carefully written question in his notebook, managing some half-coherent effort. Broadcaster Ormsby Wilkins asked a pedestrian question about cricket. Gaul remained the feature of the press conference. At the end of the conference, Alan Reid, as arguably the most senior member of the gallery, made a brief speech wishing Menzies and Dame Pattie a long and prosperous retirement and concluded 'and may your memoirs, when you produce them, Sir, be as controversial, and I hope successful, as your own long and successful career'.

Menzies thanked Reid and noted the press conference had gone on for 50 minutes, adding 'some of you might say with some justification, "Well, he ought to give us 50 minutes; he's given us mighty few press conferences." Anyhow, thank you and good luck to you.'

Gaul's overenthusiastic performance did him no harm and he went on to a successful career as a public relations consultant. As a young man, he was a member of the Labor Party, but as a consultant, he was a key adviser to a succession of Liberal leaders on election campaign tactics.

On 9 March, when the House of Representatives next met after Menzies' departure, Harold Holt moved a resolution placing on record the value the house placed on his long, able and devoted service to Australia. Holt in his speech dealt with the myth of Menzies being such an authoritarian figure that his Cabinet colleagues had little opportunity in Cabinet to consider matters that came before it. Holt said:

> As my colleagues who have sat in the Cabinet of the nation know, far from discouraging the presentation of independent view points around the table, he not only encouraged it but expected it. A great value we found ourselves deriving from his presence as Prime Minister was that as argument and debate unfolded around the Cabinet table he was able, with that calm, judicial quality of mind which is peculiarly one of his outstanding attributes, to pull the threads of an argument together...We did not always agree with his judgment, yet he would accept cheerfully and readily the decision of his Cabinet when a majority opinion was obvious.

Eggleton served four prime ministers: Menzies (for about six months), Holt, Gorton and, briefly, Fraser. He rose to the position of National Director of the Liberal Party. From the point of view of a gallery journalist, I found Eggleton one of the best. You did not have to be his mate, take him to lunch, flatter him or listen to political propaganda. For busy journalists, most importantly, he was rarely away from his desk, one floor below the gallery in his tiny office; not for him the non-members' bar. I could go directly to him in his office to put a query. If it was a Cabinet matter, Eggleton would reach into a drawer and produce a large volume, which he would briefly study.

He then would give me a run down on where a particular issue—the object of my inquiry—stood: the interdepartmental committee has reported on this to the appropriate minister; the minister will draw up a submission to Cabinet; this will be considered next week; the cost of the project is about $x million; and room will have to be found for it in what is expected to be a tight budget.

In short, you had something with a factual basis for your story. Eggleton's availability was important for journalists who were, and still are, up against deadlines.

Eggleton and Menzies became close. He told me that as Christmas Day 1965 approached, Menzies said to Eggleton, 'Laddie, I like having Christmas with the family. You know, half a day with all the family, the kids and Christmas lunch. I'm quite happy then to go off to Kirribilli House, watch the ferries going by and listen to the cricket and the tennis on the radio. Will you come with me?' Although surprised, Eggleton agreed. He spent several days at Kirribilli House with just Menzies and the housekeeper—no-one else from Menzies' staff and not a single security officer.

Over their first meal, Menzies told his press secretary of his pending retirement announcement. He discussed his Cabinet colleagues and his successor, telling Eggleton, 'Look, I have a lot of confidence in Harold [Holt] and he will be a great successor and I'm sure he will take over from me.' Menzies added he would recommend to Holt that he appoint Eggleton at least for a trial. Menzies soon after held his retirement press conference and intended his resignation would formally take effect on Australia Day, 26 January 1966. Before Menzies' resignation, a senior minister, Shane Paltridge, died suddenly. Eggleton, Menzies and the ministry flew to Perth for the funeral, spent Australia Day in Perth, and Eggleton flew back to Canberra with Harold Holt as Prime Minister.

Eggleton told the author:

> That night I slept at the famous old Esplanade Hotel in Perth with Menzies in a room on one side of me and Holt in a room on the other side. Next morning there was a knocking on my wall from the Holt side. I went and knocked on his door and he let me in, saying, 'Have you got an Australia Day message for me?' I said, 'Yes, I have (I had thought it all through) and he said, 'Good, well give it to me. I'm going to the toilet, so I'll read it while I'm in the toilet.' I thought, 'What's going to happen to my draft in there?'

Something was about to happen to Holt, which led to some of the greatest dramas in the Old Parliament House.

11. The Prime Minister Disappears

Harold Holt was fated. History will remember him for his dramatic and mysterious death off Cheviot Beach on Victoria's Mornington Peninsula, south of Melbourne, on Sunday, 17 December 1967. He had become Australia's seventeenth Prime Minister less than two years earlier, in January 1966. Apart from his dramatic death, he will be remembered unkindly for his statement at the White House, when he was visiting US President, Lyndon Baines Johnson, declaring Australia would be 'all the way with LBJ' in the Vietnam War. This is unfair. 'All the way with LBJ' had been Johnson's Senate election campaign slogan. Holt was merely being jocular and displaying to Americans he was no ignorant foreigner when it came to US politics.

Harold Holt was cursed. When elected unopposed to succeed Menzies, he had been in the House of Representatives for 30 years in Menzies' shadow—the longest wait any successor to the prime ministership has ever endured. Despite Holt's many years in senior positions in the Liberal parliamentary party, both in government and in opposition, it seemed the voting public was uninterested in him. What fame he had was as much because of his marriage to the lively and interesting Zara than for any of his own deeds.

Holt was nevertheless a popular figure, both in his own party and with the press gallery. In the gallery, he was referred to with the familiar 'Harold', not 'Holt'. Smooth, urbane and handsome—in preparation for taking over from Menzies— Holt, at considerable expense, had all his teeth capped. He was adequate, but not inspiring in the house. The words came out efficiently and the sentences were not clumsy, but somewhat like John Howard, they lacked conviction. Nor was he as eloquent as Menzies, Calwell, Whitlam, Beazley sr, Killen and many others. The author cannot remember Holt ever having a press secretary before he became Prime Minister, when Tony Eggleton moved smoothly from Menzies to Holt. In all his portfolios, Holt handled the press adroitly and charmingly.

When Holt announced his first ministry, he surprised the gallery by holding an unprecedented press conference to discuss the new Cabinet and outer ministry. Previously, prime ministers simply put out a press release listing their ministry after an election or a reshuffle, avoiding questioning as to why certain government MPs had missed out, or why newcomers had been favoured with promotion. At Holt's press conference, George Kerr (*Sydney Morning Herald*) asked why Reginald (Curley) Swartz had been promoted to Minister for Civil Aviation. Holt replied that Swartz 'hadn't put a foot wrong'. George Kerr interjected: 'Neither had he put a foot right.' Holt merely smiled.

Holt scored a stunning victory in the only election he fought as Prime Minister, in November 1966, defeating the divisive Opposition Leader, Arthur Calwell. Having lost the 1961 and 1963 elections, Calwell pleaded with the Labor Caucus not to dump him as leader, but to give him one more try. Caucus, reluctantly, agreed. Calwell declared he would fight the 1966 election on one issue: the conscription of eighteen-year-olds to fight in Vietnam. Ironically, 11 months later, public opinion turned against the war. In October 1967, Holt announced a further 1700 troops would go to Vietnam, plus a tank squadron and more helicopters, bringing the Australian forces in Vietnam to more than 8000. *The Age* commented that Holt's statement said very little to clarify the Government's belief about the course of the war:

> It did not satisfy the public nervousness that escalation may have already gone past the point of logic, it did not adequately relate our new commitment to an overall strategy, it did not indicate that the government has any view of the war's future, other than to accept Washington's decisions and accede to reasonable requests for help. All these doubts demand satisfaction during the election campaign debate. It is a pity the Labor Party has not given Mr Whitlam [who had replaced Calwell as Labor leader] a Vietnam policy, which might put Mr Holt under test.

In 1966 there was a range of views within the Labor Caucus about Vietnam. The anti-communist Right felt the war was necessary and Australian participation justified; the Left called for immediate withdrawal of Australian troops and an end to the fighting, despite Dr Jim Cairns, the leader of the Caucus left, expressing surprise that other Asian countries were not perturbed about Australian troops operating in Vietnam. He said he believed 'immediate withdrawal' would be not only impracticable but also inhumane.[1] The Left felt Cairns had betrayed them and Labor principles. This division in the Caucus explains the reference in *The Age* to Whitlam not being given a Vietnam policy to test Holt.

There was no doubt Holt was under pressure from Washington to do more in Vietnam. In 1967, President Johnson sent General Maxwell Taylor and his then civilian adviser (later Secretary of Defence), Clark Clifford, on a special mission to Canberra to seek more troops for Vietnam. Holt explained to his visitors Australia had defence obligations in other areas such as Malaysia while at the same time telling the Americans he was in favour of continued bombing of North Vietnam. This did not satisfy Clifford who later reported to Washington that Holt was not doing enough. Clifford was still unimpressed, even after Holt

---

1   COD, 28 October 1966, p. 305.

had increased the Australian effort in Vietnam to three battalions. Clifford said that in World War II Australia, with a much smaller population, had maintained 300 000 troops overseas and yet had been able to send only 7000 to Vietnam.[2]

Holt was in trouble in 1967. The new leader of the Labor Party, Gough Whitlam, was clearly besting him in Parliament at Question Time. While the majority of voters did not know this, it mattered mightily to those who sat behind the Prime Minister and the Leader of the Opposition, and Whitlam got off to a flying start. When Whitlam first faced Holt in the house, Holt said Whitlam's first speech would reveal whether he would be a better Opposition Leader than Calwell. Whitlam responded, provoking mirth on the Labor side, 'Thank you, Mr Prime Minister…Actually I always thought that you would make a better Opposition Leader than either Mr Calwell or myself.' When Whitlam became Opposition Leader, noted red baiter Bill Wentworth warned Holt the Government was almost entirely dependent upon the communist issue:

> [Although] our electoral position is excellent and I think you are a better vote-getter than Menzies…the reaction towards Whitlam is quite strong and could be overwhelming if he took a strong anti-Communist line. Under such circumstances many of our marginal seats would go at the next election and we might even lose government.[3]

Holt was criticised by many of his backbenchers for his handling of two hot issues: allegations of misuse of the RAAF VIP 34 squadron and demands for a second royal commission into the *Voyager* disaster. The former arose from mischief conceived by Labor's Fred Daly when he asked Holt, by way of a Question on Notice in November 1965, about flights in VIP aircraft and their cost. His purpose was to embarrass Calwell, who had been granted use of a VIP plane by Menzies to attend a weekend State ALP conference in Perth. As the house, unusually, had sat on a Friday, Calwell could not keep his appointment by using a commercial airline. Daly's objective was to embarrass Calwell so as to advance the cause of Whitlam becoming ALP leader. In the event, Calwell and Daly buried the hatchet before the answer to the question could be given. Calwell assured Holt that Daly would not press for an answer; in the Senate, Vince Gair, the DLP leader, asked for flight details. Government Senate leader, Denham Henty, told him, wrongly, that flight details were not recorded.

The VIP affair at its core was about misuse of taxpayers' money. Taxpayers funded the RAAF, and it was clear ministers were using the VIP squadron as a right, not a privilege. Rather than ministers travelling on commercial airlines like other Australians, RAAF aircraft were whistled up. Stories of misuse of taxpayer money by politicians, then as now, are invariably given a big splash

---

2   Frame, *The Life and Death of Harold Holt*, p. 199.
3   Ibid., p. 205.

by the media. As the probing by the ALP in the Senate continued, the issue became not so much the misuse of VIP aircraft, but the claim by Harold Holt and Air Minister, Peter Howson, that there were no records of passengers carried on VIP flights. In the gallery, it was taken for granted that the Government was covering up and undoubtedly there were records of flights and passengers.

Gorton, Leader of the Government in the Senate, in an act of seeming honesty—knowing it would damage Holt's leadership—decided to clear the air. Howson, with responsibility for the RAAF as Air Minister, was overseas. Reg Swartz, Minister for Civil Aviation, was acting Air Minister in Howson's absence and Gorton went around Swartz. He phoned A. B. (Tich) McFarlane, Secretary of the Air Department, and asked him directly whether there were passenger manifests on VIP flights. Indeed there were, said McFarlane, and, in accordance with RAAF regulations, they were retained for 12 months. On 25 October 1967, without any explanation, Gorton tabled the passenger manifests. On his return, Howson offered Holt his resignation, which was not accepted. Gorton was lauded for his honesty and, doubtless, after Holt's disappearance, it was a significant factor in the Liberals deciding that he, not Paul Hasluck, would be Prime Minister.

Since the 11 September 2001 attacks in the United States, concerns about security have led to a situation in which the RAAF VIP squadron routinely carryies MPs around Australia and overseas. Gorton became Prime Minister on 10 January 1968, taking over the ministry from Jack McEwen, who was sworn in as Prime Minister immediately after Holt's death. McEwen in turn had inherited the Holt ministry. Howson was dumped from the ministry when Gorton reshuffled it 18 days later. Alan Reid wrote that before announcing his ministry, Gorton called Howson in to the Prime Minister's Melbourne office in Treasury Gardens to tell him he would not be in the ministry.[4]

Despite the longstanding antipathy between the two, Howson said, 'Good luck to you in your new post, John', and put out his hand. Gorton rejected the offered handshake. Reid says this was the version Howson gave his friends immediately after the meeting and when he asked Howson to confirm the story, Howson replied, 'No comment'. McMahon, after defeating Gorton in the party room, restored Howson to the ministry as Minister for Aborigines—a portfolio in which he showed great energy and concern to improve the lot of Aborigines.

The *Voyager* disaster was even more damaging to Holt's leadership than the VIP affair. The destroyer *HMAS Voyager*, commanded by Captain Duncan Stevens, was cut in half in a collision with the aircraft carrier *HMAS Melbourne*, under the command of Captain John Robertson. The royal commission established by

---

4 Reid, *The Gorton Experiment*, p. 34.

Menzies found the *Voyager* was to blame, although three officers on the bridge of the *Melbourne* at the time, including its Captain, John Robertson, were also criticised. In the press gallery, the theory was that someone living had to be found to blame and Robertson was it. When he was transferred to a training establishment, Robertson resigned from the Navy.

Subsequently, an ex-*Voyager* executive officer, Peter Cabban, recorded a sensational statement to the effect that the Captain of the *Voyager*, Duncan Stevens, was a chronic alcoholic, and he cited numerous instances of the captain's sickness on a voyage to South-East Asia in 1963. In his book *Breaking Ranks*, Cabban stated Captain Stevens never drank at sea, only whilst in port, but that his recovery sometimes took several days. It emerged that Stevens was known in the Navy as 'Drunken Duncan'. Cabban would not accept the evidence to and the finding of the first royal commission. He made a most damaging statement about the heavy drinking of Stevens and this statement was taken up by Liberal backbencher John Jess, in demanding that Holt hold a second inquiry.

Holt did not know that during the drama over *Voyager*, Cabban was using as his base Gough Whitlam's Deputy Opposition Leader's office in Parliament House. Under pressure from his own side, Labor and now the gallery, Holt agreed to a debate on the *Voyager* Royal Commission on 16 May 1967. At this point, Holt had only seven months to live. The Government line was that no new inquiry was needed, and the Cabban statement was uncorroborated and irrelevant. Edward St John QC, a brilliant Sydney barrister and a loner whose independence of mind made him unusual in politics, was the key speaker. This was St John's maiden speech. The convention was and still is that MPs making their maiden speech should not be subjected to interjections.

On the conclusion of their speech, it was traditional they were congratulated on the floor of the chamber with a handshake by their colleagues and, if he was in the house, their leader. The next speaker (even though from the other side of the house) would utter a few words of congratulations to the maiden speaker— but not this time. The author was in the house for the debate. St John spoke from his seat in the back row of the house, directly behind the front bench of ministers and the Prime Minister's seat at the table.

It was a brilliant speech, methodically pulling apart the first royal commission and the Government's attempt to dismiss the Cabban statement. His speech was late in the afternoon of 16 May 1967 and was interrupted by the two-hour dinner adjournment. Resuming after dinner, St John was dealing with the assertion of the Government that Cabban's statement about the drunken behaviour of the Captain of the *Voyager*, Duncan Stevens, was irrelevant. Then this exchange occurred:

St John: Are we playing a battle of semantics? What is the meaning of the word 'irrelevant'?

Holt: What is the meaning of the word 'evidence'?

St John: I did not expect to be interrupted by the Prime Minister. We all have been invited to debate what comes to us second hand. The Prime Minister's interruption demonstrated better than anything else that this kind of matter can be sifted only by a proper judicial inquiry, by a select committee or otherwise.

The house fell silent. The Prime Minister, of all people, had breached a convention protecting maiden speakers. Worse, St John's retort had been cutting and to the point. Two days later, Holt announced there would be a second *Voyager* royal commission, despite a clear majority of Cabinet being against him, including the Attorney-General, Nigel Bowen, and Gorton. Holt was on the skids from this point on.

The second royal commission heard testimony that Captain Stevens was regularly taking amphetamines and consumed a triple brandy on the evening of the collision. The commission found this account might have been mistaken and, explicitly, that he was unimpaired by alcohol at the time of the collision. It also found that while Captain Stevens had concealed a recurrence of stomach ulcers, which should have disqualified him from command, this had no bearing on the accident. The second commission found that the accident might have resulted from *Voyager* being mistaken as to what side of *Melbourne* she was on during her final manoeuvre. It is notoriously difficult to judge a carrier's course at night by her lights, and *Melbourne* was utilising experimental red deck floodlights that might have been deceiving.

Holt's death was the most dramatic Australian political event since World War II. On Sunday, 17 December, Holt was at the family beach house at Portsea, the Parliament having risen for the year; the last Cabinet meeting finished in the early hours of Friday. Holt and four others drove to Point Nepean to watch the entry into Port Phillip Bay of Alec Rose, who was attempting an around-the-world solo journey in his yacht, *Lively Lady*. Holt suggested to the party they go to Cheviot Beach for a swim. The beach was rough and looked dangerous, yet shortly after noon, Holt, wearing a pair of lace-less sandshoes, entered the water, stating, 'I know this beach like the back of my hand'. Soon after, he disappeared in the boiling surf.

The alarm was raised. More than an hour later, three amateur skin divers arrived at the beach to begin a search, but found the sea too difficult. The largest maritime search-and-rescue operation in Australian history was mounted, with Tony Eggleton handling the media, which had hastily thrown every resource available in this holiday period into covering the sensational story. Eggleton was the obvious person to do the job and he held two to three press conferences a day until late in the evening of the following Tuesday. He became a national figure within a few days, appearing every night on TV news bulletins around the nation.

By Tuesday, all hope of finding the Prime Minister alive had disappeared. The body was never recovered, experts declaring that sea lice and crayfish would have stripped the body of all flesh within 24 hours. All sorts of ludicrous stories were to appear in the media, including Holt being picked up by a Chinese submarine and that the Prime Minister of Australia was in reality an agent of the Communist Chinese Government in Peking. Zara Holt went to the nub of the matter in dismissing the theory: 'Harry didn't like Chinese food.' Holt was a keen spear fisherman and a well-known media photo was of him in his black wetsuit, surrounded by beautiful young women. But without flippers, Holt was not a strong swimmer and he had made the mistake of going into the water wearing sandshoes, thereby weighing down his legs and making swimming difficult.

When told of the disappearance, Zara immediately inquired whether Holt was wearing flippers or sand shoes. When told it was sandshoes, she immediately declared: 'He's gone.' Suicide was soon raised as an explanation for Holt's disappearance, but colleagues such as Sir James Killen and Alexander Downer sr rejected this. Yet the suicide line was given some credence by friend and beachside neighbour Marjorie Gillespie, who was a member of the party accompanying Holt to the beach. Gillespie in an interview in 1968 rejected the idea of suicide, but in a TV documentary, *The Harold Holt Mystery*, put to air in 1985, Gillespie stated Holt 'had put himself in a situation where he was almost certain to die'. She had also revealed in 1988 that she was 'Harold Holt's lover'—a claim repeated in several magazines and newspapers. Gillespie was interviewed by journalist Simon Warrender, who reported:

> I referred to constant rumours since the Cheviot tragedy that she and Harold were having an affair. Impudently, she did not deny the rumours. 'Of course, Simon', she said 'what is your interpretation of an affair?' I told her. She said that there were various types of affairs—intimate affairs and sordid affairs and emotional affairs. Hers with Harold, she said, was an emotional affair based on 'mutual intellectual admiration and respect'.

In November 2007, with the approach of the fortieth anniversary of Holt's death, journalist Ray Martin in a Nine Network documentary, again raised the suicide theory. Martin claimed Doug Anthony, Cabinet colleague of Holt, had said it was possible Holt had committed suicide, yet in an interview with the

ABC Anthony said he did not give such an interview. Malcolm Fraser and Holt's biographer, Tom Frame, dismissed the suicide theory. Fraser, Australia's twenty-second Prime Minister and Minister for the Army in the Holt ministry, revealed Holt had been in discussions with him about the Government's future foreign policy and a Cabinet reshuffle. 'Now, if somebody is planning to jump off a cliff, they are not at the same time planning to have a major Cabinet review of the direction Australia is taking,' Fraser said.

Whatever the nature of Gillespie's 'affair' with Holt, I have always believed he went into the boiling surf because he was showing off to Gillespie. Tony Eggleton agrees with me. Holt fancied himself as a ladies' man and his actions fitted his own view of himself. I had known Holt for 15 years and was on good terms with him before his death. He, like nearly all politicians, had a positive view about the future and an ambition to play a role in it. He was certainly not suicidal and I have a previously undisclosed piece of evidence to rule it out altogether.

In the week before he left for Melbourne, Holt hosted a cocktail party for the gallery at the Lodge, either on Wednesday or Thursday. My first wife, Lesley, accompanied me to the party, where she fell into conversation with her best mate and golfing companion Joan Comans, wife of the ABC bureau head in the gallery, Jack Comans. Both had won the ladies' championship at Royal Canberra. Joan had told Lesley previously she and Holt had an affair some years earlier. Holt, playing the perfect host, came up to them with a plate offering them pieces of abalone and urging them to try his offering, explaining he had dived for the abalone himself.

Holt was full of beans, enthusiastic in talking about Zara Holt's redecorating of the Lodge—something wives of incoming prime ministers often feel compelled to do. Joan, archly, asked what the bedrooms were like. Grinning, Holt said they were fine and offered an inspection to the two women. They accepted and Holt conducted them through the Lodge and upstairs to the main bedroom. Entering, Joan said, 'Oh, two single beds, Harold, that's nice'. Sitting on one end of a bed, Joan sang to him, 'I can do anything better than you can', and a knowing Holt, sitting on the other end, sang the reply, 'No, you can't, no, you can't'. This was certainly not behaviour suggesting suicidal tendencies had gripped Holt.

12. The Influence Seekers

The Federal Government, the Public Service and the Parliament have assumed ever-greater significance in national affairs as the power of the States has waned, and are thus a target for special-interest groups. The most influential and wealthiest of special-interest groups is the Australian business community—representing businesses big, medium and small. Business claims to be enthusiasts for competition and berates unions for, among other things, wanting to have exclusive coverage of workers in business establishments. Yet businesspeople detest competition and do everything possible to wipe out competitors, be it locals or importers.

A persistent myth about Menzies was his closeness to the big end of town, but he did not go out of his way to pander to the business community. True, at the urging of the private banks, he legislated to separate the Reserve Bank from the government-owned Commonwealth Bank. The private banks had a perfectly reasonable argument. Given the sweeping powers of the Reserve to intervene in banking business, it should not have been incorporated into the Commonwealth Bank—a competitor of the private banks. Menzies encouraged Garfield Barwick to develop legislation to control potential cartels and anticompetitive behaviour. It fell to Lionel Murphy, Attorney-General in the Whitlam Government, to introduce the trade practices legislation that provided the basic weapon for the Australian Competition and Consumer Commission (ACCC) in its unending struggle with cartel power.

The struggle between the free traders and protectionists has a long history, going back to the debates leading to Federation, and was entangled in the White Australia Policy, leading to the formation of the Australian Labor Party. The protectionists and supporters of White Australia were in the ascendancy right up to the 1960s when Harold Holt cautiously began to dismantle the White Australia Policy—a task Whitlam finished.

Like most journalists, I took for granted that tariff protection for Australian industry was a given, with both sides of politics supporting the policy without question. There were only two significant business lobbies in Canberra in the 1950s: the Associated Chambers of Manufactures of Australia (ACMA) and the Associated Chambers of Commerce of Australia (ACCA)—both in the suburb of Barton, within easy walking distance of Parliament House. Both were federal organisations, as are the Commonwealth of Australia and the major political parties. ACMA's membership and funds derived from the various State Chambers of Manufactures and ACCA's membership and funds came from the State Chambers of Commerce.

ACMA was the cheerleader for the whole mechanism of the defence of Australian industry against imports provided by tariffs and anti-dumping measures. ACCA—whose membership was influential and included the banks as well as importers—mounted stiff opposition to protection. Executive Director, Ray Pelham-Thorman, a former Treasury official and a capable and determined lobbyist, led the chamber for 23 years. Bob Anderson, the CEO of ACMA, was the high priest of tariffs, and I found him to be an affable and knowledgeable contact. Tall, with a ruddy, smiling face, and popular, he was more a salesman than Pelham-Thorman, who relied on economic analysis to push his case. Menzies described him as the 'prince of lobbyists'.

Anderson, speaking for protected industries such as vehicles, textiles, clothing and footwear—indeed most products manufactured in Australia—had the political advantage over Pelham-Thorman, who represented the big end of town. The union movement was solidly behind Anderson, who had extensive political contacts, including Bill McMahon (they were friends from before the war, when keen ballroom dancers). When it came to tariffs, McMahon and Anderson were on opposite sides of the fence. McMahon was the only dissident in the Menzies ministry against the protectionist policies of McEwen.

After Anderson departed ACMA in 1977, the organisation changed its name to the Confederation of Australian Industry (CAI) and was an amalgamation of ACMA and the Australian Council of Employers' Federations (ACEF). In 1987 there was turmoil in the associated chambers. Andrew Hay, formerly secretary to Fraser Government Minister Phil Lynch, was president of ACCA. He decided to sack all the senior executives, including Howard Grant, an engineer who was recruited from the major construction company Civil and Civic. Hay believed ACCA no longer needed its specialised information services to hundreds of companies classified as associate members.[1]

By the 1970s, Taiwan had become an important export market for Australia, yet it was not extended diplomatic recognition by Canberra. The Australian Government recognised only one government in China: that which rules in Beijing. Nevertheless, the Government was anxious to assist trade with Taiwan, but could not establish an office for the Australian Trade Commission in Taipei. Soon after the Fraser Government came to power, it used ACCA as the de facto Australian Trade Commission in Taiwan. The Trade Department contracted ACCA to establish the Australian Commerce and Industry Office in Taipei. The device of ACCA in effect running the trade commissioner's service in Taipei avoided diplomatic problems with the Chinese Government. Both CAI and ACCA

---

1   Conversation with Howard Grant.

were having financial problems and finally, in 1992, the old enemies merged to become the Australian Chamber of Commerce and Industry (ACCI). By that time, the Hawke and Keating Governments had decided in favour of the free traders.

Opponents of the then system of industrial relations were scornful of what they had dubbed the industrial relations (IR) 'club'. Members of the 'club' were union officials, employer representatives and the members of the Commonwealth Conciliation and Arbitration Commission. Senior union and employer representatives were appointed by the Federal Government to the Australian Industrial Relations Commission and by State governments to the State Industrial Relations Commissions.

A pillar of the 'club' was another national body, the Metal Trades Industry Association (MTIA; now the Australian Industry Group), headquartered not in Canberra but in Sydney. The Metal Trades Award's pay and conditions flowed through to virtually all manufacturing workplaces and other industries—hence, MTIA was the most important organisation of employers under the now defunct centralised system of wage fixation. MTIA argued for the bosses on pay and conditions; ACMA was the protector of high tariffs for the bosses and workers; and the Australian Council of Trade Unions (ACTU) fought for the workers on all fronts.

Prominent members of the IR club such as Bob Anderson and legendary union leader and President of the ACTU, Albert Monk, spent a good part of Australian winters in the northern summer in Geneva, all expenses paid, attending the annual meetings of the International Labor Organisation (ILO), a UN organisation aiming to improve the labour market for workers and employers. The annual sojourn in Geneva was one of the perks for members of the club and once you were a member you were set for life. Monk was President of the ACTU from 1934 to 1943 and then again from 1949 until his retirement in 1969. Harold Holt, Minister for Labor in Menzies Governments from 1949 until 1963, was a good friend of Monk.

Menzies, like all conservative prime ministers until John Howard, was a supporter of the IR 'club'. When a serious strike arose, the Prime Minister would call on the unions and employers to go before the 'independent umpire': the Commonwealth Court of Conciliation and Arbitration and its successor from 1956, the Commonwealth Conciliation and Arbitration Commission. If a strike (or its effects) extended across State borders, it was regarded as a national strike, and Menzies and Holt believed it was their job to try to end it, not inflame it. Holt would get together with Monk to try to agree on what needed to be done on both sides—employers and unions.

'Rounds' is a journalistic term for a special area of news requiring the attention of one or more journalists: police rounds, rural rounds, shipping and aviation rounds, and so on. Industrial relations was and remains a 'round' for senior, specialist journalists in the State capitals who had good contacts in trades halls and employer organisations. When a strike became national, it was also up to the gallery to cover developments from the point of view of Holt and the Government.

Holt had no press secretary and no matter how hot an IR issue was, he would deal with the gallery directly. Many a strike did become a hot issue and communist-led unions were often involved—notably, Jim Healy and the Waterside Workers' Federation. My father was no communist, but, like many unionists, he regarded Healy as a champion of the workers, and communists succeeded in the unions because most rank-and-file members believed they were tough and incorruptible. Even though Ben Chifley used the Army to break the communist-led coal strike of 1949, this did not of itself bring about the demise of communist union leaders.

Clarrie Gaudry, the first director of the Heavy Engineering Manufacturers' Association (HEMA), established a small secretariat in Canberra. Formerly a customs official, he was hired for, among other things, his knowledge of the tariff and import quota system, which Australian industry looked to for protection from imports. During World War II, Gaudry served on Royal Australian Navy (RAN) destroyers in the Mediterranean. Known as the 'scrap-iron flotilla', these vessels were built in Britain during World War I and were at the end of their useful life.

Gaudry had some great stories. One concerned the Allies' stunning 1941 defeat of the Italian forces in the desert, when the AIF Sixth Division played a key role. More than 65 000 Italian prisoners-of-war had to be managed and fed, and RAN ships were asked to provide personnel to help. When the volunteers from Gaudry's ship got to the place where the Italians were being assembled, an army officer addressed the disconsolate Italians. 'Does anyone here speak English?', he roared. An Italian soldier pushed his way through the crowd and stood in front of him. 'Do you speak English?', asked the officer. 'Fuckin' oath I do', said the Italian. 'I ran a fish 'n' chip shop in Richmond, came to Italy on holidays and Musso [Benito Mussolini, the Italian dictator] threw me into the Army.'

Gaudry had risen to the rank of chief petty officer in charge of the radio room on his ship when a Royal Navy lieutenant seconded to the RAN asked Gaudry if he could help find a lost big bottle of black ink. Gaudry went to the door of the radio room and yelled down the corridor to the ratings in the forward mess: 'Has anyone seen the lieutenant's big bottle of black ink?' A voice from the mess boomed back: 'No, but we've seen his big, black arse.' The Britisher retorted: 'I'd watch them, Chief, they may be doing a George.' (A 'George' was a British naval term for buggery.)

Gaudry was selective about the journalists he invited to the annual HEMA dinner and, as a mate, I made the list. Although of working-class background, Gaudry insisted on dinner jackets as the dress for the dinner. Women journalists were not invited, and his friends berated him for his prejudice. Gough Whitlam was guest of honour at one of the dinners and, after his speech, was enjoying himself at the head table when a waiter, bearing a tray loaded with port, tipped the lot over the Prime Minister. Whitlam calmly got to his feet, took off his soaking trousers and continued with the dinner.

Gaudry and his successor, Richard Dowe, saw their principal role as gaining the maximum protection for their industry from import competition. The vast oil and gas reserves on Australia's North-West Shelf should have provided a great opportunity for the development of Australian heavy engineering. European companies had certainly insisted on maximum use of their own engineering industries to develop North Sea oil reserves and even during the Thatcher years in Britain, when economic rationalists commanded government policy, international oil majors seeking to develop North Sea oil fields were required to first provide the UK Offshore Supplies Office with detailed proposals for British industry participation. If contracts went to other than UK firms, developers were asked to explain.

Tiny Norway, with only 4.5 million people, was fortunate as economic rationalists were thin on the ground when the Norwegian oil fields began to be developed. The Norwegian Government legislated to ensure work on the fields had to be carried out in Norway, using Norwegian engineers and technicians. Norway today has a world-class offshore oil and gas design and engineering industry. The approach was entirely different in Australia. Multinational oil and gas companies threatened the Hawke and Keating Governments, claiming they would pull out of Australia if local industry was given any advantage in tendering for work on the shelf.

Local industry was not given a chance to compete equally, let alone given an edge over foreign companies. Australian firms competing for tenders frequently were given insufficient notice of tenders coming up, and in any case the international companies mainly gave the work to their overseas affiliates and associated companies. I kept in touch with Richard Dowe when he succeeded Gaudry (and invited women journalists to the annual dinner). Dowe fought strenuously for greater Australian industry involvement in the development of offshore oil and gas fields, but without success. Dowe regarded Woodside as his major obstacle, claiming it stymied any attempt to give local industry the slightest leg-up over the foreign competition. Dowe's attitude towards Woodside was shared by Treasurer Peter Costello, who, in 2001, cited national interest when he vetoed Royal Dutch Shell's hostile $10 billion bid to take control of Woodside, in which it had a 34 per cent stake.

In the 1980s, HEMA closed its Canberra office. What was left of the heavy engineering industry chucked in the towel—a state of affairs stemming from the lack of courage of companies within the industry and of the indifference of successive Labor and Coalition governments.

The Australian Mining Industry Council (now the Minerals Council of Australia) set up a secretariat in a handsome building on Northbourne Avenue and its founding chief executive was an old friend of mine, Paul Phillips. A former senior official in the Department of Trade under McEwen, Paul was a tall, handsome man, with greying hair combed straight back; he looked every inch the senior executive.

Phillips was a prodigious drinker and heavy smoker. He would open the office bar about 11 am for a couple of beers with his senior male staff, then head off to the Commonwealth Club bar where he would down a couple of vodka martinis before lunch with wine and coffee (with brandy), then return to the office. When the office bar opened again about 4 pm, Paul would turn up at the saloon bar of the Hotel Wellington, where he was a regular member of a large drinking school. After a middy or three at the Wello, it would be time to head home to dinner with his charming wife, Betty, for more pre-dinner drinks, wine and brandy. I never saw him the worse for wear. Phillips was also an important adviser in his public service days to the ruggedly straightforward Country Party Leader John McEwen, who, by fate, was to briefly fill the role of Australia's Prime Minister.

13. The Coalition Starts to Slide

With the retirement of Arthur Fadden in 1958, the Country Party leadership went to John McEwen (later Sir John), an Australian World War I soldier-settler. He entered Parliament in 1934 and was long recognised as one of the strongmen of the Menzies Government. As Deputy Prime Minister, McEwen was entitled to take over from Fadden as Treasurer, but McEwen had been advised Fadden had secured all the tax advantages for farmers that were possible. He decided to set up a powerful new Department of Trade. McEwen had been Minister for Commerce and Agriculture when he made the switch to Trade and therefore lost responsibility for agriculture. A new department was created—the Department of Primary Industry—and, to everyone's astonishment and mirth, the first Minister for Primary Industry was none other than the Liberal William McMahon, who had held the Social Services portfolio. Labor wit Fred Daly remarked that McMahon was the 'Kings Cross farmer'. 'All he knew about farming was growing flowers in his window box', Daly chuckled.

After the 1958 election, the Country Party won back the Department of Primary Industry, with the plodding Charles Adermann as minister. Following the 1963 election, McEwen's department was expanded into the Department of Trade and Industry—a change giving McEwen ministerial control not only of trade negotiations abroad, but also of tariff protection at home for Australian manufacturing. McEwen was seen as an arch protectionist. But his critics could not deny that had it not been for McEwen, the Australian car industry would have disappeared and much of the infrastructure of manufacturing and engineering would have been lost. McEwen told the author he wanted the manufacturing industry to have the Australian market as its base, and this solid base would allow it to achieve export success.

This seemed a sensible view and had wide support on both sides of Parliament. Most MPs remembered the Depression years of the 1930s and full employment was the rock on which all political parties' policies were based. The war had aroused a sense that Australia had to develop to enhance its economic and strategic independence and this continues as a basic policy of all political parties. As well as general approval for immigration and development of northern Australia, manufacturing was the largest employer, and politicians from both sides of the Parliament believed in protection, as did a majority of gallery journalists.

McEwen's willingness to protect the manufacturing industry naturally brought a generous flow of funds into the coffers of the Country Party. This was important, but by no means McEwen's motive. He genuinely believed, despite his party's base among farmers, that for its own security, Australia needed to develop a powerful manufacturing sector. The protectionists' domination started to slip under steady attack from the media, and farmers increasingly saw that protection for manufacturing was a burden they had to carry in the form of increased operating costs that they could not pass on in the export market.

Towards the end of the Menzies era, the first stirrings of opposition to McEwen's protectionist policies were beginning to surface. Charles Robert (Bert) Kelly, a farmer, came into Parliament in 1958 as the Liberal Member for Wakefield, and remained on the back bench until he entered the Holt ministry in 1966 as a junior minister. Because of his tireless advocacy of lower protection and criticism of the Menzies Government's protectionist policies, Bert played a far more important role on the back bench than he ever did as a minister. I remember innumerable speeches by Kelly on the tariff issue and, although he was anything but an orator, his case was well put and slowly he began to influence the Parliament and the gallery.

Another important player in the protection debate was Alf Rattigan. A former deputy secretary of the Trade Department, later Comptroller-General of Customs, he was appointed Chairman of the Tariff Board by McEwen in 1963 and remained in that position until 1979, although the organisation's title was changed to the Industries Assistance Commission (and is now the Productivity Commission). Rattigan surprised many by immediately resisting the protectionist policies of his former political master, McEwen, and he had a considerable influence on the decision of Whitlam in 1973 to cut tariffs across the board by 25 per cent. Alan Wood, when only a junior economic writer in the *Australian Financial Review*'s bureau in the gallery, was a supporter of Rattigan and was tireless in opposition to McEwen and the Trade Department.

The fundamental argument against protection was that less efficient companies or industries should not be shielded from import competition and the resources (meaning capital) being used behind a tariff barrier should be deployed to more efficient industries. This argument was convincing when movements of capital in and out of Australia were strictly controlled by the Reserve Bank. With the arrival of globalisation—permitting capital to be seamlessly shifted around the world—many formerly flourishing and protected industries have disappeared or have been substantially reduced. Sacked workers found that the capital freed up did not go to other Australian industries, but rather to China or other emerging economies. Products made in Australia thus became imports. This is leading to a resurgence in support for protection, particularly as the world slips into a global recession. The protection debate is not yet over.

In the 1960s, the Basic Industry Group (BIG) came under notice. Financed by a number of wealthy graziers, it set out to force the Menzies Government to reverse its protection policies. The financing of BIG was largely provided by Charles Russell, a wealthy Queensland grazier, who had been the Country Party

MP for the seat of Maranoa from 1949 until he was defeated in 1951. The major operative for BIG was Max Newton, who had returned to Canberra and started a newsletter called *Incentive*. Don Whitington and I regarded this apprehensively as direct competition. Fortunately, it turned out not to be. Its purpose was to argue the case against protection and McEwen's administration of the Trade Department and its readership was therefore limited. Newton had hoped farmers would subscribe to *Incentive*, but as publishers before and since Newton have discovered, farmers are tightwads when it comes to buying anything in the media. Most of them read the local paper and one of the major farm papers such as *The Land* and that is enough information for them.

BIG addressed the tariff issue from the narrow focus of its impact on the wool industry, dominated by the landed aristocracy, and McEwen used this to his advantage. Much of rural industry and those who worked in it were the beneficiaries of one form or another of government subsidy or protection. There were the statutory marketing bodies established by legislation, operating what clearly were anticompetitive systems of selling on the domestic market. Margarine production quotas were imposed to limit competition with dairy farmers; rail freight rates for hauling grain in one direction and fertiliser in the other were subsidised by State governments; and, most important of all, farmers enjoyed a variety of tax concessions, tailored for them by the Country Party. McEwen also argued that protection was needed to attract migrants who would not come to Australia if their jobs were threatened by imports. In turn, this would see population growth slowed and the domestic market for rural products would diminish.

All this was sound enough for industries such as dairying, horticulture, feed grains and, to a degree, beef and lamb. But it was not so with wool. The free-trade argument was undeniable if confined to the wool industry, with its overwhelming reliance on export markets. Protection of the Australian manufacturing industry raised wool producers' costs—not necessarily recoverable by auction selling of wool. The threat from BIG to McEwen and protection finally disappeared in the early 1970s when the wool industry agreed to the establishment of a reserve price system for wool (which eventually proved a disaster and was scrapped by the Hawke Government).

This was not the end of Max Newton. He had supporters such as Bill McMahon (thereby ensuring McEwen was an enemy) and Secretary of Treasury, John Stone. Newton was contracted to the Japan External Trade Organization (JETRO) in Sydney and was engaged in providing submissions to the Tariff Board and a general information service on tariff issues of interest to Japan. At least one senior journalist, Ian Fitchett, complained about Newton carrying out this work whilst a member of the gallery. A gallery constitution had finally been hammered out after much argument in 1966 and this provided that membership was confined to members of the Australian Journalists' Association (AJA—the journalists' union) whose duties were restricted to the 'collection and dissemination of parliamentary, government or political news'.

A number of journalists (under the lap) carried out limited non-journalistic work such as sending reports to companies of developments in Canberra of direct interest to them and advising them on public relations matters (although not directly lobbying themselves). Fitchett directly challenged Newton's right to be a member of the gallery and we all knew that this was inspired by McEwen. Fitchett was close to McEwen, who fed him with a regular flow of stories—most of them favourable to McEwen and hostile to McMahon. After a number of stormy special general meetings of the gallery, Newton agreed to resign on the condition the gallery would accept a journalist he nominated to represent him in his news service and *Incentive* newsletter.

Like all successful politicians, McEwen was a pragmatist. When it came to looking after his party, he would do the best deals possible and if he had to cross the traditional party lines, so be it. McEwen made a preference-swap deal with the Labor Party strongman and left-wing faction leader Joe Chamberlain. According to the deal, during a Senate election in Western Australia, Labor would preference the Country Party rather than the Liberals and the Country Party would preference Labor rather than the Liberals. He did the same deal with Labor Premier Vince Gair in Queensland. McEwen's press secretary, Bill Carew, told the author he was instructed to carry what Carew described as 'a bagful of brass' to Brisbane airport, where, in the bookshop of the terminal of Australian National Airways (ANA: later to become Ansett Airlines), he handed over this considerable amount of money to Gair and the preference swap was done in Queensland. This was before Gair moved over to the DLP after the Labor split.

It was Menzies who dubbed McEwen 'Black Jack', and the dour Victorian did not appear to mind when it became common in the media to so refer to him. McEwen was cursed with a terrible burden: neurodermatitis—an itchy skin condition. Bill Carew, when he travelled with McEwen, carried four pairs of extra socks because McEwen's feet would be bleeding from dermatitis. It was exacerbated by stress, caused insomnia, and insomnia added to stress, worsening the dermatitis—a self-perpetuating, awful array of maladies. It was no surprise McEwen came into office fairly late.

As Prime Minister, McEwen welcomed US President Johnson to Australia for the memorial service for Harold Holt and they hit it off immediately. Both were farmers and both were in the cattle business. Johnson invited McEwen to his Texas ranch—an invitation McEwen later took up. At the ranch, McEwen had a particularly bad time with bleeding feet and the President insisted on doing something about it. The presidential plane, Air Force One, was whistled up and McEwen was dispatched to the Mayo Clinic for treatment, where he was given cortisone. It appeared to assist him although his widow, Lady Mary, later claimed it contributed to his death.[1]

It could hardly be said that McEwen, born in 1900 and living until he was eighty, died prematurely. McEwen was a dour public figure and carried himself with great dignity in the house, although privately, in the office, he had a lively wit and his staff adored him. He assembled an impressive team to match the high-powered intellects of Treasury. The first Secretary of the Trade Department, John Crawford (later Sir John), an outstanding public servant, recruited gifted officers into the department. Unlike ministers of the Howard Government, McEwen did not object to journalists being briefed by departmental officials in both the Trade and Primary Industry Departments.

Stringing as part-time correspondent for *The Land*, I had a keen interest in what was going on in both those departments and enjoyed easy access to senior officials. One of these was Jack Campbell, who was McEwen's major adviser on developments in the European Economic Community (EEC, now the European Union). To emphasise its trading implications, the EEC was often called the European Common Market by politicians. Britain under the Macmillan Conservatives seemed intent on joining. The implications of British membership caused consternation within the Menzies Government.

Britain and Australia enjoyed preferential tariff rates for trade between the two nations under the Imperial Preference Scheme formulated at the Ottawa Conference in 1932. This was under threat. McEwen dispatched Jack Campbell to Brussels for a year and he returned with a comprehensive understanding of the politics and the bureaucratic intricacies of the developing common market. It was thought that Jack Campbell might have become the new departmental head after Crawford left the department for a new career at the Australian National University. Bill Carew told me that both McEwen and Menzies regarded Campbell as too young for such a responsibility and Alan Westerman became permanent head instead.

McEwen had dispatched Campbell to Brussels convinced the EEC had the potential to disrupt Commonwealth trade and his judgment proved accurate when Britain under Prime Minister Harold Macmillan began negotiations for the United Kingdom to join the European trade bloc. In a speech to business leaders in Brisbane in October 1961, McEwen explained his position:

> If the United Kingdom joined the Common Market on terms that now exist between the six present members, it could have devastating

---

1 Conversation with Carew.

consequences for our export opportunities to the United Kingdom. We have made this very clear from the outset. We have said, 'It is not our business to tell you how to run your own affairs. We wouldn't relish you telling us how to run our affairs. But we are partners, Australia and the United Kingdom; we are not only blood brothers, but we are also trading partners and we put it to you strongly that you ought not to go in unless you can contrive such modifications of the present arrangements as will protect our trade.[2]

The issue was to come to a head in London in September 1962 at a meeting of Commonwealth prime ministers. This was a hugely important story, not only for *Inside Canberra*, but also for *The Land*, and I wanted to get to London for the meeting. But how? *Inside Canberra* could not afford to cover the airfares and hotel and other costs. I did a deal with *The Land* that it would pay my hotel and living expenses in London if I got there. With no introduction, I talked Air India into providing me with a free return economy ticket in return for some puff pars in *The Land*.

I began to get the hang of life in the developing world on boarding my flight for London via Bombay (now Mumbai) in Sydney: all the cabin stewards were male. These jobs were far too good for women it seemed. When we got to Bombay, I was offloaded with a number of other freeloaders (mainly crews from Australian airlines). Our protests were in vain: there were fare-paying passengers who could take our seats and that was the end of the argument. About midnight, we travelled from the airport to our hotel, the magnificent old Taj Mahal Hotel on the waterfront, a reminder of the days of the British Raj. As we drove along, I was astonished to see tens of thousands of Indians asleep on the footpaths. Some had a simple canvas or plastic awning above their heads, some slept in the open on a blanket and many slept on the bare pavement.

I was thirty-three years of age, and this was my first trip abroad (leaving aside New Zealand). It drove home to me what politicians from the developing world meant when they talked about the need to lift their people out of crushing poverty. Although India was dry at the time, when we got to the hotel we all demanded a drink, only to be told by the night clerk we could not have alcohol unless we filled in a statutory declaration declaring ourselves to be alcoholics. As one, we shouted: 'Give us the forms; give us the forms.' The rooms were magnificent, with marble floors, towering ceilings and a floor space three times the size of the best hotel rooms in Australia. We spent two unforgettable days in Bombay before managing to pick up an Air India flight for the rest of the trip. The memory of India remains with me to this day.

---

2   Golding, Peter 1996, *Black Jack McEwen: Political gladiator*, Melbourne University Press, Carlton South, Vic., p. 206.

I was knocked out by London and remember my father telling me of how he walked up and down the Strand during World War I filling in time. I was walking up and down the Strand but I had plenty to fill in my time covering the conference. I was struck how at 6ft 3in, I stood out in the crowded street—a reminder of how Britain had lost so many of its finest young men in two world wars and how short food had been during World War II. The prime ministers' conference ended with no agreement and it did not matter as de Gaulle soon put a veto on British entry to the EEC. But there was no doubt in the minds of Commonwealth statesmen that Mother England had dumped her Commonwealth family and would eventually join Europe. The de Gaulle veto was a blessing, giving Australia time to turn its attention to other markets with a sense of urgency.

Alan Westerman was recruited by the Trade Department from Columbia University in the United States, where he was more or less discovered by the then Trade Commissioner for New York, Eric McClintock, who later became the Chairman of Woolworths in Australia. Westerman was highly regarded by McEwen, in part because he was an expert on shipping costs and at that time the shipping cost of wool was creating concern in the Government. It was as a result of Westerman's knowledge of the various shipping conferences that McEwen forced the government-owned Australian National Line—then basically serving only the Australian coast—into the European shipping conference. McEwen explained to the Parliament that this gave the Government a 'window' into the financial operations and the costing methods of freight price setting by the conference lines.

Westerman also encouraged McEwen to apply pressure to the shipping companies to use the new method of shipping products in containers. Malcolm Summers in the Trade Department played a major role in the development of the containerisation trade and later became head of the Department of Shipping. In the published diaries of Peter Howson, a minister in the Menzies, Holt, McEwen, Gorton and McMahon Governments, Howson tells[3] of having a drink with Sir Roland Wilson, who was about to retire as Secretary of the Treasury: 'His [Wilson's] epithets on Westerman were almost unprintable.' McEwen would have been most gratified had he heard this. Westerman's job was to confront Treasury, not to please it.

McEwen was Australia's eighteenth prime minister and his tenure was short: 19 December 1967 to 10 January 1968. Michael Page in *Prime Ministers of Australia* sums him up well: 'John McEwen was what used to be known as a "black Scot".'[4] He was a tall, strong man with hair and eyebrows as black as crows' wings; upright in every sense of the word, aggressive, ruthlessly determined to get his own way and inflexible in defence of Country Party policies.

3   Howson, *The Howson Diaries*, p. 230.
4   Page, Michael 1988, *The Prime Ministers of Australia*, Robertsbridge, London and Sydney.

Everyone knew him as 'Black Jack'. Born in 1900 at Chiltern in Victoria, he was orphaned at seven and, like many great figures before him and since, he was brought up by his grandmother. He volunteered for the Army when he was eighteen and would have gone to the Western Front had the war lasted, but in the event he did not leave Australia. He was, nevertheless, entitled to a soldier-settler's block provided by the Government for returned soldiers.

Given the humble circumstances of his childhood, his achievements in politics were prodigious. He entered the Federal Parliament in 1934 representing the Victorian seat of Echuca and, during his long career, which ended in 1971 when he resigned, he represented Indi and then Murray. After only three years in Parliament, he was Interior Minister in the Lyons Government and was in the Cabinet of every non-Labor government from then until his retirement.

In his short tenure as Prime Minister, he was responsible for a political earthquake: blocking William McMahon's bid to become Prime Minister after the death of Holt. McEwen, like Menzies, wanted Hasluck to replace Holt. Two days after Holt disappeared, Governor-General, Richard Casey, swore in McEwen as Prime Minister. McEwen had told Casey he intended to keep the Holt ministry unchanged until the Liberal Party had elected a new leader, when he would stand aside as Prime Minister. At a press conference in Parliament House after his swearing in, McEwen made it clear his appointment was not conditional on these undertakings. The gallery was hot on the heels of the sensational development that McEwen had told senior figures in the Liberal Party that the Country Party would not join a coalition with McMahon as prime minister. Alan Reid[5] recorded the following exchange at a press conference:

> Question—Mr. McEwen, are you prepared to say publicly, as you have apparently said privately, that you will not accept Mr. McMahon as a Prime Minister, as Leader of the Liberal Party.
>
> McEwen—Yes, I say to you I have told Mr. McMahon that neither I nor my Country Party colleagues would be prepared to serve under him as Prime Minister. Mr. McMahon knows the reasons. My senior Liberal Party colleagues not only know the reasons, but knew the reasons before Mr. Holt's death.
>
> Question—Do you disclose the reasons?
>
> McEwen—No, I will not.

McEwen explained he had had to decide whether to disclose his opposition to McMahon before the Liberal Party room met to elect its new leader and expose

---

5 Reid, Alan 1969, *The Power Struggle*, Shakespeare Head Press, Sydney.

himself to the charge of seeking to influence the outcome. On the other hand, McEwen went on, if he remained silent and McMahon was elected, this would produce 'a very serious national crisis', with the Country Party refusing to form a coalition under McMahon. Like many of his ministerial colleagues, McEwen detested Billy McMahon, whom he regarded as deceitful, a liar and the main leak in Cabinet to the anti-Country Party Packer press. In the gallery, McMahon was known as 'Billy the Leak'. The NSW Liberal Party was affronted that their (and Packer's) man was being denied the political leadership of Australia, but was powerless to do anything about it. When Gorton was elected as Holt's successor as Liberal leader, McEwen, as was inevitable, ended his 21 days in the highest office in the land.

Going right back to Federation, until the arrival of television, the major daily papers in the various States exerted most media influence on politicians from both sides of the Parliament. The Menzies era was a time of comparative social, economic and political stability. Apart from the odd upheaval and close election outcome, the country seemed happy to let Menzies go on and on, but when Menzies went, change was in the wind. The influence of the daily newspapers on voters diminished with the development of television and radio news and current affairs and, after the death of Holt, the impact of the electronic media on politics accelerated.

In the early 1950s, the papers from the two biggest States obviously had the greatest political clout. Although the Herald and Weekly Times' morning Melbourne paper, *The Sun News Pictorial*, had the largest circulation in the nation, the group's Melbourne *Herald*, the only afternoon paper in Melbourne, was the first paper Victorian MPs, including Menzies, looked to. *The Age* in Melbourne (controlled by the Syme family) was important. In Sydney, the venerable broadsheet the *Sydney Morning Herald*, flagship of the Fairfax group, and Frank Packer's tabloid, *The Daily Telegraph*, although having a greater circulation, shared political influence. Anti-Labor and anti-union, *The Tele* was the most overtly politically biased major paper in Australia. My father would never read *The Tele* and was appalled that unionists made up the bulk of its readers. In the gallery, the bureaus serving these Sydney and Melbourne papers were similarly regarded as having more clout with the Government and Opposition than other bureaus.

The ABC bureau was of little significance in the early 1950s, and, for some time after the dawn of television, Jack Comans ('Como' to everyone) was bureau head of the national broadcaster. Although a very good tennis player in his youth, Como was, around the gallery, slow moving and slow talking. He would join other journalists for the morning vigil at the top of the stairs in King's Hall to catch moments with people such as Artie Fadden. No story ever emerged as a result.

Comans eschewed speculation on, or interpretation of, news. Unless a news item came from a press release or an official announcement, there would be no report at all on the ABC. Colin Parks remembers coming from the ABC in Adelaide to join the ABC's gallery team and introducing himself to Comans in the ABC office. Comans told Parks he had a piece of advice to offer and the junior from Adelaide leaned forward, expecting some invaluable tips about covering politics. Comans' words, as Parks remembers them, were: 'There are a lot of pisspots around here. Stick to beer and you'll be all right.'

During the 1960s, the first bastardisation case at the Duntroon Military College was a major news story. Senior cadets, it emerged, were bullying junior cadets. Reporters rushed to Duntroon to report the story. Not Como. Tony Ferguson was producer or director (I am not sure which) of the ABC's highly successful *This Day Tonight* (*TDT*), an evening TV current affairs program. We both started our journalistic career as cadets on the *Daily Mirror*. Tony told me how he was on the phone to Comans asking him to get a crew and reporter over to Duntroon for a piece on the bastardisation scandal. Comans refused, saying this was not the type of story the ABC covered. Ferguson was furious. He even appealed directly to the then General Manager of the ABC, Talbot Duckmanton. To Ferguson's astonishment, Duckmanton refused to give Comans any direction, telling Ferguson he completely agreed with Comans' decision not to cover the story.

Parks and a number of other old hands, including myself, took part in an oral history conference with historian Michael Richards at Old Parliament House on 8 December 2004. Parks' comments gave a feel of the atmosphere in the old building and what it was like to work there and how difficult Comans could be:

> The nature of this building was such that the whole building and everyone in it was a source. You could walk into this building at nine in the morning and you could sniff something. You could feel an atmosphere that something was going on. It was a quickened pace or: what are those two talking about? Those people are enemies so what are they talking about? Doormen were always a very good source in this place. I remember walking in one Monday morning and saying to the bloke on the Reps door—George I think—'Did you have a good weekend?' 'No, I've spent the whole bloody weekend working', he said. I asked, 'What do you mean, the place isn't open?' and he said 'No, I had to work here all weekend because they're cleaning out [Defence Minister, Malcolm] Fraser's office. The bloody sheilas' boxes—all weekend I had to carry them out to the car'…Very funny, I thought. So I reported it dutifully to the head man, Jack Comans, who said 'No, that's bullshit, just bullshit.' Anyway, two hours later, Fraser announced his resignation. I mean, we were so far ahead of the story it didn't matter, yet we didn't report it.

Jack as head of the bureau had the last call on whether stories, which were un-sourced, should be reported. It was all 'bullshit'—because he didn't get it officially.

Parks later became press secretary to Prime Minister Bob Hawke and moved on to success as a political lobbyist in Canberra for some of Australia's largest companies.

It was against this background that in 1972 Ken Begg from the ABC's Sydney office was dispatched to Canberra as political correspondent. Begg, in an interview with the author, said there had long been concern among the senior editorial managers that the Canberra bureau was not getting on top of some of the Canberra stories. One instance was when John Gorton voted himself out of office on the day of Bill McMahon's challenge. The ABC did not report it for several hours.

Begg told the author: 'There was great frustration because commercial radio was starting to operate in the Canberra gallery and they were reporting these issues, they were reporting the gossip and the speculation and putting great pressure on the ABC, which was getting left behind.'

The ABC also recognised it had to start putting some people into the Canberra office who had experience in both radio and television news and current affairs. The catalyst was change—change in the nature of politics, the changing nature of reporting and the fact that technology was starting to impact on the reporting of politics at both the State and the federal level. Begg found that Como was of little help to him in learning the ropes. He took Begg aside and said: 'I can't give you any of my contacts; it would be a betrayal of their confidence.' Begg said: 'I later found out that Comans' contact was a bloke who used to work for some National Party senator. Como used to drink with him down in the non-members'—a hopeless bloke.'

Begg remembers the election night of 10 December 1977, long before the ABC had the services of electoral experts such as Antony Green, and Comans was the inhouse expert, but hard to pin down. Begg recalls:

Jack, at 9 o'clock on election night, said, 'Labor will shit it in', and departed for the Canberra Club at Canberra's Civic Centre. That was his analysis—'Labor will shit it in'—so we had 47 radio bulletins and television bulletins to do and he just disappeared. The chief sub at the time was screaming, saying, 'Where the fuck is Labor shitting it in? What am I supposed to write, "Labor will shit it in" for the 10 o'clock bulletin?' That was Jack; he just disappeared. Of course, far from shitting in, Whitlam was trounced by Fraser.

Despite Begg's difficulties with Comans, the ABC was well on its way to being the dominant bureau in the gallery. In 1967 the current affairs radio program *AM* began and relied heavily on Canberra content. Even today, listening to *AM* is a must for politicians, political journalists and many more Australians. Radio current affairs was further beefed up with *PM* and *The World Today*. This gives the ABC the ability to comprehensively cover a big story right through the day. Nothing in commercial TV/radio, then or now, goes anywhere near touching this service. The ABC is now easily the most important bureau in the gallery, reaching more Australians via radio, television and its online service than any other media organisation.

To the credit of ABC management, it has for decades provided the Canberra bureau with adequate, well-trained and experienced journalists for TV and radio. One was Michael Willesee, son of the Foreign Minister in the Whitlam Government. He came to Canberra in the 1960s as the first representative in the gallery of the (now long gone) WA paper the *Perth Daily News*. Young, handsome and witty, he was recognised for his talents by the ABC and became the Canberra representative of *This Day Tonight*. With just the right amount of aggression, without appearing overbearing or unfair, Willesee was one of the best interviewers on Australian TV. I was much older than Mike, yet I learned a lot from him about TV journalism—something of great value in my role as the sole and part-time representative of the Ten Network in the gallery.

In his oral history, Begg touched on the pressures on ABC journalists, particularly those reporting politics, either in Canberra or in the State capitals. He contrasted this with his experience later in commercial TV when he left the ABC to head the Seven Network's gallery staff. Politicians from all parties, but particularly the party in government, pressure ABC journalists, or senior management, or sometimes both. Speaking of his years with the ABC in the gallery, Begg complained 'everything in those days was about balance'. He told of how McMahon in the 1972 campaign 'assassinated' his Cabinet by saying, in effect, he had to do half the work because his ministers were too lazy. (I remember this story well and it was one of the sensations of the campaign.) Begg reported the story yet it did not go to air until 11 pm because the TV news editor at the time, Keith Fraser, without consulting Begg, was convinced he had got the story 'terribly wrong'. Begg went on:

> Back in the Seventies we were living in a time of balance, where you had to have the same amount of words [for each side]. If you had 45 words for the Labor Party, you had to have 45 words for the Liberal Party, 15 for the DLP and 15 for the National Party. If you had a wide shot of the Prime Minister and a close up of the Opposition Leader, then the next night you had to reverse. So we lived in that silly time of everything having to be balance and lines had to be counted and the ABC was, and

is today, under great pressure. So I was more aware of pressure in the ABC as a public broadcaster than I ever was in the commercial world. I was very aware Talbot Duckmanton [then ABC General Manager], was under heavy political pressure, particularly at election time.

Since Begg's time, the pressure on the ABC has become greater. Much of TV and radio news/current affairs is about the doings of government, particularly its failings, hence the government of the day is the leading critic of the ABC. The fact that a government gets something right is not nearly as newsworthy as something it gets wrong. This is an iron law of journalism, whatever the media.

Neil Andrew (Wakefield, SA), a good fellow, if somewhat naive, was Speaker of the House for some of the Howard Government era. He once said to me: 'Rob, I used to subscribe to *Inside Canberra*, but it could never find anything good to say about the [Howard] Government.' I explained to him the job of the gallery was to attack the Government, of whatever political colour. Nearly all (not all) politicians seek power and these are the ones holding powerful jobs in a government—from the Prime Minister down. Wishing to continue in power, they do not want the media to know details of how they will achieve this. Our job is to discover the bastardry they are up to. The wielders of power are the ones we cannot trust, not the Opposition.

14. Labor Out of the Wilderness

In March 1963, *The Daily Telegraph* published a bombshell picture of the Opposition Leader, Arthur Calwell, and his deputy, Gough Whitlam, waiting in the dead of night outside the Kingston Hotel for 36 members of the specially convened ALP National Conference to vote on the Menzies Government's legislation for a US naval communications base at North West Cape in Western Australia. This gave Whitlam a powerful weapon in his mission to transform the Australian Labor Party into a democratic national institution. Many inside and outside the Labor Party today would argue it is far from a truly democratic party. This is fair criticism, but when compared with the Liberal Party (Australia's most successful postwar party), the Labor Party is far more democratic. Under Prime Minister John Howard, who over four parliamentary terms assumed the role of an elected dictator, the federal parliamentary Liberal Party was less democratic than ever.

Whitlam's achievements were at least as great when in opposition as when he was Prime Minister. Whitlam ranks with Menzies as one of Australia's most significant political leaders. Menzies came back from his failed prewar career to unite the dispirited and impotent conservatives and overthrow a socialist Labor government that appeared to have a stranglehold on power. Whitlam brought together a divided and hopeless Labor Party to return it to power after its longest period in opposition, and changed politics profoundly.

To the astonishment of the nation, Whitlam was sacked by the Governor-General, Sir John Kerr, on Remembrance Day, 11 November 1975, despite having the confidence of the Lower House of Parliament both before and after his sacking. Whitlam saved Australia from a constitutional crisis by accepting the dismissal and fighting it unsuccessfully at the ballot box. His government lasted just a month short of three years. A year and five months after his election, he retained office in the 1974 double-dissolution election, when a young Sydney Liberal, John Winston Howard, was elected to represent the electorate of Bennelong.

Whitlam was born on 11 July 1916 into a comfortable middle-class family. His father, Fred Whitlam, was the Commonwealth Crown Solicitor and although he was President of the Young Men's Christian Association of Canberra, Whitlam's strong Christian faith did not influence his son towards a similar bent. Gough Whitlam, an avowed atheist, found this was no handicap to attaining the highest position in the country. When Whitlam was only a boy, his mother suffered a concussion in an accident, leaving her hard of hearing, and the family learned to speak to her slowly and clearly.[1] This assisted Whitlam to develop his measured

---

1 Conversation with Whitlam.

and clear style of public oratory. He attended three primary schools in Sydney and two secondary schools in Canberra before graduating from the University of Sydney (BA, LLB).

He joined the Sydney University Regiment when Germany invaded Poland and the Royal Australian Air Force (RAAF) when Japan bombed Pearl Harbor, serving in northern Australia in aircraft protecting Australian convoys and attacking Japanese positions in the islands. A navigator with the rank of flight lieutenant at the end of the Pacific War, he was a crewmember of the only British Empire aircraft at MacArthur's headquarters in Manila. His wartime experiences carried on into civilian life. Whitlam always noted in his diary all his flight details: the airline (be it a civilian or a RAAF VIP aircraft), flight numbers, type and registration of aircraft. In August 1945, he joined the Labor Party, and he was admitted to the NSW Bar in 1947. Fortunately, although failing to win the State seat of Sutherland (NSW) in 1950, he won the federal seat of Werriwa (in the western suburbs of Sydney) in a by-election in November 1952.

Evatt, by the end of the 1950s, was obviously crumbling, both mentally and physically. In what must have been one of the most extraordinary and foolish acts by any State government, the Heffron NSW Labor Government appointed Evatt Chief Justice of New South Wales. On 7 March 1960—with Evatt having gone to the Bench—Arthur Calwell, aged sixty-four and with 20 years in Federal Parliament behind him, finally rose to the top of the Labor Party. Whitlam, then only forty-three and qualifying as 'young' in politics at the time, unexpectedly and narrowly defeated Eddie Ward in the ballot for deputy leader. Fellow Labor MP Les Haylen described Ward as an unusual 'Labor ranter'—meticulously dressed, his iron-grey hair swept back from his forehead: 'He looked like a dentist ready to drill. He had a rocket take-off—not for him the preamble, the body of the speech, the lead-off and the peroration. He was airborne from the moment his hand hit the table.'

I found Ward, despite his forbidding manner, approachable and witty. Ward first entered Parliament in 1931, and, although earlier a supporter of Jack Lang, the mortal enemy of Curtin and Chifley, Ward had been in every Cabinet from Curtin's to Chifley's last in 1949. He had contested the deputy leadership in five previous ballots going back to 1946 and unsuccessfully challenged Evatt's leadership in 1958. He had every reason to be bitter about losing to a blow-in, Whitlam, who had been in Parliament for barely eight years. As a young man, Ward was a professional boxer, fighting 10 rounds at Sydney Stadium—only one level below the boxers fighting the main event.

Tall and still looking athletic, even in his fifties, Ward was so enraged at missing the deputy leadership he swung a punch at Whitlam in the Labor lobby, right outside Whitlam's office. The blow grazed Whitlam's lip, and he swung around, rushed through his office door and locked it, leaving a fuming Ward outside. After losing to Whitlam, Ward suffered a heart attack—putting him out of Parliament for more than a year. He returned in 1963, and, yarning to him, Eric Walsh asked him when he first knew he was crook. Ward's joking reply was, 'When I missed Whitlam with that punch'.

Having won the deputy leadership of his party, Whitlam had to wait another seven years before he became Labor leader, on 8 February 1967. Whitlam was responsible for introducing the system of shadow opposition ministers into the Australian political system and one of his first initiatives as Labor leader was to allocate shadow ministers to the front bench of the Labor opposition—the Caucus executive. Until then members of the executive often made contradictory public statements on policy issues, such as industrial relations, giving the Coalition parties grounds for portraying Labor as a divided party. The outlook for Labor was bleak when Whitlam took over in the wake of Harold Holt's crushing defeat of Arthur Calwell in the Vietnam War election of 26 November 1966. Yet in only four years and nine months, and after overcoming immense internal difficulties in his party, Whitlam was elected Prime Minister on 2 December 1972. When Whitlam took over the leadership of the party, the Liberals and Country Party had ruled for more than 17 years.

Having entered Parliament as the MP for Werriwa, Whitlam had to live in the electorate, and the family moved from their comfortable home, with Cronulla Beach nearby, to Cabramatta—then regarded as a long way out in Sydney's west. The policy proposals (Whitlam referred to them as 'the program') were the most detailed and sweeping ever put forward by any national political leader, before or since. Included was a plan for extension of the sewerage system in the outer suburbs of major cities, leading DLP Senator Vince Gair later to deride Whitlam as a politician whose main interest was in the provision of sewers.

In fact, Whitlam had tapped into the concerns of voters out in the west—the first federal leader to do so. When the sewer was connected to the Whitlam home, the family had a celebratory party. It did not take long for gallery journalists to notice the tall, new member with considerable oratorical powers, a quick wit and some bright ideas. With his wife, Margaret, a charming and lively woman who matched her husband's considerable intellect, they were a standout couple.

In the author's experience, no party leader had better relations with gallery journalists than Whitlam, and if they wandered into his office, they were welcome. If they could not converse with Whitlam, there was always someone lively on his staff with whom to gossip. Most journalists were aching to see the back of Calwell, who had become a tragic figure.

Whitlam's press secretary/speechwriter, Graham Freudenberg ('Freudie', as he was known throughout Parliament House), barely made average height, wore glasses and dressed in a standard business suit and tie; he could have been mistaken for an accountant. With his usual candour, Freudenberg wrote that '[w]ith good cause [John] Menadue [then Whitlam's private secretary] had some reservations about my suitability as a press secretary. Apart from my irregular habits, he could see that the demands of the job were changing rapidly.'[2] 'Freudie' and his great mate Peter Cullen (staffer to the wily Victorian veteran Labor senator Pat Kennelly) were valued customers in the non-members' bar.

Freudie was, and probably still is, a night person, writing speeches after midnight and turning up to the office at midday. Whitlam was punctual, punctilious, energetic, a morning and night person and expected similar attributes from his staff—except Freudie. They hit it off and together bested on the floor of Parliament every Liberal leader after Menzies. Freudenberg was rarely in the advisers' box on the opposition side of the house, following every word of Whitlam as he delivered an important speech penned by his speechwriter.

Unable to stand the tension, Freudenberg would instead be in Whitlam's office, listening to the speech on the chamber's communications system, while pacing up and down chain-smoking. His intellect and powers of argument, coupled with his easy bar-room personality, had much to do with the gallery journalists being largely so pro-Whitlam when their proprietors certainly were not. When the non-members' bar closed half an hour after the Parliament rose for the night, inevitably there would be a troupe of journalists invited into the Opposition Leader's office for drinks from Whitlam's bar. Whitlam was all but a teetotaller and would normally have gone home for the night. Lorraine Hoare, one of Whitlam's secretaries, asked her boss on several occasions to give her the key to the office bar so that it would not be drained by Freudenberg and members of the gallery. Whitlam declined, aware of his speechwriter's great value as a link to the gallery.

After a bitter struggle with the ALP Left and finally attaining the ALP leadership, Whitlam was able to put forward in his 1972 election policy a proposal for aid to private schools on a needs basis. It was based on the same argument used decades later by Mark Latham as Opposition Leader that aid should not be given to wealthy private schools, but allocated on the basis of need. In the lead-up to the 1972 election campaign, Mick Young and prominent Catholic layman Arthur Rolfe met Bishop Carroll and Monsignor T. O. Wallace to put to them that the Church in New South Wales should make a statement that the Labor policy was acceptable, as was the Liberal policy of blanket aid, irrespective of the individual needs of schools. This was exactly the opposite message conservative Catholic bishops were putting out—that only the Liberal policy was acceptable.

---

2 Freudenberg, *A Figure of Speech*.

Carroll made an important speech accepting the Whitlam policy and stating the policies of both parties were acceptable and could be expected to evolve through time. Eric Walsh played a vital role in alerting the gallery that Carroll had said there was no longer a reason to vote against Labor on the basis of state aid. And this was the message the media carried the next morning. The curse of the DLP was finally lifted from Whitlam, by his own actions in putting his political future on the line and with the help of people such as Carroll, Rolfe, Mick Young, Walsh and Freudenberg. The gallery, with some personal ambivalence, was closely following developments in the struggle within the ALP on state aid. Many in the gallery were Catholics, educated in the system and supportive of the argument by the Church. It was a strong one: that Catholic parents were being denied justice by a tax system requiring them to pay their share of upholding the state school system, even though their children were not using it. A lesser number of journalists had a background of GPS schools and were also sympathetic to the Catholic argument.

In the author's experience, Eric Walsh, as press secretary, influenced the Prime Minister of the day to a greater extent than any other in the role, even exceeding the influence of the legendary Don Rogers, who was press secretary to both Curtin and Chifley. Walsh was not a 'spin doctor', but rather he created 'news' favourable to the Whitlam Government—a prime example being the work put in on Bishop Carroll. Then he sold the importance of the news to key gallery political commentators. Walsh started in journalism as a cadet on *The Tweed and South Coast Daily* at Murwillumbah, in northern New South Wales, and came into the gallery when he joined the *Mirror* as bureau head, following the departure of Kevin Power.

I came to know him well from this point. Walsh at that time was 20 or more years younger than other bureau heads such as Jack Allsop (Sydney *Sun*), Harold Cox (Melbourne *Herald*) and Ian Fitchett (*The Age*). After five years on the *Mirror*, he left to join *The National Times*. Walsh, a lapsed Catholic, had all the charm of the Irish, plus a keen interest in good food and drink, and at one stage in his career as a consultant, he was proprietor of a restaurant in Kingston, ACT, not far from Parliament House, named EJ's. He was later to be a partner in a restaurant of the same name in exclusive Macquarie Street, Sydney. Above all, he was a top journalist with an extraordinary array of contacts. Walsh left the *National Times* when Mick Young, who as National Secretary was then running the ALP campaign for the 1972 election, invited him to join the Whitlam team. Walsh's salary came directly from party contributions made by Richard Crebbin of Marrickville Margarine, who supported Labor in the hope of ending the restriction on margarine production imposed by State legislation setting a quota on production.

This was a Country Party device to protect the dairy industry, and, as not many dairy farmers voted Labor, it was thought Labor might be willing to put an end to quotas. And it worked. John Menadue tells of the tricks the Whitlam staffers were up to in the lead-up to the 1972 election.[3] Mick Young and Walsh set up a front organisation, 'Businessmen for Change of Government', which was put forward as a genuinely independent organisation aimed at getting rid of the McMahon Government. It was a sham. Sim Rubensohn, the brilliant advertising man running Labor's advertising campaign, provided a tame businessman from the Jewish community, Patrick Sayers, to head the organisation. Walsh prepared the press ads, and Rupert Murdoch, who was backing Labor in the election, ran the ads for free in his papers and funded payments for those run in other newspapers. Although the gallery did not know these details, my memory of the time is that journalists were not completely taken in. Nevertheless, it was an effective gambit.

Walsh joined the Prime Minister's staff as press secretary after the defeat of McMahon on 2 December 1972, and played a significant role in the early days of the Whitlam Government as it came to grips with a federal bureaucracy that had not served a Labor government for 23 years. Whitlam and Walsh soon got a taste of public service obstruction. Graham Freudenberg, nominally Whitlam's press secretary, was in fact his speechwriter. He was not keen on the press secretary role and, when Walsh came onboard after the election, Freudenberg decided he would move out of Whitlam's office to the Prime Minister's Department, just across the road in West Block, and would remain in his role as speechwriter. Sir John Bunting, Secretary of the Prime Minister's Department, had a problem with this: there was no position for Freudenberg approved by the Public Service Board. Whitlam dismissed this as bullshit and told Freudenberg to get on with his move.

Although Freudenberg moved into the department, still Bunting would not bend. Well into February, three months into the Whitlam Government, Freudenberg, sitting at a desk in the department, opened a drawer and found a letter from Bunting to Keith Sinclair, an ex-editor of *The Age*, who had been hired to give the Liberal Prime Minister Bill McMahon public relations advice. Peter Wilenski, private secretary to Whitlam, fronted Bunting on this letter, demanding to know why the department was still paying a person hired to give advice to the defeated McMahon and, worse, the department was freezing out Freudenberg. Walsh says Bunting was 'sick' with embarrassment and lamely explained that 'he [Sinclair] was one of us'.

From then on, Walsh pushed Whitlam to get rid of Bunting and he finally did when Walsh suggested that John Menadue, Whitlam's private secretary when

---

3   Menadue, John 1999, *Things You Learn Along the Way*, David Lovell Publishing, Melbourne.

Whitlam was first deputy leader of the ALP and then leader, should head the Prime Minister's Department. Whitlam was hesitant about moving Bunting. His father was a senior public servant and Whitlam had grown up with the tradition of an independent, non-political public service. He was also concerned he would inevitably be accused of politicising the Public Service by appointing Menadue. From 1967, Menadue was the senior executive in Australia for News Limited, and Rupert Murdoch was quite happy that his headman was leaving to become the Prime Minister's principal adviser.

As a public servant, Menadue could only be seen as coming from the Labor side. Not only had he been private secretary to Whitlam for seven years, he had also been an unsuccessful Labor candidate for the southern NSW seat of Hume in 1966. I was a friend of Menadue, who was well known and liked by the gallery. The Opposition accused Whitlam of politicising the Public Service and the allegation was widely reported but did little to harm Whitlam's standing with ordinary voters. In any case, the senior ranks of the Public Service were widely regarded as being 'politicised' simply through serving Liberal prime ministers for so long. Given Bunting's attitude towards Freudenberg, the Public Service— at least at the permanent-head level—was reluctant to accept the election of a Labor government. Menadue wrote:

> Bringing an outsider to such a senior position, who was personally associated with him [Whitlam] and into the Public Service, which was supposedly politically neutral, was risky. It wasn't politically neutral in my view. With its service to conservative governments for 23 years it was steeped, however unwittingly, in traditional ways of thinking and doing things. It was culturally, if not politically, conservative. But I had a label on me. There was an assumption that senior public servants were neutral and I wasn't. The difference as I saw it was that I was open about my position. Furthermore, I had always been sceptical of the person who says I am non-political. A person who is non-political accepts the status quo and is not attracted to political action to change it. That person, in my view, is conservative and should acknowledge it.[4]

The problem Whitlam and his staff encountered with Bunting was not the only instance of the Canberra mandarins finding difficulty in accepting a Labor government. On Sunday, 3 December 1972, the day after his election victory, Whitlam rang McMahon and said he would like to see as early as possible: Bunting, head of the Foreign Affairs Department; Sir Keith Waller, head of the Defence Department; Sir Arthur Tange, head of the Attorney-General's Department; Clarrie Harders and the Chairman of the Public Service

---

4   Ibid., p. 120.

Board, Sir Alan Cooley. Graham Freudenberg notes: 'The fraught omission was Sir Frederick Wheeler', head of Treasury, who would be the source of grave problems for Whitlam in the 'loans affair'.[5]

Waller, in his Sunday afternoon discussion with Whitlam, suggested Australia should continue to abstain on several important resolutions due to come before the UN General Assembly that week. In his book, Whitlam recorded his response: 'I thought otherwise. To abstain would be to pass up the opportunity to demonstrate at the highest international level that there was indeed a new Government in Australia, with new polices and new attitudes.'[6]

One of the matters to be voted on was a highly sensitive resolution regarding Rhodesia (now Zimbabwe)—then not governed by the black majority, but by the white-minority government of Ian Smith. In 1971 only Portugal, South Africa and Britain voted against this resolution. Portugal, ruled by the dictator Antonio Salazar, was determined to hang on to its colonies in Africa and elsewhere. South Africa was still ruled by a racist apartheid government and Menzies believed the continuation of the hated apartheid system was a domestic matter and not one to be discussed at Commonwealth Heads of Government meetings. Britain was of course a colonial power. Australia, New Zealand, France and the United States were among nine countries abstaining.

Against this background, it was preposterous that Waller should advise Whitlam to continue Menzies' policy of abstaining and not join the 102 countries, including India and the countries of the Association of South-East Asian Nations (ASEAN) in our region, voting for the resolution. After several hours of discussion with the departmental heads, Freudenberg records, Whitlam called into the meeting his opposition staff who were to continue in the Prime Minister's office: Jim Spigelman, Dick Hall, Eric Walsh and Freudenberg. He declared to the mandarins: 'I take full responsibility for these men. I vouch for them and they are not to be subject to security clearances.' Freudenberg believed this illustrated that Whitlam was not free of Labor's deep-seated suspicions of the Australian Security Intelligence Service (ASIO). Sir Arthur Tange was one mandarin not prepared to hide his suspicions about the Labor Government's staffers.

Clem Lloyd came to Canberra as I did, but much later, for the *Daily Mirror*. Clem was a respected journalist, yet at heart a scholar, during his journalistic career accumulating an impressive variety of degrees. He was a big man, with a generous girth, and his hobbies were food and drink. Lloyd could not drive and got around Canberra in taxis, or with a lift from his many friends. I asked him once why he did not drive and he said, simply: 'I tried it once, but was no good

---

5   Freudenberg, *A Figure of Speech*.
6   Whitlam, Gough 1985, *The Whitlam Government 1972–75*, Penguin, Ringwood, Vic., p. 14.

at it.' This was the statement of an honest man. For a male to declare he was no good at driving would be regarded as an admission of failure. Clem did not see it as that—just an explanation.

Lloyd's prodigious appetite for good food was legendary among his friends. He found himself, on a trip to Taiwan, on his own in a restaurant and ordered Peking duck—a dish prepared for at least four. When he had polished it off, the kitchen staff gathered around him and applauded. Lance Barnard, Whitlam's loyal deputy, was Defence Minister in the first Whitlam Government. Lloyd had been adviser/press secretary for seven years when Barnard became Defence Minister. Equipped with a powerful intellect, Lloyd could interpret politics as well as anyone, including Whitlam.

Eric Walsh told the author that at the Sunday meeting of department heads the day after the 1972 election, Tange, the Defence Minister, told Whitlam the new government could not end conscription because it would not get through the Senate, where there were five DLP senators, suggesting national service could be ended only by legislation. Veteran Fairfax journalist Brian Toohey, then an adviser on Barnard's staff with Lloyd, gave the author an account of a discussion he had with Tange the next day. Tange, without an appointment, turned up to see Barnard at his Parliament House office at 9 am. Toohey read a brief that Tange was to put to Barnard and at the end of the brief was the advice, on a single page, that conscription could not be ended other than by legislation. It transpired that Tange wrote this page. Toohey told Tange, before ushering him into Barnard's office, that this was unsatisfactory, explaining to Tange the Whitlam Government had settled on a perfectly legal way to end conscription. Tange rejected Toohey's offer to explain the plan.

The idea for avoiding legislation came from the Parliamentary Library and was uncomplicated: the Army Board comprised Barnard, the head of the Department of the Army and the Army commander, and simply by signing a piece of paper, the board members could give every conscript in the Army an honourable discharge. Lloyd and Toohey had already established that the Defence Department had no objection to this method of ending conscription, nor did the Department of the Army, the top brass in the Army and the Department of Labour and National Service, which administered conscription. Further, Lionel Murphy, the Attorney-General, had approved the scheme. Toohey believes Tange was not in favour of conscription, but would not accept it was the role of ministerial staffers to instruct him on such matters.

The episode provided yet another example of why the Whitlam Government doubted the ability of the entrenched bureaucracy to work with Labor. Another blow-up between Clem Lloyd and Tange occurred before Lloyd resigned in disgust from Barnard's office. Part of Labor's election policy in 1972—conceived by Lloyd—was to merge the departments of Defence, Army, Navy and Air and Supply into one department: Defence. Naturally, the top brass in the three services objected to this. Instead of having their own separate minister to fight for more money for their service within the Government, they would have to go cap in hand to the Defence Minister. Tange did not like the policy, principally because he was not consulted about it and it slimmed down his bureaucratic empire.

Soon after the election and the dust-up with Tange on the means to end conscription, Clem Lloyd received Barnard's permission to issue a press release (under the minister's name), announcing the amalgamation of the various service departments would proceed. Tange's reaction was immediate: he stormed into Barnard's office demanding to know why he had not been consulted about the release. Toohey, who was present, told the author Lloyd seized the back of Tange's suit collar with one hand and lifted him off the floor and facing the exit door. Lloyd, while achieving this considerable feat of strength, explained Tange was not consulted because it was 'fucking election policy'. Returning Tange to the floor, Lloyd said: 'We'll now go straight to Gough Whitlam's office and sort this out.' Cowed, Tange replied this would not be necessary and departed. Little wonder he was after revenge.

Lord Carrington, the British Defence Minister, visited Australia on 19 January 1973 for talks with his counterpart, Sir Arthur Tange, and Barnard. Tange regarded himself as a law unto himself in defence and told Barnard that Lloyd could not attend the discussions with Carrington. Although Carrington's staffers attended the meeting, Barnard buckled and Lloyd was excluded. In disgust—not with Tange, but with Barnard—Lloyd resigned. From then on, Barnard's reputation was seriously damaged within his party and the gallery, yet with Whitlam's backing he remained Deputy Prime Minister until Labor narrowly won the 1974 election and Caucus dumped him for Jim Cairns.

The episode provided yet another example of why the Whitlam Government doubted the ability of the entrenched bureaucracy to work with Labor. Toohey was not getting along with Barnard and soon after was offered two jobs: Treasurer Frank Crean wanted him to join his staff and Max Walsh, then running the *Australian Financial Review*'s Canberra bureau, wanted Toohey as a journalist. Barnard then got huffy about Crean poaching his staff. Toohey decided to refuse to work for either minister and took up Walsh's offer.

Mick Young, more than any other, deserved the credit for getting Whitlam into power. Young was burly, broad shouldered, curly haired, and one of the last important Labor figures who started on the shop floor—in his case, as a shearer. He became an organiser for the AWU, then SA State Secretary of the ALP, and, at a crucial time in Labor's history, Federal Secretary. Through Eric Walsh, Young's greatest mate, I got to know Mick well and spent many a long lunch with him. He played a key role in the 1970 federal ousting of the left-dominated Victorian executive whose purists believed it was more important to cling to Labor's 'principles' than gain office.

Whitlam had to get rid of this obstacle and, with Young, he succeeded. Young was also his most important ally in breaking the tradition of the '36 faceless men' running the national conference and instructing the parliamentary party how to vote, even though the leader and deputy leader of the parliamentary party were not delegates to the conference. Whitlam and Young turned all this around with the federal and State parliamentary Labor leaders not only being given delegate status at the national conference, but with the federal parliamentary leader also having the most important role of any delegate.

The conference—previously an instrument of the State secretaries—was expanded to a far larger and more democratic body of several hundred. Most importantly, the conference was open to the media. Young was highly regarded by the gallery and brilliantly ran the initial national conferences—open to the media and the public. The media enjoyed a spacious press room and was provided detailed daily coverage of the conferences and debates. Today, even when Labor is in opposition, the national conference is the most important party event on the calendar for the media.

This is in sharp contrast with the deservedly meagre coverage given the weak and meaningless equivalent: the Federal Council of the Liberal Party. It has no power to impose policy on the parliamentary Liberal Party and is a mere talking shop. John Howard accepted a proposal by Lynton Crosby, Federal Director of the Liberal Party, for a Liberal federal conference of several hundred delegates— similar to the size of the Labor national conference, but unlike the Labor model, with no power to impose policy on Liberal MPs. Held in Brisbane in 1998, it was a flop, devoid of media interest, and was never tried again.

Mick Young, more than anyone I know (even Eric Walsh), seemed to know hundreds, if not thousands, of people in politics, business, the unions and academia, and was respected by them. Unlike many politicians, Mick was generous with his time and money and if a PR mate wanted Young to have lunch with a client, Mick would oblige if he could. With his mates—whether lobbyists, gallery members or politicians—he shouted in turn and often paid more than his share of a lunch or dinner. This sort of generosity is not the general rule of politicians, many of whom believe part of the perks of the job is to be wined and dined.

Menadue[7] gives a firsthand account of events leading up to Whitlam's 1972 election win when Rupert Murdoch was supporting Labor and Gough's team was desperate to keep it that way. At the time, Menadue was CEO of News Limited. His account of a social event that almost went wrong reveals Whitlam could be difficult about his relations with Murdoch:

> About three weeks before the election, Mick Young and I spoke to Rupert about a social cruise on the harbour with Gough. He thought it a good idea. He was coming back from overseas and was in Australia for a few weeks before the campaign. He is always on hand for elections; he can't keep away. Mick and I organised the boat but weren't sure who was paying. But we couldn't get Gough to be in it. 'I'm too fucking busy to see Rupert. I'm too fucking busy'. We continued to press him, but as a concession he offered, 'I'm not going but will Margaret [his wife] do?' I don't think Margaret was consulted at all. We finally persuaded him that he had to come along for the boat ride. In the end it worked well and Gough was courteous and relaxed. Rupert paid for the boat.

Young entered Parliament in the 1974 double-dissolution election as MP for Port Adelaide. When Whitlam finally left the scene, Young was Senior Vice-President of the ALP and Shadow Minister for Employment and Industrial Relations in Opposition Leader Bill Hayden's Shadow Cabinet (he was a good friend of Hayden's). Additionally, Young held the key position of Manager of Opposition Business in the house until Hayden, out of the blue, removed him from this role.

Alan Ramsey, then Hayden's press secretary, authored the chapter 'The Hayden years: 1976–82' in *The True Believers—The Story of the Federal Parliamentary Labor Party*. He wrote: 'Hayden took this [Leader of Opposition in the house] from him after one too many of Mick's long lunches and a growing concern that not a lot was happening in the development of employment policy.' I broke the story of Young's demotion in *Inside Canberra*, and Hayden, who has a naturally closed and suspicious nature, blamed Young for leaking it to me. Hayden was wide of the mark as I was given the yarn by Tony Ferguson, then in the ALP National Secretariat.

In 1983 Young was in hot water with the establishment of the Hope Royal Commission into foreign intelligence operations in Australia. Justice Robert Hope had been appointed in 1974 by the Whitlam Government to conduct a royal commission into Australia's intelligence services and, for this reason, the Hawke Government turned to him. The genesis of the second royal commission

---

7   Menadue, *Things You Learn Along the Way*, p. 110.

was information given the Government by ASIO that Soviet Embassy KGB spy Valeriy Ivanov had been attempting to recruit National Secretary of the ALP, David Combe, as a mole inside the Labor Party.

Like Mick Young, Combe was a prominent Labor identity in South Australia, and, due to Young's influence, he succeeded him as National Secretary. The Hawke Government was in serious trouble: not even in government for a year and its very future was threatened by the spy scandal. Cabinet, with Young in attendance, decided to expel Ivanov and to establish a royal commission. Held in Canberra, it was a sensational news development and was given maximum media coverage for months, particularly when Hawke was in the box giving evidence for 20 consecutive days. ASIO had information that Combe had been talking to Melbourne businessman Laurie Mathieson about trade with the Soviet Union.

Laurie Mathieson and his partner Bruce Fasham were big in trade with Russia and were clients of Young's closest friend, consultant Eric Walsh. Young tipped off Walsh so that he could warn Mathieson of the imminent appointment of a royal commission. ASIO then passed on the news to Hawke that Young had tipped off Walsh, who did not then know that Mathieson was an ASIO informer. Mathieson and Fasham occupied lavish offices in St Kilda Road, Melbourne, and Walsh advised them to have a sweep of their offices to ensure they were not being bugged by ASIO. The cream of the joke was that Fasham also was an ASIO informer and neither of the partners knew this about each other.[8]

Hope's terms of reference were extended to allow investigation of Young's leak, forcing his resignation from the ministry. Ultimately, Hope vindicated the Hawke Government's handling of the Combe–Ivanov affair and cleared Combe and Young of any wrongdoing. Young reclaimed his portfolio—temporarily filled by then Aviation Minister, Kim Beazley—in the ALP National Secretariat by January, after a spectacular own goal by the Federal Opposition.

Only a week after Justice Cross found Ian Sinclair had made claims that were not only untrue, but that he also knew to be untrue, the National Party elected Sinclair as its federal leader. In that instant, the Opposition's political attack over falling standards of ministerial propriety was blunted. The Government used the Sinclair findings to deflect attacks on its own conduct. Opposition Leader, Andrew Peacock, railed in vain that returning Mick Young to a national security role was like 'putting Ned Kelly in charge of the Reserve Bank' or 'locking up Dracula in the blood bank'. Bob Hawke pressed on with Young's rehabilitation under the political cover afforded him by the Nationals.

---

8   Conversation with Walsh.

Then Minister for External Affairs and Trade, Gareth Evans, in 1995 delivered the inaugural annual Peter Wilenski Memorial Lecture, established by the Australian Institute of Policy and Science to honour its former director. Evans referred to Wilenski's career as 'breathtaking in its range and level of accomplishments', and described Wilenski as 'the little egg-headed Jewish kid who came to Australia from Poland as a refugee in 1943'. Wilenski died of cancer a year earlier aged only fifty-five. Richard Hall, press secretary to Whitlam in opposition, confidently prepared for victory over McMahon in 1972. Hall recommended Wilenski as chief of staff and spelt out Wilenski's truly impressive academic credentials. 'Christ, he's a professional student' was Whitlam's first dismissive comment, but Wilenski got the job when Labor came to power.

Eric Walsh told the author they did not really hit it off. Wilenski was a small, quiet man—'egg-headed', as Evans described him—and moved quietly. He frequently appeared unexpectedly from behind the Prime Minister, evoking the exclamation from Whitlam: 'Don't fucking slither.' Suffering from a severe bout of pneumonia, Wilenski took no part in the 1974 election campaign. Whitlam, who like many of the top politicians seemed immune from illness, was impatient with staff off sick and, after the 1974 election, he got rid of Wilenski, sending him off as special adviser to the royal commission on the Public Service chaired by Dr H. C. (Nugget) Coombs.

Wilenski was brilliant. At only twenty-four, he was Resident Medical Officer at Sydney's Royal North Shore Hospital, going on to become head of the Department of Labor and Immigration in 1975. Fraser removed him from this post. In 1983 he was appointed Secretary of the Department of Education and Youth Affairs; then Chairman of the Public Service Board; followed by appointment as Secretary of the Department of Transport and Communications in 1987–88. On the Public Service Board and in the Transport Department, he struck a blow for public health that had far wider ramifications than he could then have imagined. *Serving the Nation—100 years of public service* was commissioned by the Public Service Commission to mark the centenary of the Commonwealth Public Service, and it chronicled Wilenski's successful campaign to ban smoking in government departments, instrumentalities and on Australian airlines.

The downside was that it led to public servants standing outside their office buildings smoking, when they should have been working. It eventually led to a smoking ban in virtually all buildings, public and private, and it is now spreading to a ban on smoking outdoors in public places, such as football stadiums and beaches. At the end of the Cold War, as Gareth Evans said, 'a defining moment in international affairs and a time of extraordinary readjustment in the UN itself', Wilenski in 1989 was appointed Australia's Permanent Representative to the United Nations and in 1992 he was appointed Secretary of the Department of Foreign Affairs and Trade, dying while still in that position.

Totally uninterested in sport, Whitlam was out of the ordinary. Menzies started the ball rolling as the first prime ministerial cricket 'tragic'—besotted by the game but a hopeless cricketer as a young man and promoting himself as a keen sports fan. Harold Holt was a keen spear fisherman. Gorton was not particularly into sport as a political tool, although his press secretary, Owen Lloyd, convinced him to go to North Bondi, put on lifesaver's cap and rush into the surf for the cameras. As Prime Minister, Hawke assiduously cultivated his image as an all-round sports participant in cricket, golf and yachting; both Howard and Rudd confessed to being 'cricket tragics' and enthusiastic followers of the game. Although her husband was not interested in sport, Margaret Whitlam represented Australia as a swimmer at the 1938 Empire Games in Sydney and his offspring were keen on sport; Whitlam had to be coaxed by his staff to attend sporting events.

Nevertheless, he simply had to attend a function organised by the Australian Olympic Committee, and Mick Young accompanied him to point out who were the champion athletes present. Reluctantly, Whitlam agreed to Eric Walsh's idea of attending the Miracle Mile classic trotting race at Harold Park in Sydney as guest of honour of the committee. Whitlam, a food enthusiast, enjoyed the lavish smorgasbord. Starting time came for the big event and the committee and guests moved to the viewing area overlooking the track and close to the winning post. The race was a thriller and excitement reached fever pitch as the field came around the last turn and headed up the straight, with the whips cracking and the huge crowd roaring. Walsh looked around for Whitlam. There he was at the far end of the big committee area, his bum pointing towards the track while he continued to demolish the smorgasbord.

Melbourne was a contender for the centenary 1996 Olympics, marking the first Modern Olympics in Athens in 1896, and word had gone out from the Foreign Affairs Department that staff at foreign postings were to do all they could to lobby on behalf of Melbourne. Whitlam happened to be in Jakarta and the then Ambassador, Phillip Flood, arranged for Whitlam to be present at a function he was hosting for top government people in the hope of influencing them to support Melbourne. Flood correctly believed that Whitlam—so well known in Asia—would be a good ally for Melbourne's cause. Whitlam (an authority in his own right on classic Greek history) had not been apprised of this. Flood joined Whitlam, who was conversing with Indonesian Government identities, and said something along the lines of 'Mr Whitlam, we were talking about what would be the best city for the 1996 centenary Olympics'. Whitlam replied: 'It should be Athens.' Dead silence.

Michael Delaney, aged only twenty-four, joined Whitlam's office as private secretary to the Prime Minister in January 1973, on secondment from the Public Service Board. Delaney was educated by the Christian Brothers, then won a scholarship to Latrobe University, working full-time at any job he could get: builder's labourer and service station attendant, among others. Delaney came to Canberra after winning a place in a competitive field as a graduate trainee in public administration and joined the Public Service Board.

The Prime Minister's office in the north-east corner of the Old Parliament House had been refurbished, although it was still cramped for a staff of about 10. (Later, Howard and Rudd had more than 40 staff.) Delaney remembers it as a well-organised office, ruled by Whitlam, who was, as he had been all his life, obsessive about getting things done. The character of the office and its operations, Delaney believed, were extensions of Whitlam's experience as a long-term Leader of the Opposition. Whitlam expected high standards from his staff and they would normally be in the office by 8 am (except Freudenberg), and when the Parliament was sitting, would not get away until 10–11 pm. Like most ministerial and opposition staffers, Whitlam's staff generally had rushed meals in the non-members' dining room (known by all who used it as 'the sheltered workshop', although with hindsight it was excellent: plain food and cheap).

Graham Freudenberg's skill as a subeditor played a part in the Fraser Government settling on *Advance Australia Fair* as the national anthem. Long before Paul Keating initiated the move to a republic, the Whitlam Government decided to ditch *God Save the Queen* as the anthem, arousing outrage among monarchists and joy among republicans. At the time, the feminist movement—with some influence on the Whitlam Government—had demanded political correctness and terms such as 'chairman' and 'fisherman' were to be avoided and replaced with 'chair' or 'chairperson' and 'fisherperson'. But what to do about the words in *Advance Australia Fair*: 'Australian sons let us rejoice'? 'Australian sons and daughters, let us rejoice' would be ridiculous. Perhaps only a complete rewrite would accommodate the feminists.

Freudenberg removed the gender issue with the simple device of changing one word, 'sons', to 'all'. So we now sing, 'Australians *all* let us rejoice'. The Whitlam Government commissioned the largest-ever unofficial poll to gauge voter preferences for a new anthem, and, in 1977, the Fraser Government undertook a non-binding plebiscite asking voters to show their preference. The Freudenberg version of *Advance Australia Fair* won easily, with 43.29 per cent of the vote over *God Save the Queen*, *Waltzing Matilda* and *Song of Australia*. If the decision had come down to preferences, *Waltzing Matilda* (which received the second-highest vote: 28.28 per cent) might just have won outright. As a point of interest, judging by support for *God Save the Queen*, the Australian Capital Territory was the most disloyal Territory, giving the then anthem, *God*

Save the Queen, only 6.65 per cent. Of the States, the old anthem was most popular in Western Australia, with 23.17 per cent, and least popular in New South Wales, with 15.32 per cent.[9]

Delaney was required to read all the newspapers before getting to the office. Whitlam would be up at 4 am in the Lodge reading the papers. Delaney remembers failing his paper-reading chore and an angry Whitlam told him: 'If you can't get them read by the time you arrive here, like I do, don't bother turning up.' A crisis in the newspaper-reading routine came in 1973 when Delaney moved from Queanbeyan to a house in the Ridgeway on a 3 ha block. The Ridgeway is on a hill to the north-east of and overlooking Queanbeyan and was only a 15-minute drive from Parliament House.

Although Delaney lived only a kilometre or two from the centre of the town, the newsagent with the monopoly control of newspaper retail sales refused to deliver Delaney's papers because he was 'out of town'. Worse still, he had no phone since the Post Office—then operating a telephone monopoly—wanted $5000 dollars to construct a phone line to the property and Delaney simply could not afford it. That figure was not much less than what he had paid for his block. Whitlam fumed: not only was his private secretary without newspapers, he could not be contacted. Delaney, who had learned the intricacies of the bureaucracy when in the Public Service, had the task of getting the machinery of government busy first thing each day on whatever Whitlam wanted done arising from the morning news. This involved furious working of the phone from his home contacting senior officials, briefing them and explaining what the Prime Minister wanted.

This all had to be ready for Question Time in the early afternoon. In his usual 'crash through or crash' style, Whitlam got busy. He contacted Fairfax to complain about the treatment of Delaney and a second newsagency in Queanbeyan was licensed, which delivered the papers to Ridgeway and halved the value of the original newsagency business. Next, the Post Office was instructed to supply Delaney with a phone immediately, and, arriving home, he found his phone connected to a line strung on gum trees all the way up the side of the Ridgeway. There was no charge—just part of the work the Post Office was required to carry out for the Prime Minister's office. Delaney has carried the 4.30 am morning newspaper-reading obsession with him throughout his career in the private sector, including in his present position as head of one of the most important national small business groups, the Motor Trades Association of Australia.

Communication difficulties faced by busy prime ministers until the 1990s cannot be comprehended today, except by the elderly, and mobile phones were

9 *Parliamentary Handbook.*

yet to appear in Australia. Frank Crean (father of Simon), first Treasurer in the Whitlam Government, disliked flying and would, if possible, be driven between Canberra and his Melbourne office in his chauffeured Commonwealth car. At one point, Whitlam was in Brisbane and urgently needed to speak to Crean, whom he believed was in Canberra, but could not be raised. Eric Walsh was asked to find out where the Treasurer might be and the press secretary returned to tell the Prime Minister Crean had left his Parliament House office about a certain time headed for Melbourne.

'The bastard's in Benalla', Whitlam fumed. Walsh had never heard of Benalla (between Wangaratta and Melbourne), but Whitlam, who possessed an encyclopaedic knowledge of Australian towns, gained as both a politician and an air force navigator, guessed Benalla was about where Crean would be. Michael Delaney, a Victorian, was ordered to get busy: phone the Benalla Police Station with the number plate of Crean's car and instruct the police to intercept Crean with the message to urgently phone the Prime Minister. It worked and was not the first time Whitlam called on the services of the police for similar duties.

A corridor of small, cramped offices ran off the reception area of the Prime Minister's office and here Delaney, Jim Spigelman and Peter Wilenski toiled for long hours. Whitlam referred to this as 'the Polish corridor'. Spigelman was senior adviser for legal and constitutional matters and freedom of information— both lively political issues. Labor's victory in December 1972 returned it to office federally for the first time since Menzies defeated the Chifley Government in the same month in 1949. It was the best day for Labor since the end of the war and was achieved entirely by the leadership Whitlam had given the party, yet for Caucus it would be business as usual, whether Labor was in office or not.

Whitlam was constantly reminded that Caucus ruled the roost. Caucus elected the ministry as it had since the early years of Federation and the Prime Minister allocated portfolios. In 1956 Menzies had followed the Westminster practice of a ministry with an inner Cabinet. There were 15 ministers in this Cabinet. Whitlam wanted to continue this system, but was defeated back in April when Caucus—by 34 votes to 33—ruled that Whitlam would have a Cabinet consisting of all members of the ministry. Had Caucus considered this after the election, Whitlam might well have won.

He now faced the burden of a Cabinet of 27: the members. Even worse, ministers (and particularly Lionel Murphy) would not abide by the Westminster practice of supporting a Cabinet decision once made, whether or not each minister had agreed with the decision. They were quite prepared to go to Caucus and overturn Cabinet decisions and inevitably Cabinet leaked like a sieve to the media. Every minister had a press secretary, many of whom regarded defence of their boss their major role, not serving the Labor Government. Factional opponents of their boss were more frequently the targets of press secretaries than the Liberal opposition, who regarded the non-members' bar as an ideal place to sell their minister to the gallery and knife the minister's Caucus opponents.

With 27 ministers in the Cabinet, inevitably much time was wasted on repetitive debates and Whitlam's exasperation was palpable. Moss Cass, a short, dark, intense man from the Victorian Left faction, was a medical practitioner before he entered Parliament. As Minister for Environment, Cass publicly advocated the decriminalisation of marijuana smoking. About the same time, Cass's wife (in the Melbourne *Age*) bemoaned the loss of conjugal rights the wives of federal parliamentarians endured.

Soon after, at the weekly Cabinet meeting, Cass argued with Whitlam about some issue, telling the Prime Minister, 'The trouble with you, Gough, is that you know nothing about the grassroots of the Labor Party'. Whitlam retorted: 'Moss, you know a lot about grass and your wife apparently knows something about roots, but you know fuck-all about the grassroots of the Labor Party.' Whitlam could be bitchy. Cass passed by Whitlam and Bill Hayden walking down the government lobby, and, nodding to Whitlam, Cass said: 'Morning, Leader.' Out of earshot, Whitlam said to Hayden: 'I'm glad he spoke. Now we know his face from his arse.'[10]

Cass was a stern defender of the environment when it was regarded an issue of only secondary interest by the elite. (Incidentally, Peter Howson, a junior minister in the short-lived McMahon Government, was the first Federal Minister for the Environment.) Cass and Whitlam were in tune on environmental protection. Cass was not prepared to accept the standard views on motherhood issues, such as the high priority governments traditionally gave to assisting farmers, and when a huge flood rolled down the Darling River, a journalist asked Cass what he was going to do for farmers. Cass replied: 'Flood plains are for floods.'

The Health Minister, Doug Everingham, a medical practitioner, was another interesting non-conformist in the Whitlam Government, coming into the spotlight when, as the member for the Queensland electorate of Capricornia (a major centre for the sugar industry), he declared that sugar was 'a second-class food and a third-class poison'. Yet it did not seem to do him much damage in his electorate. Spelling reform was a particular hobbyhorse of the Health Minister and he proposed renaming his department the Health Department, involving an expensive change of government stationery, various forms and amendments to legislation. Whitlam commented: 'He's m-a-d in the h-e-d.' Whitlam wrote to Everingham, telling him that spelling reform was not part of his portfolio duties. He addressed it to 'Dug' and signed it 'Gof'. The department retained its name.

10   Conversation with Eric Walsh.

Everingham turned out to be a resilient politician; elected to Capricornia in the 1967 by-election; losing it in 1975 with the defeat of Whitlam by Fraser; winning again in 1977; he retired in 1984. Graham Freudenberg wrote that there was a widely held view that Everingham was vulnerable in the by-election because of his atheism and views on communism.[11] Although a non-believer himself, Whitlam had unsuccessfully opposed Everingham's preselection. He issued an edict to Everingham: that he not issue public statements unless approved by Whitlam, and he had to curb his addiction to writing indiscreetly honest letters to newspaper editors.

Whitlam and his press party were to visit Everingham at his home, named 'Ingersoll' after the nineteenth-century American crusading free thinker. Freudenberg was worried that the 'smart alecs' from the Canberra gallery would note the name of the house and 'revive the atheism thing'. Jack Stanaway, whom we all knew well because of his days in the gallery, was then working for the Queensland ALP and, hearing of Freudenberg's concern, he ordered Everingham to take down the name plaque of his home. Everingham refused, saying, 'Jack, I've done everything you and Gough have asked me in the campaign. I've shut up. I haven't written any letters. But this is my home and that name stays. Some things are sacred.'

Barbara Stewart from Whitlam's staff was stationed in Rockhampton for the election and realised voters in his electorate had high regard for Everingham. As a medico, he had operated his own private, personal version of Medibank for needy patients, seven years before Bill Hayden established it nationally. Everingham easily won the election, but, unknown to everyone in Parliament House, Gough Whitlam was soon to have much more to worry about than the personal foibles of Doug Everingham.

---

11   Freudenberg, *A Figure of Speech*, p. 89.

15. Darkness Descends on Whitlam

An important factor in the downfall of the Whitlam Government was the affair involving the Deputy Prime Minister, Dr Jim Cairns, and Junie Morosi. The media could not get enough of the yarn—splashed as a 'bombshell sex story'. Cairns' colleagues in the Caucus and journalists in the gallery were, to say the least, surprised. Until then, it had been assumed that Cairns and his devoted wife of many years were inseparable. Morosi turned up, out of the blue, becoming a regular visitor to the office of the Leader of the Government in the Senate, Minister for Customs and Attorney-General, Lionel Murphy. She was a stunning beauty, slender, with beautiful black hair—in short, a knockout. Morosi was not on Murphy's staff but the general view around Parliament was that Murphy was 'knocking her off'.

Murphy came to the Parliament as a NSW Senator in 1962. His promotion was rapid: Leader of the Opposition in the Senate in 1967 and Leader of the Government in the Senate when Whitlam came to power in 1972. With his promotion came a more commodious office, allowing him, when the Senate rose for the night, to host some of the best parties in Parliament House. Frequently, the parties would, in the early hours of the morning, move to Murphy's fine house in Arthur Circle, Forrest—an exclusive address. Lionel's gorgeous wife, Ingrid, a former model, was the hostess. No matter how late the party, Murphy would be in Parliament House next morning bright and early. A big, powerful man, he had the rolling gait of a sailor and, like many successful politicians, had an iron constitution. As early as his mid-forties, a spectacular whisky nose—red and well veined—dominated his features. Murphy's female staff—all invariably attractive—would work on his nose with pancake make-up for his TV appearances, which was a demanding and skilled task.

Murphy introduced Jim Cairns to Morosi and he was besotted. At this stage, the Opposition did not try to make anything of the affair. Press secretary Eric Walsh asked Whitlam what he thought about Cairns and Morosi. Whitlam replied: 'He's c**t-struck at sixty.' One night after the Senate rose, Morosi and Cairns were in Murphy's office; with Whitlam overseas, Cairns was the acting Prime Minister. The couple decided to spend the night together at the Lakeside Hotel, on the northern shore of Lake Burley Griffin, just across Commonwealth Avenue Bridge. But how were they to get there? That very day, the Commonwealth car drivers were on strike. With no Commonwealth car available to take the lovers to the Lakeside, Murphy had the answer: Trevor Wright, Murphy's private secretary, would convey them in his well-worn Holden. Morosi and Cairns sat in the backseat, with Wright as the chauffeur, and off they drove, not knowing that on that very night police were hunting a dangerous prisoner who had escaped from Cooma jail, some 100 km to the south.

Halfway across Commonwealth Avenue Bridge, a police roadblock halted the party. Trevor, who had been enjoying the party in Murphy's office, was aghast. The breathalyser loomed, but no, a policeman shone his torch into the back seat of the Holden and sighted the acting Prime Minister. 'I'm very sorry, Sir', said the policeman, 'go ahead', which they apparently did, in more ways than one. It also transpired that ASIO was desperately searching for the acting Prime Minister that night—without success.[1]

While the media and the Opposition both knew of the dramatic crossing of the lake by the lovers in Trevor Wright's car, Morosi came into the sights of the Opposition for different reasons. The Department of Treasury was appalled when Cairns, as Treasurer, appointed Morosi as his office coordinator. It had long been the boast of Treasury (with some justification) that it gave the Treasurer a quality of service and backup that no other department, including the Prime Minister's Department, could match. Morosi was totally unqualified and, within weeks, despite the best efforts of others on the Treasurer's staff, Cairns' office was a shambles.

The Opposition, in late 1974, began to question Cairns' employment of Morosi, who, with her husband, had been involved in several failed companies. On 4 December 1974, John Howard—elected in May that year as the MP for Bennelong on Sydney's North Shore—raised in Parliament the issue of 'a well-publicised appointment' to Cairns' staff.[2] Adopting the Uriah Heap approach, he assured the house he was not raising the matter in 'an acrimonious personal sense, but as a matter of concern to this Parliament'. Howard did not mention Morosi's name. He said he had information that companies 'of which that person and her husband' were directors, officers and/or shareholders were currently being investigated by the NSW Commissioner for Corporate Affairs. Howard said: 'I raise this matter because I know that such an investigation will prompt an immediate investigation by the government', adding that he would be 'very relieved to know that there is no substance in the information', but believed his information was reliable.

The next day in Question Time in the house, Whitlam said that, as a result of the newspaper reports of that morning, he had raised the Howard statement with Cairns and the Treasurer had asked him to get in touch with the Premier of New South Wales 'to secure the fullest and earliest account of any investigation'. Yet although according to Whitlam Cairns had asked that he (Whitlam) seek a full investigation by the NSW Government of Howard's allegations against Morosi, Cairns gave her full clearance in a personal explanation to the house at the end of Question Time:

---

1 Conversation with Trevor Wright.
2 CPD.

I am quite satisfied that Miss Morosi is a person of very considerable ability, character and integrity…I am not going to be influenced by newspaper campaigns which have an element of the scurrilous and an element of the irresponsible. I suggest to honourable members that if I had chosen a man or even a woman who was not good looking, perhaps nothing would have happened.

This was the big story of the day on the last day of parliamentary sittings for the year. Cairns was digging in and, although the issue raised by Howard failed to turn up anything damaging to Cairns, it added to a deepening sense of gloom in Caucus. The end was near for Cairns and, for that matter, for the Whitlam Government. On 4 June 1975, Cairns misled the house by denying the existence of a letter, signed by him, to a Melbourne businessman offering a brokerage fee for the raising of a government loan. The letter did exist and Cairns had signed it. People I knew well in Treasury had been telling me for weeks that Morosi had created havoc in the Treasurer's office and Cairns was probably telling the truth when he said he had no recollection of the letter. Yet he could hardly offer Morosi's incompetence as an excuse and Whitlam had to sack him.

Cairns owned up to the Morosi affair in an interview with John Cleary on ABC radio in September 2002, when he was eighty-eight. When asked by Cleary, 'Did you go to bed with Junie Morosi?', Cairns replied, 'Yes'. Richard Ackland was in the *Australian Financial Review*'s bureau in 1975 and he later edited an acidic magazine, *Justinian*, which circulated widely in the legal profession. After Cairns' confession, Ackland authored an article in the *Sydney Morning Herald* pointing to the hypocrisy and lies the lovers had told about their relationship. For example, they had both sued *The National Times*, a Fairfax publication, for alleging what Cairns later confessed to. Ackland's article reported that on 18 October 1982 in the Supreme Court of New South Wales Cairns was asked before a jury if he had ever had an adulterous relationship. He replied, 'No, never'.

The National Times published an interview with an American director of Morgan Stanley, Dudley Scholes, who referred to Cairns' 'girlfriend, Morosi'. Cairns claimed the remark gave rise to a defamatory imputation that he was 'improperly involved with his assistant, Junie Morosi, in a romantic or sexual association contrary to the obligations of his marriage and to that of Miss Morosi'. Morosi told the jury: 'I felt insulted, angry, upset and hurt. It was very demeaning to me as a woman [to be called a "girlfriend"].' The jury found that the imputation did arise from the article in *The National Times*, but that it was not defamatory. Claiming the jury's finding was perverse, Cairns and Morosi went to the Court of Appeal. Justice Hutley at one point remarked: 'The fact that so intelligent and glamorous a woman as Miss Morosi [Mrs Ditchburn] developed a romantic interest in him may raise his standing in public eyes.' Cairns and Morosi lost the appeals with costs awarded to Fairfax.

Trevor Wright, Murphy's private secretary and an officer of the Customs Department, had been private secretary to Don Chipp, Customs Minister in the McMahon Government, and nobody raised the slightest question that this should exclude him from working for the Labor Government. Since Federation, officers from a minister's department normally were seconded as ministerial private secretaries. There was also a small group of 'professional' private secretaries specialising in this position and working for ministers irrespective of their party. Cliff (Nobby) Clark and Frank Hinchelwood were two I remember. For example, Menzies' private secretary, Geoff Yeend, was seconded from the Prime Minister's Department. After the death of Curtin, Chifley was both Prime Minister and Treasurer, as well as Leader of the House, and an officer from the Prime Minister's Department was seconded as his private secretary and an officer from Treasury was his private secretary for that portfolio.

The non-political Commonwealth Public Service not only administered the nation (at the direction of the Cabinet), but also was the advisory body to the Government. The adviser to ministers was the secretary of his department and, in practice, other senior officers from the department would come to Parliament House to brief their minister. This system gradually changed on the election of the Whitlam Government to the point where, under the Howard Government, ministers relied almost entirely on their hugely expanded personal, and mostly partisan, staff for advice. There were exceptions. Howard sought advice from his departmental secretary, Max Moore Wilton (whom he had recruited from the private sector), and Treasury remained virtually unchallenged as the adviser to the Treasurer.

On 17 July 1973, Gough Whitlam and his Minister for Overseas Trade, Jim Cairns, announced the historic decision to slash tariffs across the board by 25 per cent, provoking attacks by unions. To his great credit, Bob Hawke, then both National President of the Labor Party and President of the ACTU, supported the tariff cut. *The Age*[3] reported, according to a poll it had taken, tariff cuts had been 'widely, if cautiously, welcomed throughout the nation'. All newspapers supported the decision. The *Australian Financial Review* said 'it was a vast step towards national maturity and a move that will greatly strengthen Australia's international bargaining position when (and if) long-awaited GATT [General Agreement on Tariff and Trade] negotiations begin later this year'. Whitlam had appointed Alf Rattigan (later chair of the Industries Assistance Commission) to head a committee and give a recommendation on the tariff cut.

Rattigan believes the tariff decision enabled the Liberal–Country Party Coalition in 1978 and 1979 to secure, in the GATT negotiations, concessions benefiting

---

3   24 July 1973.

the export of agricultural products to Europe, Japan and the United States.[4] By now, the average gallery member, who had regarded trade and tariff policies as second-rung 'economic' stories and not all that important, had to refocus. Given *Inside Canberra* had a strong readership in manufacturing, Don and I had long been following the protection debate and were far from enthusiastic about reductions in protection.

The author is still to be convinced that the rush by Australian governments, both Coalition and Labor, to have the most hairy-chested free-trade policies in the world is necessarily in the best interests of the nation. Many of the world's most vibrant economies—the United States, Japan, China and Germany—have not gone nearly as far as Australia in embracing abolition of protection for manufacturing, and rural and service industries. Successive Australian governments should have done far more to lessen the impact of tariff reductions by, for example, greater support for training and skills and more assistance for technological innovation to maintain the competitiveness of Australian industry.

Bringing independence to Papua New Guinea is one of Whitlam's proudest achievements and in *The Whitlam Government*, Whitlam explains how in the 1950s Labor was inhibited by Calwell's attitude towards Papua New Guinea.[5] Calwell spelt out his policy in a speech to the Australian Institute of Political Science Summer School in January 1958:

> The Labor Party desires to maintain the status now existing in Dutch New Guinea, in our own Territory and in Indonesia, by an agreement for security against external attack and for uplifting the welfare of the inhabitants of the area. So that I shall not be misunderstood by not being explicit enough, I repeat the views I expressed in 1950 in the House of Representatives on the Indonesian claim to Dutch New Guinea: 'The Indonesians have no claim whatsoever to Dutch New Guinea, whether on ethical, historical or any other grounds; they have no more claim to Dutch New Guinea than they have to Siam, Colombia or anywhere else.' If we allowed the Indonesians into Dutch New Guinea, there would be no hope of holding the northern portion of Australia and the fate of this country would be sealed and certain.

Calwell's view at this time was the majority view—of not only the Labor Party, but also the Liberals and, more importantly, the Australian population. History has proved Calwell wrong, yet the Indonesian takeover of West Papua today is unsettling the area. The hostility of the local inhabitants to foreigners mounts as Jakarta pursues a policy of mass 'transmigration' of Indonesians to the province from other parts of the archipelago. Australian governments, from Menzies

---

4   Rattigan, G. A. 1986, *Industry Assistance: The inside story*, Melbourne University Press, Carlton, Vic., p. 170.
5   Whitlam, Gough 1985, *The Whitlam Government 1972–75*, Penguin, Ringwood, Vic., p. 72.

on, had to deal with a drive in the United Nations after the war by the newly emerged independent countries such as India, backed by the United States, for an end to colonisation. It was the refusal by Washington to back the objections of the Dutch and the Menzies Government to an Indonesian takeover that forced the Dutch out.

I met Michael Somare, the man who was to become the first PNG Prime Minister, at a party in Eric Walsh's O'Connor house in the early 1960s. Born in 1936, Somare is the son of a village policeman and his education included time in a Japanese-run primary school after the Japanese invasion of Papua New Guinea. Before becoming Prime Minister of Papua New Guinea, Somare developed a network of influential Australians. With the departure of Calwell, Whitlam proceeded with his plans for independence for Papua New Guinea, and, on 1 December 1973, the territory gained self-governance, followed by full independence on 16 September 1975. Veteran ABC journalist Graeme Dobell, for many years the foreign affairs/defence correspondent for Radio Australia, wrote that in the mid-1960s, the Australian Cabinet debated integrating Papua New Guinea into Australia and granting the people a form of Australian citizenship.[6]

Whitlam had marked out his policy priorities in his historic visit to China in July 1971 as Leader of the Opposition. The first priority was getting out of Vietnam and the second was recognition of the People's Republic of China. His first overseas visit as Prime Minister was not devoted to knee bending to the great powers. He visited New Zealand in January 1973, Papua New Guinea and Indonesia in February and India in May before Mexico City, Washington, DC, and finally Ottawa for the Commonwealth Heads of Government meeting in August.

On Whitlam's official visit to Papua New Guinea, the press party got a taste of Whitlam's quirky sense of humour. The Prime Minister's party visited Mendi in the Highlands, where he was guest of honour at a spectacular gathering of the tribes. Warriors adorned in fantastic traditional dress danced and chanted in the 'sing-sing' display, while the Prime Minister's party looked on. A tribal elder approached Whitlam and solemnly presented him with what looked like a club or a large walking stick, with elaborately carved snakes—a symbol of long life—and topped with a large knob. Whitlam turned to Walsh and asked: 'What do I do with it, lean on it or strap it on?' Unsurprisingly, the response produced muffled laughter from the press party.

On 11 November 1975, Michael Somare stood beside a radio in Port Moresby, listening to the account of how the Governor-General, Sir John Kerr, had

---

6   Dobell, Graeme 2000, *Australia Finds Home: The choices and chances of an Asia Pacific journey,* ABC Books, Sydney, p. 134.

dismissed the Whitlam Labor Government. The Prime Minister of the newly independent Papua New Guinea turned to an aide and said with a grin: 'We've only just cut them loose and they've already stuffed it up.'[7]

As Opposition Leader, Malcolm Fraser had promised he would not use the Senate to block supply unless there were 'reprehensible circumstances'. The Whitlam Government was doomed by the loans affair, which Malcolm Fraser found a convenient 'reprehensible circumstance' and secured the agreement of the Governor-General, Sir John Kerr, to sack Whitlam. The loans affair could be described as many things, including stupid and irrational, but not 'reprehensible'. No corruption was ever found, nobody ever lent any money, or paid any money—nor was it illegal in the letter or spirit of the law.

What precisely Fraser saw as 'reprehensible' was that Rex 'Strangler' Connor, the Minister for Minerals and Energy, and the Deputy Prime Minister, Jim Cairns, knowingly misled the house. On 4 June, Cairns denied in the house the existence of a letter he had signed to a Melbourne businessman offering him a commission if he could raise loans overseas. Whitlam dismissed Cairns from the ministry on 2 July 1975, and, in the house, said it was a tragedy for his party, its leader and the Deputy Prime Minister.

With his respect for the institution of Parliament, Whitlam had done his duty and sacked both Cairns and Connor. Caucus had the power to object, but did not. Yet Fraser still found it was 'reprehensible', even though Whitlam had acted strictly in accordance with Westminster practice. It was Fraser and Kerr who were guilty of 'reprehensible' circumstances. In retrospect, if Whitlam had been as clever as John Howard was years later, he would have survived. The house, Cabinet and Treasury would have been kept in the dark about the loans affair and Whitlam would have used television to declare that black was white and nobody had told him anything was wrong. Howard, of course, was never told anything was wrong, be it children overboard or the scandal of wheat-for-oil trade dodges operated by the Australian Wheat Board.

The loans affair arose because of the efforts by Connor and his departmental head, Lennox Hewitt, to raise cheap Arab money for national projects such as gas pipelines. The secretive Connor was at heart an old-fashioned socialist. Clyde Cameron, Minister for Labor and a Whitlam hater, was responsible for Connor meeting a Pakistani middleman, Tirath Khemlani, who claimed he could raise the funds. The Treasury previously had sole responsibility for raising loans abroad for the Commonwealth and, correctly, believed it was being bypassed. Fred Wheeler, Treasury Secretary, was rightly suspicious of Khemlani and of Connor's secret dealings.

---

7   Ibid., p. 134.

Whitlam correctly suspected that Treasury would try to undermine the Government. Like others in the gallery, I was the recipient of leaks from Treasury to the office of the Shadow Treasurer, Phil Lynch, via either his press secretary, Brian Buckley, or his private secretary, Andrew Hay. They did not reveal the sources of their leaked information, but there is no doubt it came from Treasury. Wheeler had 'old mates" access to a network of international finance houses that filled him in on Khemlani's dubious operations. The media seized on the dispute between Treasury and the Government, portraying it as a major scandal.

Had it not been for Connor and Cairns misleading the Parliament, the affair could have been confined to the business section of newspapers. The media portrayal of Khemlani certainly had racial overtones: here was this funny little Pakistani who ate peanuts, trying to sell a Labor Government access to loans so he could make a huge commission. On 20 May 1975, Whitlam told Connor that he was to stop all attempts to raise money. Secretly, he refused and was even sleeping alongside the teleprinter in his office in the hope that someone, such as Khemlani, would find the money and Connor would be proved right.

Bob Sorby, now a NSW judge, then principal adviser to Connor, informed John Menadue of Connor's defiance of the order to give up on the loan. Sorby was a friend of the author and a former gallery member with the *Australian Financial Review*'s bureau, specialising in coverage of the mining and energy industries. After his gallery years, he became an adviser to Paul Keating, and the Labor Opposition's spokesman on minerals and resources. Later, Sorby was a political adviser to Prime Minister Bob Hawke, and he told me how worried Hawke was about Keating's attempts to undermine his prime ministership. Menadue[8] recounts how he and Clarrie Harders, Secretary of the Attorney-General's Department, had warned Whitlam that Connor had a lot more correspondence about loans than he had disclosed.

Menadue, together with Bill Hayden, the new Treasurer after Cairns' departure, quizzed Connor about the additional correspondence. Menadue observed that Connor looked sick and anything but a 'strangler'. His answers were unsatisfactory and Whitlam told Menadue on 15 October—nearly five months after Connor was told to stop his loan activity—to go to Connor and get him to resign. Menadue protested this was not his job, but Whitlam persisted. 'He [Whitlam] was intimidated, as others were, by Connor,' Menadue wrote. Connor told Menadue to 'piss off'. Whitlam finally spoke to Connor and secured his resignation—a shattering blow to the Government, coming on top of the dismissal of Cairns.

---

8   Menadue, *Things You Learn Along the Way*, p. 146.

In February 1975, the Whitlam Government appointed the Attorney-General, Senator Lionel Murphy, to the High Court. Despite a long history of political appointments to the Bench and the postwar appointment as Chief Justice of Sir Garfield Barwick (Attorney-General and Minister for External Affairs in the Menzies Governments), Murphy's appointment aroused immense resentment from the anti-Labor side of politics. As a lawyer, Murphy was fully qualified for the High Court and as a minister he had an outstanding record of achievement in a few short years. In March 1973, with his press secretary, George Negus, by his side, Murphy, as Attorney-General, caused a sensation by raiding the Melbourne headquarters of ASIO.

Labor was deeply suspicious of ASIO—for good reason: it had for years spied on Labor MPs, union leaders and general identities on the left of politics. Murphy was dissatisfied with answers he had received from ASIO about the activities of fascist Croatian terrorist groups operating in Australia. He was responsible for important legislation, including the establishment of the Family Court of Australia, the *Trade Practices Act* and the *Racial Discrimination Act*. Don Whitington, a mate of Murphy's after he became Attorney-General and Customs Minister, found him a source of good copy for *Inside Canberra*. Don and I enjoyed many lunches and dinners with Murphy—an entertaining and informed conversationalist on many topics. At Sydney University, he combined a Bachelor of Law Degree with a Bachelor of Science. One of the weaknesses of postwar Cabinets has been their domination by lawyers and the lack of representation of people with skills that really matter such as social workers, scientists, engineers and businesspeople.

So incensed were the Liberals at Murphy's elevation to the High Court that, in an act of bastardry and spite, the NSW lightweight Premier, Tom Lewis, tore up a longstanding convention dealing with filling Senate vacancies. The Constitution gives the power of filling vacancies to the Parliament (in effect, the Government) of the State the departed Senator represented. It had long been a convention that the vacancy would be filled by the nomination of the party of the departed Senator. Rather than adhere to the convention, Lewis appointed Cleaver Bunton, a former Mayor of Albury, as a non-Labor replacement.

This was important, since the Senate numbers were unchanged by the 1974 double-dissolution election. The Coalition did not have sufficient numbers to block supply and, to everyone's surprise and despite Lewis's despicable act, Bunton voted with the Government on supply. It was the death of Queensland Labor Senator Bert Milliner that instead led to the dismissal of the Whitlam Government. Tom Burns, then leader of the Queensland parliamentary Labor Party, insisted that the replacement should be Malcolm Colston, who had just missed election in 1974. Colston eventually made it into the Senate, ratted on Labor in 1999 and disgraced himself when it was revealed he had been rorting his travel allowances, after initially blaming his secretary.

In an act far more reprehensible than what Fraser could find against the Whitlam Government, the Queensland Premier, Joh Bjelke-Peterson, tossed convention to the wind and appointed a complete unknown to replace Milliner: Albert Field, who despised Whitlam, yet was claimed by Bjelke-Petersen to be a Labor man. Graham Freudenberg is critical of Labor tactics, despite the dirty tactics of the Queensland Premier.[9] He believes if Labor had been more flexible on this matter of principle, the Coalition could have been denied the vital extra vote. Burns rejected an invitation from the Bjelke-Petersen Cabinet to submit a panel of names. There is, of course, no guarantee that, had the panel been provided, the awful Bjelke-Petersen would suddenly act decently. Although appointed to fill the vacancy, Field failed to take his seat in the Senate.

A High Court challenge was launched and he simply absented himself from Senate sittings. The 1975 double-dissolution election aborted any political career he might have had. His failure to turn up in the Senate was no help to Labor. Because a Labor nominee did not fill the Bert Milliner vacancy, the Coalition in the Senate had the numbers to block supply. 'They did it over a dead senator's corpse', declared independent SA Senator Steele Hall, a former leader of the SA parliamentary Liberal Party (1968–70), describing how supply was blocked. Although Fraser was the beneficiary of Bjelke-Petersen's act of bastardry, he in effect admitted the unfairness of how he got to the Lodge by passing in 1977 the Constitutional Alteration (Senate Casual Vacancies) Bill to ensure casual vacancies are filled by representatives of the same political party as the senators they replace.

Supply was to run out on 20 November. The Senate repeatedly sent the supply legislation back with the demand Whitlam call an election. Whitlam refused, with the total backing of his party and, privately, the near-unanimous support of the gallery. The Government was making arrangements with the banks for temporary assistance should supply run out. The Whitlam camp and most members of the gallery believed Fraser would not be able to hold his troops solid in the Senate as the pressure came and several would crack. It would require only one to do so for the budget to pass. Fraser stalled a vote in the Senate, knowing that in the event of being asked to actually reject supply, several of his senators would rebel. Graham Freudenberg and many others believe Fraser was about to lose these senators in the very week that Kerr dismissed Whitlam.

John Menadue, CEO of News Limited's Australian operations before heading the Prime Minister's Department, wrote of Rupert Murdoch's highly partisan actions in supporting the Kerr dismissal.[10] In the gallery there was much discussion about Murdoch's behaviour and News Limited journalists in Sydney held

---

9   Freudenberg, *A Figure of Speech*, p. 176.
10   Menadue, *Things You Learn Along the Way*, pp. 156–7.

several stoppages as a protest against Murdoch's stand. What was not generally known was the childhood connection between Fraser and Murdoch. Fraser's father grazed the Victorian Western District property 'Nareen' and Murdoch's father, Keith (later Sir Keith), owned an adjoining property. As small children, Malcolm Fraser and Rupert Murdoch shared the same nanny.

With the crisis building, Menadue organised a lunch with Murdoch and News Limited head, Ken Cowley, in a Kingston restaurant on 7 November 1975. Complaining to them both about the coverage of the crisis, he told Murdoch he had cancelled his subscription to *The Australian*. 'This didn't put him [Murdoch] off his lunch,' Menadue says. On 11 December, Menadue made a written record of the lunch five weeks earlier, and he wrote:

> Rupert Murdoch told many of his friends that Mr. Fraser had informed him that the Governor-General had given him [Fraser] an assurance that if he hung on long enough there would be a general election before Christmas…although I have no direct information. He did tell me, however on 7 November that he was quite certain there would be an election before Christmas and that he would be staying in Australia until this occurred. He was very confident of the outcome of any election and even mentioned to me the position to which I might be appointed in the event of the Liberal victory—Ambassador to Japan.

Murdoch was right about that. Menadue was appointed as Ambassador to Japan and Murdoch could only have got that information from Fraser. When Murdoch later denied this account of the lunch, Menadue stated: 'I stand by it.' Having known Menadue well since the 1960s, the author has not the slightest doubt his was the truthful account.

Books have been written about Kerr's dismissal of the Whitlam Government— the most dramatic peacetime political incident since Federation. It became a talking point, somewhat like the assassination of US President John Kennedy: 'where were you when it happened?' I was in the non-members' dining room at lunch with Don Whitington and some other journalists when David Halpin, a ministerial press secretary, rushed in, ashen face. 'We've been dismissed by Kerr', he said. Those at the table retorted 'bullshit'. 'No, it's true, there's a statement in the boxes', said Halpin. We all rushed from the dining room. On the front steps of Parliament House, one of the shortest and most historically important speeches ever made in Australia came from Whitlam.

On the road directly in front of Parliament House, a gathering crowd of tourists and public servants watched Kerr's secretary, David Smith, who had mounted the front steps, read the proclamation of the Governor-General dissolving Parliament. The steps behind Smith were crowded with journalists, MPs and staffers. Whitlam was slightly behind the Governor-General's secretary, looking over his shoulder. Smith ended the proclamation with the words 'God save the Queen'. Whitlam, exuding confidence, stepped forward and declared:

> Well may we say 'God save the Queen' because nothing will save the Governor-General. The proclamation you have just heard read was counter-signed by Malcolm Fraser, who will undoubtedly go down in Australia's history from Remembrance Day 1975 as Kerr's cur…Maintain your rage and enthusiasm through the campaign for the election now to be held and until polling day.

Apart from the boos at the mention of Fraser, all this was said to wild applause and cheers. Many voters maintained their rage, but not enough to save Whitlam at the election. A greater number decided not to vote for a prime minister dismissed by the Governor-General. It might not have been clear to voters just why he was dismissed, but the very fact of the dismissal was fatal to Whitlam. There had never been any doubt Kerr had the reserve power to dismiss a government; Whitlam at no stage contested this. The argument was about the circumstances and justification of the use of this ultimate extreme power.

After his dismissal, Whitlam asked for and received two motions of confidence from the House of Representatives, and the Speaker, Gordon Scholes, rushed to get to Kerr a motion carried by the house reaffirming Whitlam as Prime Minister. How could it be that the Governor-General could sack a prime minister who retained the confidence of the house? Here was a constitutional crisis, with the Prime Minister twice reaffirmed in his position by the house after being sacked by the Governor-General. Scholes, upon arriving at the gates of Government House in his official car, was locked out. The gates were shut and were not to be opened.

A very angry Speaker returned to Parliament House and delivered a fiery speech denouncing this treatment. It was not until late in the afternoon that Kerr finally agreed to see Scholes. When he did, Kerr dismissed the motion of confidence in the Government as irrelevant, because he had already dissolved the Parliament. There was no constitutional provision for this action to be reversed, nor was there any constitutional provision for the Governor-General to ignore motions of confidence in his prime minister.

Whitlam had accepted that the ultimate judgment had to come from the people. There is no doubt in my mind that Kerr's action was unforgivable: he deceived his prime minister, which he later admitted, saying he knew if he had warned Whitlam he was thinking of dismissing him, Whitlam would have beaten him to the punch and advised the Queen to sack Kerr. Whitlam denies he would have contemplated such an action. Kerr should at least have told Fraser he would make no decision until the Senate had actually voted, one way or another, on supply instead of continuing to block it.

Apart from Fraser, the principal defender of Sir John Kerr's outrage was and continues to be Sir David Smith, but to borrow Mandy Rice-Davies' immortal quote, 'he would say that, wouldn't he'. Smith owes his knighthood to his luck. He was in the clerk's job in 1972 as Secretary of the Executive Council—a position below that of the Parliamentary Liaison Officer, in itself only in the middle ranks of the Prime Minister's Department. Smith was sent to Government House as Kerr's official secretary in 1973 and was attached to the Queen's household at Buckingham Palace in June–July 1975. In 1990, he was created a Knight of the Royal Victorian Order—an award within the Queen's personal gift.

Smith received the honour in recognition of his services to the Crown, both in Australia and in services rendered at Buckingham Palace. He owed this to former Labor leader Bill Hayden who was Governor-General courtesy of Prime Minister Hawke. Although the granting of imperial honours was barred by the ALP platform, Hayden as Governor-General personally intervened, urging the Queen to grant Smith the knighthood. Murray Tyrell, who preceded Smith as the Governor-General's secretary, was equally lucky in getting his Royal Victorian knighthood when the Coalition was in power. Tyrell was a lowly clerical assistant in the fourth division when he made it to Yarralumla, and the knighthoods for both Tyrell and Smith were treated as a great joke in the Prime Minister's Department.

It is no surprise, then, that Smith is a fervent monarchist and he probably got his gong as a result of a push from Bill Hayden. In spite of the fact Hayden would not have got the job as Governor-General but for Bob Hawke, Hayden renounced the policy of the party he owed so much to and, at the time of the republican debate, he outed himself as a monarchist. In the eyes of many Labor people, this marked the lowest point of Hayden's career.

In the wake of the sacking, some in Caucus raised the option of blocking supply to Fraser, who had guaranteed to Kerr he would have it passed. Whitlam rejected this on the grounds that, having fought the issue of the Senate blocking supply, it could hardly now adopt the same tactics used by Fraser. Clem Lloyd wrote the chapter on Gough Whitlam for *Australian Prime Ministers* in which he states there was some discussion by ministers about the prospect of Kerr using the Army if he was frustrated in this way. Labor minister Les Johnson recalls Whitlam asking Defence Minister, Bill Morrison, 'Who's got the army?' and Morrison replying, 'They do'.[11] Whitlam wrote that he believed Kerr would have used troops if Labor had attempted to keep the Parliament going.[12]

---

11 Grattan, Michelle (ed.) 2000, *Australian Prime Ministers*, New Holland, Frenchs Forest, NSW.
12 Whitlam, Gough 2005, *The Truth of the Matter*, Melbourne University Press, Carlton, Vic.

More than three decades on, the constitutional provisions and the reserve power of the Governor-General that led to the dismissal of the Whitlam Government are unchanged. The reserve power will probably be unchanged until Australia decides to become a republic, and even this would not alter the key point of the dismissal: the power of the Senate to block or reject supply. Removal of this power by a referendum would fail and it could not possibly gain the support of a majority of voters and a majority of the States. The smaller States would never agree. In 1987, Queensland Democrats Senator Michael Macklin, in a Private Member's Bill, put forward a workable solution to the supply problem. Macklin's proposal did not remove the right of the Senate to block or refuse supply, but rather, it changed the outcome should supply be blocked.

In short, if supply for a particular year is blocked or defeated, the amount of supply available to the Government for that year would revert to the appropriation of the previous year, thus not denying the Government sufficient money to carry out its ordinary executive services. Nor would Macklin's measure interfere with the double-dissolution provisions of the Constitution designed to deal with disagreements between the two houses. Although dying on the Senate notice paper, Macklin's bill still contains the core of an idea to fix the supply issue.

16. A New Home

Fraser won the December 1975 election with a swing of 7.5 per cent, surpassing Whitlam's effort in 1969 and bested only by the 7.9 per cent swing John Curtin achieved in 1943. Labor representation in the House of Representatives crashed from 66 seats to 36. Fraser was anything but a popular prime minister in the gallery—most believing he came to power, if not by a conspiracy between the Governor-General and Fraser, at least by highly dubious constitutional means.

Given widespread community concern at the Whitlam sacking, the size of Fraser's win was unexpected. This was a misjudgment by the gallery, including the author. Fraser owed his landslide win to a majority of voters taking note that the umpire, Kerr, declared Whitlam unfit to govern. The gallery believed Fraser had soiled his reputation and, if he had been patient, he would have won legitimately at the general election expected in late 1977, or early 1978. The experienced frontbench team he had behind him—most having been ministers in the McMahon Government—was of considerable assistance to Fraser in the election campaign. Labor was in for a long period of turmoil and tears.

The Country Party went through a series of name changes: National Country Party from May 1975; National Party of Australia in 1982; and in October 2003, simply The Nationals. For much of the postwar period until 1983, The Nationals had a powerful group of ministers, headed for much of the time by John McEwen. In the Fraser Cabinet, Doug Anthony was Deputy Prime Minister, with other Nationals ministers being Ian Sinclair and Peter Nixon (the latter close to Fraser). Phil Lynch was Treasurer—a reward for his work in keeping the loans scandal going. John Howard, elected to the house only in May 1974, made it to the shadow ministry in March 1975, and in the Fraser ministry was in the junior portfolio of Business and Consumer Affairs. He was widely regarded in the gallery—and by the author—as the leading nerd in the Liberal Party, with a limited political future. Howard, a Methodist from the western suburbs of Sydney, remained living at home until he was thirty-two, and was dismissed as just another bore from the Young Liberals. How wrong we were.

What we should have realised was that Howard had the patronage of John Carrick, who, as State Secretary, ran the Liberal Party in New South Wales, and Sir Frank Packer. Following McMahon's failure, Howard was groomed as the heir to McMahon's position as the up-and-coming federal MP destined for the top job in Canberra. Carrick, a member of the Sydney University Regiment, was selected in World War II for Sparrow Force—a 1400-man unit assigned to resist the Japanese advance on Timor. The Japanese landed thousands of troops by parachute and the Australian force was overwhelmed. Captain (later Sir John) Carrick was sent to Changi Prison in Singapore and survived about a year on the Thai–Burma railway. Of medium height, lean and sharp-featured, Carrick was elected to the Senate in 1971 and became a senior minister in the Fraser Government. On an official visit to Tokyo, he was congratulated on his ability to speak Japanese by a Japanese minister, who asked where he had learned the language. 'I was a guest of the Emperor' was Carrick's response.

After a land scandal, Phil Lynch was stood down and Howard's career skyrocketed. Fraser decided to give him the Treasury portfolio in November 1977—an extraordinary promotion for someone who had been in Parliament only a mere three years and had limited ministerial experience. (Lynch was later cleared by an inquiry and returned to the ministry, although not to his former role as Treasurer.) Part of the deal Fraser did with Kerr was that, on being sworn in as Prime Minister, he would maintain a stopgap ministry until after the 1975 election, exactly the same shadow ministry he led, and this included Don Chipp.

Fraser dumped Chipp from the ministry after the election and Chipp reacted by forming the Australian Democrats, which after the 1980 election held the balance of power in the Senate. The Democrats' gradual decline began in 1999 when Democrat leader, Meg Lees, supported Howard's goods and services tax (GST) on condition that food be excluded. The rank and file of her party was opposed to the GST. The 2007 election marked the end for the Democrats, when they failed to elect any senators. The Australian Greens replaced them as the balance-of-power party.

I knew Fraser well after he entered Parliament in 1955 as the Liberal MP for the western Victorian seat of Wannon. He owned 'Nareen', a large property in the Western District of Victoria, and it was no surprise he had more affinity with the Country Party than with the Liberals. I was stringing for the Stock and Land group of farm papers and was interested in Fraser's struggle—unsuccessful in the end—to keep wool sales in Portland, in his electorate. At the time, there were wool auctions in many country centres—most long since gone.

His colleagues and most in the gallery regarded Fraser as an aloof, cold country squire with no interest other than the pursuit of power. *Sydney Morning Herald* political journalist Peter Bowers wrote that Fraser's visage bore a remarkable resemblance to the mysterious Easter Island statues. Cartoonists leaped on the idea as presenting them with just the right caricature of the Prime Minister. His apparent aloofness and difficulty meeting people was a reflection of an innate shyness, but he overcame his shyness with his ruthless ambition to climb the greasy pole of politics. Fraser, far more than Menzies, tended to want to get his own way in Cabinet, and interfered more in other ministers' portfolios than any Liberal prime minister before him.

I paid regular calls on Walter Ives, head of the Department of Primary Industry, when the department was housed in what were called the woolsheds: temporary, wooden, single-storey buildings in Barton, demolished long ago. Ives was a big fellow with a distinguished mien and a sharp sense of humour and he was a keen political judge and a wine buff. Ives agreed with many in the gallery and a number of Liberal ministers that Fraser, the farmer, was closer to Doug Anthony and Peter Nixon than to Liberal ministers and thus belonged in the National Party. Most of my contact with Ives was when deputy National leader, Ian Sinclair, was his minister. Fraser infuriated the head of the department by phoning officers, such as division heads, not only going over Ives' head, but Sinclair's too.

Ives was appalled by Sinclair's notorious lack of punctuality. Turning up late was the norm for Sinclair. He would be 15 or more minutes late for meetings of the Agricultural Ministers' Council—federal and State ministers for agriculture— and would not have read the agenda, let alone the papers his department had carefully prepared for him. Doug Anthony, rather than Sinclair, took over the leadership of the National Party from McEwen because 'Black Jack' supported Anthony.

McEwen was angered by Sinclair's habitual lateness at the weekly meetings of National Party ministers—a few hours before Cabinet—to discuss the Cabinet agenda, which was supplied in advance so they could plan tactics. A story went around—possibly apocryphal—of Sinclair climbing into a Commonwealth car outside Parliament House, running late for his flight and urging the driver to get him to the airport with all possible speed. On the way the driver asked Sinclair whether he had played sport before entering politics. Sinclair replied he had played rugby for Sydney University. 'Well', inquired the driver, 'who went on for you up to half time?' Despite this weakness, Sinclair was a capable minister and a smart politician and the best of the Nationals' ministers, including McEwen, as a performer in the house.

An article in the *Australian Financial Review* by Andre Morony,[1] a former Treasury officer, revealed another example of Fraser's insistence on being informed of important issues in the portfolios of other ministers. The Reserve Bank was not at that time fully independent and the Government set interest rates after consultation with Treasury and the Reserve. According to Morony, in 1982, the Cabinet agreed, after considerable hesitation, to an auction system for the sale of short-term government bonds. With an auction system, the market would, if left alone, set the rates.

---

1   10 December 2007.

The Treasurer, John Howard, delegated his power to Treasury officials to accept or reject bids to Treasury and it was understood that whatever the interest rate—except in exceptional market circumstances—it would be accepted. Morony claimed a senior Treasury official, to whom he gave the fictitious name 'Kevin', received a copy of a letter from Fraser to Howard for his action. The Fraser letter stated all tenders had to be referred to the Prime Minister for approval. 'Kevin' declared this would wreck the auction system and that 'those bastards' (in Fraser's department) had put him up to it. Kevin decided to 'lose' the letter, threw it in his safe and forgot about it. Fraser was not acting in any way unlawfully and was perfectly entitled to issue his instruction to Howard. Had Kevin's defiance of a direct instruction from the Prime Minister been discovered, he should have been sacked out of hand.

David Barnett, an experienced journalist, opened the first permanent Australian Associated Press (AAP) office in the gallery. When Fraser failed in his first challenge to the then Opposition Leader, Bill Snedden, Barnett sought out Tony Staley, one of Fraser's principal supporters, and said something along the lines of 'Bad luck, mate, better luck next time and I hope you pull it off'. When the second attempt succeeded, Tony Eggleton, then running Fraser's office (and soon to run the Liberal Party's Canberra headquarters as Federal Secretary), decided that Barnett should be press secretary to the new Opposition Leader, and Fraser agreed.

The 'doorstop' interview was well understood overseas when Fraser became Prime Minister, but not in Australia. Journos (and particularly radio and TV reporters) would await the arrival or departure of politicians from their offices or conferences, or wherever they might be, to ask questions. Politicians could either stop briefly or simply give a 'no comment' and walk on. Barnett put the idea to Fraser that the gallery could doorstop him each morning, prior to him entering his office through a door on the eastern side of Parliament House. Barnett told the author that Fraser initially did not like the idea but finally agreed.

Importantly, as well as introducing the doorstop, Barnett began the now standard practice of providing a transcript of the doorstops to the gallery. Morning-paper journalists disliked the doorstop and were not prepared to come into the office before 8 am on most days, but at least the transcript gave them everything that had been said. The doorstop—now simply known as 'the doors'—has long been a standard procedure, with TV and radio journalists stationed outside the entrances to both the house and the Senate to record 'grabs' from various politicians on the issues of the morning.

It began to dawn on the gallery towards the end of his occupancy of the Lodge that Fraser was by no means the snooty, old-fashioned Tory whose only mission was to keep Labor out of office. The author asked Barnett why the gallery, including myself, was so surprised by Fraser's record: the saviour of Fraser Island; an environmentalist; champion of multiculturalism; a key player in the overturning of white colonial rule in Rhodesia; a fierce opponent of apartheid in South Africa; not to mention his tireless opposition, in retirement, to the central tenets of John Winston Howard. Barnett's observation was that it illustrated 'the great depth of superficiality of the Canberra press gallery'. 'They looked at this bloke', Barnett continued, 'they considered his background, and they allocated him to a pigeonhole'.

Barnett's point is well taken, although I believe the gallery never forgave Fraser for his role in the dismissal of Whitlam. Barnett was later to become a worshipper of Howard. Fraser and Howard detested one another after Fraser supported Peacock as Liberal leader after Fraser lost the 1983 election. Barnett, then a casual journalist and farmer, was one of the exclusive group Howard invited to a Sydney Harbour cruise with US President George Bush when he visited Australia. With his wife, Pru Goward, Barnett wrote an authorised Howard biography that could hardly be described as searching.

Barnett believes Fraser's biggest mistake was not to move on deregulation of the economy. According to Barnett, Fraser 'got pissed off with all of this. I mean nobody said when he was there that you should deregulate the economy, you should free up the interest rates, you should reduce tariffs, you should abolish the Arbitration Commission; everybody said the opposite.' The author disagrees; there were proponents of deregulation and low tariffs in the Fraser Government—notably, Phil Lynch and John Howard. When Lynch was Treasurer, the Industries Assistance Commission recommended sweeping reductions in protection for the textiles, clothing and footwear (TCF) industries. Fraser baulked; TCF was deeply embedded in the Australian economy.

It was not just a city industry in Labor-held electorates; far from it. More than 80 per cent of federal electorates had at least one TCF establishment. In some regional areas, it was the most significant employer and an important employer of migrant women. Lynch told me that in one long Cabinet discussion about what do to about protection cuts, Fraser asked, 'But what about Marshall [Baillieu]?' As well as being a member of one of Victoria's best-known and wealthiest families, Marshall Baillieu was the Liberal member for La Trobe, an electorate where TCF was an important employer. Lynch thought this reaction of Fraser's was pathetic, but nevertheless Fraser prevailed and the recommendations of the commission were greatly watered down—much to the relief of the majority of members of the house.

In all my years reporting Parliament, I have only had two parliamentarians I would describe as mates: Mick Young and Ian Macphee. There are dozens of MPs who were acquaintances and many with whom I have had a warm professional relationship and admired. But Young and Macphee were my only close friends among them. It is not a good idea for political journalists to become too close to politicians. My own experience is that it does, even subconsciously, steer you away from areas where you would have to publish critical material against them.

Yet, neither Young nor Macphee gave me any great scoops—nor did I look for them. Young resigned from the Hawke Cabinet in February 1988, disgusted with allegations he had not followed rules on handling campaign donations during the 1987 election. He was later cleared of any wrongdoing. Apart from his friendship with Young, Hawke valued his shrewd political brain and pleaded with him, to no avail, not to resign. Young gave up drinking at this time and started a successful career as a political lobbyist.

Macphee was targeted by the Liberal Party right, with the support of Howard, and, like Young, was a loss to his party when David Kemp defeated him in preselection for the seat of Goldstein. Kemp went on to enjoy promotion under Prime Minister Howard. The editorial in the Australian Communist Party's newspaper, *The Guardian*, of 10 May 1989 is a fair summing up:

> Macphee's successful opponent [Kemp] is an advocate of extreme right wing polices and his pre-selection is a victory for those who are pushing the Liberal Party to a more and more hard right position. Ian Macphee was the most consistent of the small 'l' Liberal members and his defeat is a calculated attack on the policies and values he has upheld. John Howard, by failing to support him during the course of the ballot, underlines his real support for the extreme right wing.

A lawyer, Macphee was educated at Sydney University and the University of Hawai'i and, before entering Parliament, was director of the Victorian Chamber of Manufactures and as such, a friend of Australian industry. Both he and Young served as Immigration Minister (Macphee in the Fraser Government and Young in the Hawke Government). Mick told me he thought the immigration portfolio was the most difficult of all. 'Wherever you go someone is tugging at your sleeve begging you to intervene and let relatives into Australia.' Both Macphee and Young had the advantage of John Menadue as Secretary of the Immigration Department. The three were champions of multiculturalism and of a strong immigration program, as were Whitlam and Fraser. This was enough for Howard to become an enemy of Macphee and, even more so, Macphee was a card-carrying member of the 'industrial relations club'—a group despised by Howard.

When Macphee became Minister for Employment and Industrial Relations in the last Fraser Government, it gave Howard even more reason to get him out of Parliament. Also targeted by the Liberal right were other moderate Liberals such as Senator Peter Baume and Senator Chris Puplick. The treatment of these moderates sits awkwardly with the repeated claims by Howard that the Liberal Party was a 'broad church'. It was broad only if an MP was a Howard supporter, or if moderates crossed over to him, as did Robert Hill and Amanda Vanstone and, most notably of all, Phillip Ruddock.

At least in the Fraser years there was a place for the moderates as well as those on the right, even the mad right. Macphee was far more in the Menzies tradition than Howard and, like Menzies, believed in the arbitration system. Macphee also believed the path to growth, productivity improvement and a better life was through encouraging cooperation between capital and labour—a view that was anathema to the right. It is no accident the Macphee's view of the world is widely shared in Europe (particularly in Scandinavia) and has been the foundation of the success of many European nations.

A brain clot killed Don Whitington in 1977, and was a blow to me, not only emotionally, but I had to review how to carry on without him. He was my tutor, friend and partner and, like his wife, Helen, all who knew him well were shocked. Don was survived by Helen (nee Scott) and two sons and a daughter from his first marriage. Don met Helen when she was on the staff of Bill Snedden, one of Don's best contacts in the Liberal Party. Mick Young made certain Don's death was recorded by making a short statement in the house regretting his passing. Following Don's death, I went into partnership with Bob Freeden, a friend of Don's who had worked on the *Northern Territory News* after Don and Eric White founded the paper. Bob published a number of newsletters from Sydney and when he retired I bought out his half of *Inside Canberra*.

My son was also named Robin, as was my father—which in retrospect was probably not a good idea—and, like me, answered to Rob, while my father was known as Bob or Bobby. My son joined me in the press gallery, providing a news service for Sydney radio station 2CH. He did all the news work without my assistance and I did the easy part: a couple of minutes' commentary for drive time. I would sign off 'this is Rob Chalmers' and decided he would sign off as 'Rob Chalmers junior'. If I rang Gough Whitlam—then out of politics—I would generally open with, 'It's Rob Chalmers, Gough'. The great man knew who I was but inquired 'Senior or junior?' Rob and I continued with the 2CH news service for some 10 years until the station put its own staff in the press gallery.

With insufficient capital and staff, I made the mistake of expanding my business and, in addition to *Inside Canberra*, published newsletters on primary industry, the stock market, transport, defence and state politics as well as *The Guide to Federal Parliament* with biographical and contact information about every MP and senator. Some of these I wrote and edited; some were written and edited by part-time writers. Ken Randall and I were joint publishers of *The House Magazine*, published each week the Parliament was sitting; it was an unashamed copy of the successful magazine of the same name at Westminster. Designed to appeal to backbenchers, each issue had a front-page caricature, or sometimes a photo, of a backbencher with a sympathetic and light-hearted profile inside.

Ed Rollgejser, our clever artist, drew the page-one sketches of MPs, based on their hobby or favourite sport. Joggers would be in running gear, or, if tennis players, they would be in a tennis setting. This idea was popular with MPs and they were keen to be featured. Ken and I wrote the various articles, and my second wife, Jenny Hutchison, provided the bulk of the magazine. This was a detailed listing of progress of legislation and the details of the business of both chambers, plus reports on activities of parliamentary committees. All MPs and the departments of the Parliament received the magazine free, with revenue coming from business subscribers and advertising.

I handled the hairiest job of chasing up advertising. Qantas was a regular advertiser, yet paid not with cash but international air tickets, which you cannot eat. We could take advantage of free flights but Ken and I strained our bank balances with travelling expenses overseas. A few subjects were so dull it was hard to do a lively sketch and profile, but most MPs are interesting, with diverse interests. Koomarri, our printer, was a charity assisting handicapped people in Canberra to find work and our association with Koomarri went on for several decades. In the end, the competition from the Internet—providing much information for free that was the basis of *The House Magazine*—was too much and we ceased publication.

The Malcolm Fraser story is also the story of the failure of Bill Hayden, the Hamlet of postwar politics. After initially spurning the leadership of the Labor Party after the defeat of Whitlam in 1975, Hayden's chance of reaching the top was snatched from him eight years later. Like us all, Hayden had his strengths and weaknesses: he was one of the Whitlam Government's most successful ministers (Social Security Minister and later Treasurer; as well as Foreign Minister in the Hawke Government) and then Governor-General. He could not handle the toughest job in politics, Opposition Leader, and this was what prevented him being elected Prime Minister. Like Howard, Hayden was deeply suspicious of many around him. I knew Hayden on a professional basis when he entered Parliament in 1961 as the MP for Oxley, Queensland. Mick Young resigned as ALP National Secretary in 1973 and was parked in Whitlam's office as a political adviser until he could take over as the MP for Port Adelaide at the following election.

At one stage, when Hayden was away from Canberra with the Parliament not sitting, he occupied Hayden's unit at Swinger Hill, where I lived with Mick for a few weeks. Defeated by Fraser in 1975, Whitlam offered the leadership to Hayden—the obvious candidate—and he refused. Hayden, according to his press secretary, Alan Ramsey, was deeply worried about finding himself unemployed. He did not stand for election to the Labor front bench and departed the political scene (although not resigning from Parliament) to get a law degree. Hayden mustered up enough courage to return to politics when Kim Beazley sr resigned in disgust at the Whitlam leadership, and Hayden was elected to the front bench vacancy. Fatally for Labor (and this was as much the fault of Caucus as Whitlam), the 1977 election came around on 10 December with Whitlam still leader.

He managed a tiny swing of 1.1 per cent to Labor—not nearly enough, given the swing of 7.4 per cent to the Coalition in the 1975 election.[2] Hayden finally challenged Whitlam for the leadership and narrowly lost, with 30 votes to Whitlam's 32. Within a fortnight, Whitlam resigned the leadership and Hayden became leader by 36 votes to 28 over Lionel Bowen.

Hayden was not a convincing political leader and made a serious error when he fell out with one of his greatest and most influential supporters, Mick Young. At the time, Young had two shadow roles, Employment and Industrial Relations, and also occupied the key role of Leader of Opposition Business in the house; Hayden relieved him of the last. Alan Ramsey said in the chapter on Hayden in *True Believers* it was because of 'one too many of Mick's long lunches and dissatisfaction of what was not happening in the development of employment policy'. Nobody else had noticed this policy failure (if indeed there was one). As for the long lunches, Young was an important Labor identity who had played a key role in Labor's historic 1972 victory.

Young found long lunches with a wide variety of friends in business, unions, public relations and advertising were a means of discovering what was going on, not to get pissed. Hayden could have done with some long lunches himself but lacked Young's easygoing Irish charm. Young was popular and well known in the gallery and throughout the Labor Party. Young complained he had learned of his demotion as leader of the house not directly from Hayden, but from 'a journalist'—namely, me. Hayden claimed he had told Young a few days earlier, but I had the story in *Inside Canberra* before Hayden told Young. I got the tip from my former *Daily Mirror* colleague Tony Ferguson, who was then handling media relations at John Curtin House, the ALP federal secretariat.

Fraser won the 18 October 1980 election partly because of Labor making a mess of policy on capital gains. A Caucus committee had been debating a wealth tax for some time, giving Fraser the opportunity to portray Labor as

---

2   These are estimates of the two-party preferred vote by Malcolm Mackerras. The actual swings were not available until the 1983 election.

preparing to introduce a capital gains tax. Hayden denied this, but all too late. Nevertheless, Hayden more than halved Fraser's majority, paving the way for the 1983 election win by his nemesis, Bob Hawke, who entered Parliament only in the 1980 election as the newly preselected member for the safe Labor seat of Wills. Hawke was not a standout performer in Parliament and appeared unable to get the hang of life as a parliamentarian. He obviously missed ordering people around and, most of all, his network of mates was of no particular help to him as an MP. Nevertheless, from then on Labor politics was all about when and if Hawke would displace Hayden.

Fraser forced the resignation of Phillip Lynch from his seat of Flinders over dodgy land deals, partly involving land with the intriguing name of Stumpy Gully. This was soon after the Watergate scandal brought down US President Richard Nixon, and Gough Whitlam might have been the first in the world to appropriate the suffix when he described the Lynch affair as 'Landgate'. Peter Reith won the Flinders by-election for the Liberals in December 1982 and later had a ministerial career full of controversy in the Howard Government. From then on Hayden was doomed and, as it turned out, so was Fraser. Mick Young supported the move against Hayden not in any sense to get even with his former friend. Mick told me he believed that Hawke, with all his faults, was the most popular public figure in Australia at the time and had a far better chance of winning the election than Hayden.

Peter Walsh rang me, asking, incredulously, if I thought Caucus could be foolish enough to dump Hayden for 'that fraud Hawke', and (wrongly) I said Hayden would survive. John Button, a rock-solid Hayden supporter, agreed that Hayden had to go to give Labor a chance at the next election. To ensure this, he went quietly. Button, together with Hawke and Lionel Bowen, sealed the final deal with Hayden, including a guarantee that Hayden's staff would be looked after and that Hayden would become Minister for Foreign Affairs. Hawke agreed to all of Hayden's demands, although Lionel Bowen, then Shadow Foreign Affairs Minister, did not find it at all agreeable. When Hawke came into office, Bowen received second prize: Deputy Prime Minister and Minister for Trade. Hayden decided he wanted another promotion—this time as Governor-General—and asked Hawke for the job.

Perhaps still burdened by a sense of guilt about replacing Hayden as ALP leader, Hawke obliged. With the retirement of Sir Ninian Stephen as Governor-General in February 1989, Hayden took up residence at Yarralumla and stayed there until a month before Howard won the 1996 election. A mere 15 days before Howard won the 1996 election, Sir William Deane, appointed by Keating, took up residence in Yarralumla as Governor-General, and he proved to be one of the most popular Queen's representatives since the war, but was not at all liked by

Howard. A senior bureaucrat close to Howard assured me Deane would not, as head of state, open the 2000 Sydney Olympics. I was assured Howard insisted this would be his role.

He was wrong and Deane declared the Games open, but Howard still got in on the act. At the opening ceremony, when the camera pulled away for a wide shot of the dais, there, a few metres behind the Governor-General, seated where it was assumed senior Olympic officials would be, were instead the smiling Howard and wife, Janette. At the Olympics, Howard's insatiable appetite for the TV cameras was obvious. Courtesy of the Seven Network (then with exclusive TV coverage of the Games and controlled by Kerry Stokes), Howard appeared nightly, prominent in the audience at events where Australia was likely to win gold. Stokes at the time was ingratiating himself with Howard as changes in the Government's TV policy were mooted.

On the morning of 3 February 1983, scoop artist Laurie Oakes put to breakfast radio the story that Fraser would call an election that day. Hayden had already made up his mind to resign the leadership in favour of Hawke, yet Fraser did not know this. He thought a bloody challenge from Hawke was still the likely outcome. Yet by mid-morning at a meeting of the Caucus executive in Brisbane, Hayden resigned. After the terms and conditions had been finalised, Hayden and Hawke found themselves alone in the meeting room. Paul Kelly wrote that, at this point, Hayden was overwhelmed by the events and broke down. Hawke wept with him.[3]

Shortly after, Fraser left for Yarralumla to seek from the Governor-General, Sir Ninian Stephen, a double dissolution of the Parliament for a 5 March election. This meant that all the senators, not half of them, would also face the electors. Fraser knew before he left that Hayden was in trouble, but believed Hayden would resist Hawke to the end. I remember waiting outside the Prime Minister's office in the government lobby with a big contingent from the gallery. A press conference had been called for 1 pm that day and everyone knew it was about the election.

Sir Ninian would not be rushed. He was having lunch with the Polish Ambassador and Fraser was sent off empty handed. The gallery was waiting expectantly outside his office but Fraser had nothing to tell us. Hayden had announced his intention to resign after Fraser left for Yarralumla. He had also made a now famous comment that 'even a drover's dog' could have won the election against Fraser. In the end, after Stephen had been punctilious about granting a double dissolution of both houses, Fraser held his press conference about 5 pm, after his hoped-for Caucus bloodbath had proved a chimera. He

---

3   Kelly, Paul 1984, *The Hawke Ascendancy*, Angus & Robertson, North Ryde, NSW, p. 386.

had been ambushed by the ALP. Instead of facing Hayden, whom Fraser had defeated in the 1980 election, suddenly he was up against the most popular public figure in Australia.

In the last week of the March 1983 election campaign, Fraser and Opposition Leader, Bob Hawke, each separately addressed the National Press Club—a highlight of the campaign, and now an important tradition in Australian politics. I was President of the club and Fraser, as the guest of the club, had a pre-lunch drink in the boardroom. Like all prime ministers, Fraser found it incomprehensible that anyone could believe his political opponent would be a better prime minister than himself. He asked me if I thought 'this fellow Hawke' could beat him and when I replied I believed he would, he seemed surprised.

In the 1980s, I was lucky enough take a fortnight's all-expenses-paid visit to Sweden with a press party organised by a mate, Matt O'Brien, who was then working with George Kerr in the Canberra office of International Public Relations. The RAAF was looking to replace the Dassault Mirage III jet fighter. Sweden was in the race with the Saab 37 Viggen (Thunderbolt), a single-seat, single-engine, short–medium-range fighter and attack aircraft. I realised Australia was being outperformed by countries such as Sweden.

With the Cold War still dominating world politics, Sweden, with about half Australia's population, was far more advanced. The Cold War continued and the Russian 'bear' was nearby. Across the Gulf of Bothnia was Finland and beyond that the Soviet Union. Sweden designed and manufactured its own frontline military aircraft, had a defence force more capable than Australia's and was a world leader in high-tech electronics and engineering. The men were handsome, the women gorgeous and every Swede I met spoke excellent English. It was a punishing trip, with our hosts from Saab entertaining us every night until late and then up early for the official part of the visit.

The Australian press party visited the Swedish Department of Defence, where a much smaller civilian staff than the Defence Department in Australia managed a far superior and better-equipped military. Parkinson's Law was alive and well in Australia, but not, apparently, in Sweden. We visited the first Swedish Air Force squadron to be equipped with the latest Viggen. The commanding officer of the base and his deputy drove us around in two cars. It struck me then that it would be unimaginable for such an important officer of the RAAF to act as a driver for visitors. At the mess for drinks, the CO then explained that as it was Sunday, there was no staff on. Nevertheless, he looked after the drinks and took over bar duties. Again, this sort of behaviour would be unimaginable in the RAAF. I was beginning to understand how the Swedes could hold their own in a tough world. The RAAF shunned the Viggen and, predictably, chose the far more expensive F-18 Hornet from the United States.

British journalist, author, satirist, media personality, soldier-spy and later Christian convert Malcolm Muggeridge visited Australia in 1976. George Kerr accompanied him to the Snowy Mountains Hydro-Electric Scheme, where Muggeridge, on his portable typewriter, wrote an article for one of the British newspapers. Asked by Muggeridge to edit the piece, George found it a brilliant piece of writing with not a comma out of place. Muggeridge also told Kerr what he believed was the best joke he had heard in Australia, which goes like this: a shearer won the lottery and took his shearing mates to celebrate at the Bandywallop pub. A mate asked him, 'What are you going to do with your money, Jack?' 'Ah,' said Jack, 'I've never been to England, so I'll take a trip.' 'And what route will you take?' asked his mate. 'Oh,' said Jack, 'I'll take the missus. She stuck to me in the Depression.'

Almost no-one in Caucus admired or liked Bob Hawke when he came to power. He was regarded as arrogant, boastful, self-indulgent and a bad drunk. This was the near-unanimous view of friend and foe alike, yet he won four elections (1983, 1984, 1987 and 1990) and was one of Australia's best prime ministers. He chaired a talented Cabinet, achieving more in economic reform than any other government before or since. Despite this record, he suffered the ultimate humiliation—unique to him—of being sacked by Caucus after winning four elections.

Hawke was a bad drunk and, worse, refused to shout in turn. He was lousy. 'Wouldn't shout in a shark attack', in the bar-room vernacular of the time. Ian Macphee, when Director of the Victorian Chamber of Manufactures and as such a member of the 'industrial relations club'—as was Hawke as ACTU President—enjoyed the annual perk that was the meeting of the International Labour Organisation (ILO) in Switzerland. Delegates stayed at the best hotels in Geneva, all expenses paid. Macphee told me how the Australian ILO delegates decided to all meet in one of the popular bars and ambush Hawke. It was arranged everyone would be in the bar before Hawke was due and on his arrival he was to be greeted with the combined demand 'It's your shout, Bob'; finally, he had to shout.

Barry Cohen, later Environment Minister in the Hawke Government, played a round of golf at the Monash club in Sydney with Hawke when he was ACTU President. As they were about to depart the course, Cohen told Hawke how much he had to pay as his share of green fees, lunch and hire of the buggy. Hawke said, 'I don't pay'. Cohen insisted and finally extracted the money from him.[4] It was typical Hawke; he did not expect to pay for anything. As Prime Minister, he was automatically an honorary member of the Royal Canberra Golf Club (as were governors-general). Hawke exercised his rights with alacrity, often playing

---

4 Conversation with Cohen.

early in the morning with his driver and Australian Federal Police bodyguard. Hawke did not even consider paying green fees for his guests, as club members were required to do.

Hawke fancied himself as an accomplished punter. He did not hesitate to phone prominent people in the racing game, such as trainers Ernie Smith and Colin Hayes and owner Jack Ingham, for their tips. Bookmakers found it hard to get him to pay his losses. A Hawke acquaintance says that around the Sydney betting community he was known as the 'Wonga Pigeon'—apparently a nervous bird that would not settle. Hawke was also a noted womaniser and sexist with it. At one stage, a Cabinet minister having an affair with a staffer—a particularly thin journalist—was the subject of gossip around the gallery. Hawke was greatly interested. 'I don't know what you see in her, mate. Every time you fuck her, she'd rattle,' he quipped, accompanied by that distinctive Hawke laugh.

Hawke's future second wife, Blanche d'Alpuget, in her insightful biography *Robert J. Hawke*, revealed what most Australians did not know: Hawke was a serial womaniser. His high opinion poll popularity rating rose even higher. For whatever reason, he was certainly attractive to women. Hawke was a prominent Labor figure at Gough Whitlam's triumphant 'It's Time' 1972 election campaign launch at the Blacktown Civic Centre, in Sydney's west. In the euphoria following the launch, women were literally flinging themselves at Hawke. (In what follows, I have drawn material from d'Alpuget's writings.)

Hawke's vanity was obvious. I was President of the National Press Club when Hawke was guest of honour at the club's annual charity day and hit off from the first tee for the TV cameras. It was a terrible shot, but that did not matter, the cameras were only shooting him on the tee, not tracking where the ball finished up. Nevertheless, he insisted on at least three more swings, until he hit a half-decent shot. Hawke was insensitive to the reaction of others to his words. As President of the ALP, he chaired a national conference in Perth, where it was apparent to all that he was bedding a female taxi driver. At 9 am one day, Hawke was at his place as chairman on the head table, obviously still the worse for liquor, and testy. In the presence of TV cameras and 300 or so delegates and observers in the hall, Hawke declared, 'Delegates, you'll have to stop wanking'.

Hawke's father, Clem, regarded Bob as 'his special son' and his mother, Ellie, thought he was her special baby. He was always the centre of attention, and competition between the parents later turned to rivalry for the boy's attention. A relative, d'Alpuget reports, believed Hawke could play his parents off against each other, learning when very young 'how agreeable it was to be a cynosure'. This, says d'Alpuget, could be the origin of his later success in seeking and gaining publicity.

Hawke ran an excellent election campaign in 1983 and it was no contest: Hawke, far and away the most popular public figure in the nation, against one of the most unpopular, Fraser. Bill Hayden and Labor made a mess of the issue of a capital gains tax in 1980. The Fraser message was that if Labor came to power, citizens should hide their money under the bed because Labor wanted to get its hand on their wealth.

In the 1983 campaign, Fraser tried a similar tack, declaring Labor could not be trusted with money. Hawke retorted that if Fraser meant the money should go under the bed again, this could not happen, since this was where the communists were—a reference to the continued efforts by the non-Labor parties to brand Labor as allied with communists. Fraser could not frighten voters in 1983, nor persuade them that Hawke could not be trusted. Seven years and three months after the dismissal of the Whitlam Government, Bob Hawke brought Labor back into power with a decisive win on 5 March 1983.

Hawke was well known to the gallery and disliked before his election victory. The consensus was he would not last as Prime Minister and at his core was a preening show pony. Again, this was a gallery misjudgment. Even after his resounding victory, Hawke's rival was seen as his Treasurer, Paul Keating, who was in good standing with the gallery. Keating had received a big laugh prior to Hawke's victory, referring to him as the 'silver bodgie' (a bodgie was an expression from the 1950s and 1960s meaning a young man with long hair and a love of pop music who chased girls and was generally a social pest).

Hawke's close relations with the Hungarian migrant tycoon Peter Abeles—known far and wide as 'the beast of Budapest', or simply 'the beast'—was a matter of abiding interest to the gallery and everyone in politics. Even as Prime Minister, Hawke rang Abeles every day and would do apparently anything for him. Speculation ranged from Abeles blackmailing Hawke to outright corruption. None of it was true. Once again, d'Alpuget has the answer: Hawke's desire for a father figure, nurtured by his devotion to his father. All of Hawke's real friends were much older than him.

George Rockey, a Hungarian migrant who together with Abeles built Thomas Nationwide Transport (TNT) into the largest transport company in Australia, treated Hawke like a son. Apart from Rockey's tailor attending to Hawke's suits, Rockey even chose Hawke's underwear. D'Alpuget writes: 'It seems as if, in his earliest years, an emotional stage was set and roles allotted to actors and that the play was performed again and again.'[5] Allowing Rockey to choose his underwear, I believe, reflected Hawke's extreme vanity and an obsession about his appearance. Throughout his life, he has given close attention to his hairstyle

---

5   d'Alpuget, *Robert J. Hawke*, p. 9.

and, when he greyed, he at least looked distinguished. Hawke was sensitive about his height: he was not tall, about average height, yet he would claim to be tall and wore shoes with higher heels than standard.

Peter Abeles was a remarkable achiever. Born in 1924 in Budapest, he was, during the war, forced into the Hungarian Jewish labour battalion in the German Army. In 1947 he migrated to Australia with £4000 given to him by his father, and knocked about in various odd jobs, including selling paperback novels and clothing. His friend and fellow Hungarian George Rockey arrived in 1959 with £400 and they linked up. They bought a truck each but could not make a go of it until they hired professional drivers. They founded Alltrans in December of that year and, in 1954, they opened Sydney Coal Merchants.

In *Robert J. Hawke*, d'Alpuget[6] reveals that they began to encroach on the business of coal giant Sir Roderick Miller by undercutting his price. Abeles approached Miller for a price-fixing deal whereby he and Rockey would have one-third of the Sydney market. Miller responded by sending Sydney Coal Merchants and Alltrans broke by buying every mine supplying Abeles and Rockey. Only 14 years later, they bought out Miller and, moving in on TNT, by the 1970s, they had a global transport business.

Abeles was a big man, tall, hair brushed straight back, always smoking an expensive Havana cigar. His friendship with Hawke was hardly life-long; he did not meet Hawke until after the latter had attained the presidency of the ACTU on 10 September 1969. Abeles was obviously seeking influence within the trade union movement for his business enterprises. What stands out about Abeles' dubious business tactics was an aversion to competition. What he had proposed to Miller was later to become the criminal offence of cartel behaviour under the *Trade Practices Act*. Throughout his co-ownership of Ansett Airlines with Rupert Murdoch, Abeles' objective was to avoid competition. In March 1998, John Menadue, Chief Executive of the then government-owned Qantas (then without domestic routes), put to the Hawke Government the idea of a 'tricycle'.[7]

The scheme was to amalgamate Qantas, the government-owned domestic carrier Australian Airlines (formerly TAA) and the New Zealand Government-owned Air New Zealand. The NZ Government planned to privatise Air New Zealand and the Hawke Government was anxious to privatise Australian Airlines and Qantas. Menadue saw the tricycle proposal as facilitating privatisation, with a public float of the merged entity in the first quarter of 1989. The tricycle would be a stronger competitor in the Pacific against the US mega-carriers United and

6   Ibid., p. 236.
7   Menadue, *Things You Learn Along the Way*, p. 268.

American Airlines. The Transport Minister, Gareth Evans, was enthusiastic, but Abeles and Murdoch were not. In the end, so many concessions were demanded on behalf of Ansett that Qantas abandoned the tricycle idea.

Yet oddly, in the end, Hawke delivered the blow that led ultimately to the collapse of Ansett: the dumping of the cosy two-airline policy, invented by Menzies, which gave the government airline, Australian Airlines, and the privately owned Ansett Airlines a duopoly over the domestic market. Senator Denham Henty, in 1964 Aviation Minister in the last Menzies Government, once delivered a notable malapropism in the Senate. Meaning to refer to the two-airline policy, he managed the 'two-line air policy'. It was much more than a two-line policy and was backed by an army of bureaucrats in the Civil Aviation Department.

These officials ruled that everything had to be the same on both airlines: fares were normally identical and schedules controlled. Regulations even ensured meals were the same. If one airline decided to offer a new style of sandwich, bureaucrats decided whether this was allowable under the regulations. Abeles and Murdoch fought hard to retain the two-airline policy but its death was inevitable. The only concession the joint owners received was the right of Ansett to operate on international routes. Ansett ventured into this entirely different and competitive market on a number of Asian routes, but could not compete with Qantas and other foreign airlines.

Hawke was transformed when he came to the prime ministership. His hedonism, wantonness and aggressiveness were shed. Like Curtin, and emulating his hero, John Curtin (who also had a serious problem with alcohol), he went off the grog and appeared to stick to it. But Hawke remained sensitive and emotional. During at least two press conferences I attended, the Australian Prime Minister broke down weeping, his eyes and nose gushing, a picture of desolation. One followed the slaughter of demonstrators in Tiananmen Square in Beijing in 1989; the other was when he poured his heart out about the drug problems with which his daughter Ros struggled.

His popularity with voters was such that he could get away with comments that, in later years, no politician could copy. Asked by a journalist if he knew the price of bread (or it might have been milk or butter), he said he had no idea and had never been inside a supermarket, ending the discussion with, 'Hazel does the shopping'. There were always people anxious to help him. Rockey and Abeles invariably could be relied on, while others organised his ascension to the presidency of the ACTU, his preselection for the safe seat of Wills, and his defeat of Hayden. As Prime Minister, he had excellent staff offering good advice, and he listened. His special knack for dealing with the media was instinctive.

Peter Barron was a key political adviser. I knew Barron well, from when he came to the gallery representing the afternoon Sydney *Sun*, before joining the *Daily Mirror* bureau. In 1975, he was in the Media Department when Jim Spigelman (later Chief Justice of New South Wales) was the permanent head and his minister was Senator Doug McClelland, father of Rudd Government minister Robert McClelland. Malcolm Fraser, on winning the 1975 election, abolished the Media Department and Barron was without a job, until Neville Wran, still in opposition, invited Barron to join his staff. The period with Wran led to Barron teaming up with Hawke. Barron and another political adviser and former State Secretary of the Victorian ALP, Bob Hogg, were blunt in advising Hawke and if he made a mistake, he was told in no uncertain terms that he had stuffed up.

For example, it was revealed in January 1985 that Hawke, without consulting his ministers, had in 1983 told US President Ronald Reagan he would adhere to the agreement the Fraser Government had entered into for assisting the United States to monitor test firings of the MX missile. The missile was designed to shoot down Soviet intercontinental ballistic missiles attacking the United States, and in testing, they would crash to earth in Australian waters. At this time, Labor was strongly supporting disarmament objectives and right across the party there were demands that Hawke withdraw his undertaking. Barron applied the pressure on Hawke, who agreed to withdraw his undertaking only days before his scheduled formal prime ministerial visit to the United States and a meeting with Reagan.

During Question Time, Barron sat in the advisers' box on the floor of the house and only metres from the Speaker's chair, from where he would pass Hawke quick notes of advice. Hawke enjoyed the theatrics of Question Time and had a high opinion of how well he handled the Opposition's questions. Answering one question, Hawke overcooked his reply and a note came from Barron: 'You're talking too much.' Hawke read the note, threw it on the ministerial table among his papers and quietened down for the rest of Question Time. A staffer, who picked up Hawke's papers and saw the Barron note, recounted this incident to me. It is hard to imagine any adviser having the authority and confidence to give such blunt advice to any other prime minister.

Achieving fundamental change to Caucus's attitude to the power of a Labor Cabinet was one of Hawke's major achievements. With considerable support from ministers, including John Button and Gareth Evans, Caucus conceded the principle of collective Cabinet responsibility for its decisions by every member of Cabinet—something denied to Whitlam. In the Whitlam Government, Cabinet member Lionel Murphy exercised what he saw as his right to appeal to Caucus to overturn a Cabinet decision he had opposed. Caucus also agreed to Hawke's demand for an inner Cabinet with junior ministers outside Cabinet. For the first time, Caucus effectively conceded that, indeed, all members of Caucus were not equal.

Whitlam had failed to gain the agreement of Caucus on an inner Cabinet and had an unwieldy Cabinet of 27 to deal with. Neal Blewett, Health Minister in the Hawke Government, contributed a chapter, 'The Hawke Cabinets', to *The Hawke Government, A Critical Retrospective* and summed up the Hawke approach to his Cabinet:

> Cabinet ministers ruled over relatively autonomous fiefdoms, with the Prime Minister maintaining a strategic supervision and concentrating on a few high-priority issues, while leaving his ministers relatively free to develop and implement their policies. Only if a minister got into trouble or his policy antagonised his fellow minister, or of course, when he or she needed significant money, would the Prime Minister and Cabinet swing into action.[8]

This was remarkably similar to Menzies' style of chairing Cabinet. When the Hawke Government came to power, Whitlam's difficulty with public service mandarins resistant to change was in the minds of ministers. Labor had been out of power for eight years and the Public Service had settled back into the comfort of a Coalition government, although Malcolm Fraser had not been as easy, or reliant, on the Public Service as had Menzies, Holt, Gorton and McMahon. In December 1983 a white paper, *Reforming the Australian Public Service*, was published. This was hardly a hot news item, yet the reforms were among the considerable accomplishments of the Hawke Government.

Michael Delaney, formerly with the Public Service Board and private secretary to Prime Minister Whitlam, was in charge of the white paper project. Hawke had a mandate for public service reform and intended using it. The central aim of the white paper was to place ministers firmly in control of their departments. 'Permanent heads' of government departments were renamed 'heads' and were put on contracts.

A new concept, the Senior Executive Service (SES), was formed to replace the Second Division of the Public Service—the rank immediately below the department head. Outsiders could apply for public service positions, which were advertised, and the concept of promotions based on seniority was finally laid to rest. The Hawke Government aimed to rotate heads of departments every five years into another department. The Chairman of the Public Service Board was required to raise the rotation with departmental heads and their ministers

---

8   Ryan, Susan and Bramston, Troy (eds), *The Hawke Government: A critical retrospective*, Pluto Press Australia, North Melbourne, p. 76.

about possible placements and would report to the Prime Minister if necessary. Ministers were in a more powerful position: they could engage consultants to work on projects nominated by the minister; and these consultants could work in departments, with the agreement and supervision of the department head.

A significant change was to allow ministers and other MPs to employ their own staff under terms and conditions applying in the Public Service. Tenure would be at the discretion of ministers and MPs and would be related to the period a minister or MP held office. As a consequence, staff were vigorous partisan warriors, fighting behind the scenes for their bosses. The number of staff members was up to the Prime Minister. When the Parliament moved into the spacious permanent building on Capital Hill, staff numbers rocketed. Not surprisingly, although this was an extra burden carried by taxpayers, the Opposition agreed with most of the implementing legislation for the changes.

Prominent lawyer John Button, a small man, jockey-sized, neat and precise in his movements and his words, with sparkling eyes matching his impish humour, reinvigorated federal industry policy. The scholarly Race Mathews, Whitlam's chief of staff, introduced him to me at Button's Melbourne home during the 1972 election. Mathews contested and won the outer Melbourne seat of Casey, holding it until his defeat in 1975, and later had a successful career in State politics in Victoria and then in academia. Button entered the Senate at the 1974 double-dissolution election and went on to become one of longest-serving ministers in the Hawke/Keating Governments.

From the formation of the first Hawke Government until his resignation from the Senate immediately after the 1993 election, Button was Minister for Industry and did more for the Australian manufacturing industry than any minister in this portfolio before or since. In the face of resistance from unions and industrialists, he was responsible for industry plans for the vehicle, TCF and information technology (IT) industries, which saw them revive and succeed, despite a program of tariff cuts for all industries.

Because of union influence within the ALP and the unions' opposition to tariff cuts, Button was anything but the most popular figure in Caucus, yet he succeeded with the total support of Hawke, Keating and ACTU Secretary, Bill Kelty. Not that his relationship with all three of them was always harmonious. More than most ministers I have known, Button was direct and honest in public comments—often to the embarrassment and rage of his colleagues and Paul Keating in particular. Naturally, he was much liked by the media.

I knew Button well and in 1985 he phoned asking that I come to see him. When I walked into his office, he was at his desk writing away furiously, explaining it was a speech he was to give that night to a business group. I inquired why he was writing the speech when he had staffers and people in his department to write speeches, or at least put together notes. Most ministers' speeches were written in this way, but not Button's. When he gave a speech—invariably first class and humorous—they were his words, not those of a speechwriter.

Putting down his pen, he explained he was considering appointing David Charles to the vacant position of head of his department. He understood I knew Charles and he wanted my opinion of him. Button said he was not prepared to just rely on the opinion of bureaucrats. I often had lunch with Charles, who was already a senior public servant with a successful career in the Commonwealth Public Service; our conversations were invariably about politics and policy issues. With an honours degree in economics (from Monash University) and having studied at the London School of Economics, Charles should have been what came to be described as an economic rationalist. The Treasury employed plenty of adherents to this dogma and opposed any sort of assistance for industry.

Charles did not agree. Although a supporter of lower tariffs, he was a pragmatist and was interested in anything that could assist the development of the Australian manufacturing industry. I assured Button I had the highest regard for Charles. Button was obviously pleased, telling me he had asked another mutual friend, Ian Grigg, of his opinion and Grigg had also endorsed Charles. Grigg was a former public servant and private secretary to Bill McMahon, and was CEO of the car industry lobby, the Federal Chamber of Automotive Industries. Charles was appointed secretary, although I never discovered whether our endorsement made a difference.

This must surely have been the only instance of a minister asking a journalist for advice about a senior public service appointment. John Button wrote the chapter on the history of industry policy in the Hawke Government in *The Hawke Government: A critical retrospective*, edited by Susan Ryan and Troy Bramston. The chapter details the fascinating story of the various plans, such as those for the car and TCF industries, Button was responsible for and the difficult negotiations involved. Yet nowhere in the essay does he refer to his feats in industry policy, or even the fact he was Industry Minister, instead referring to what 'the Government' had done.

Unbeknown to Andrew Peacock, the Liberal leader after Malcolm Fraser lost the 1983 election, Bob Hawke and National Party Leader, Doug Anthony, had come to a deal to expand the size of the House of Representatives from 123 (virtually unchanged since 1949) to 148. The National Party was running out of electorates it could reasonably win. Increasing the numbers in the house automatically required the necessary expansion of the Senate from 10 senators from each State to 12 (s. 24 of the Constitution says membership of the Lower

House shall 'as nearly as practicable' be twice the number of senators). The expansion of the Senate improved the National Party's chances of hanging on to its seats in the Upper House.

This presented a problem: where were the 25 additional MHRs to be housed? There was simply no room for additional offices for 25 more MHRs and the move to the permanent parliamentary building was five years away. The bureaucrats in Parliament House persuaded the Speaker, Harry Jenkins, and the President, Doug McClelland, that the press gallery should be moved out of Parliament House to offices at the nearby Hotel Canberra—a five-minute walk away.

In 1974, Tooheys Brewery's lease on the hotel expired and the Whitlam Property Minister, Fred Daly, and Tooheys could not come to an agreement on a new lease. The hotel closed operations and public servants were moved in: the bedrooms became offices. There would be no problem finding ample space in the former Hotel Canberra to accommodate the gallery. Peter Barron, Hawke's adviser, soon came to hear about this development and informed Hawke. Hawke went ballistic. Like all prime ministers, Hawke wanted the gallery close at hand and able to be whistled up at a moment's notice. Jenkins and McClelland were instructed to immediately drop this idea, or they would be out of a job when Caucus next met.

Here was a problem. There was no chance of Hawke allowing the gallery to be moved out of the building, yet no room existed for the new MPs. The answer was to build temporary, two-storey office space in the gardens on the house side connected by a covered walkway to the first floor of the Parliament, bridging the side road alongside the building. Each office, although 'temporary', was far roomier and more desirable than the cramped MPs' offices in the parliamentary building. Senior opposition MPs such as Ian Macphee moved into the new offices, leaving the cramped offices in the parliamentary building to new MPs. The press had once again demonstrated that, even in the Parliament itself, it had far more clout than backbench parliamentarians.

As the move to Parliament's permanent home on Capital Hill neared, the sense of anticipation throughout the old building was tinged with regret. The endless debates about what site should be selected for the permanent home were over, although the fate of the old building was still to be settled. To keep it, even if slimmed down to its 1927 dimensions, would clearly interfere with the view along the great 'central axis' designed by Burley Griffin, running from the permanent Parliament House to the top of Mt Ainslie, directly to the north. Many, including the author and former Clerk of the House, Norman Parkes, believed the old building should be demolished.

One idea was to demolish all but its façade and move it to one side, away from the central axis, as happened with the statue of King George V. In the end, it was decided to retain the building and clean up its rear—still in view from the front of the permanent Parliament House. There had been a proposal to build the permanent Parliament on the slight hill, Camp Hill, immediately behind the provisional building. If this had proceeded, the old building would have been demolished. Menzies' concept would have had the permanent Parliament built on the central axis, on the southern shore of Lake Burley Griffin. He envisaged the Prime Minister greeting Her Majesty for a royal occasion, when she stepped from the Royal Barge that carried her upstream from the Governor-General's residence at Yarralumla.

The final decisions for the permanent Parliament House were settled during the Fraser Government. The Hilton Hotel bombing on 13 February 1978 alarmed Fraser and he insisted that, for security reasons, ministers be accommodated in a separate wing on the southern end of the building, far removed from the front of the building where tourists and visitors entered. At one stage, it was proposed that the media would be barred from accessing the ministerial wing altogether, but when they got wind of this, the gallery kicked up such a fuss it was dropped. Members of the gallery have free access to the ministerial wing, which importantly also houses the Prime Minister's press office.

Thanks to Fraser, the Prime Minister's office has absolutely no outlook. On the western side of the building, particularly on the top floor, there are magnificent views of the Brindabella Mountains in the distance to the west, with the diplomatic area of Yarralumla in the foreground and the Woden Valley stretching away to the south. My gallery office has such a view. Yet the Prime Minister's office windows provide a view onto an enclosed, empty courtyard—a waste of space and used only for the Prime Minister's press conferences. There are many other areas in and around the building for press conferences.

The gallery owes a lot to Paul Keating. The Speaker, Bill Snedden (later Sir Billy), and the President of the Senate, Condor Laucke (later Sir Condor), co-chaired the joint select committee investigating the design of the new Parliament House and its report was to be vital to the final design agreed to by the Parliament. Snedden did not want the gallery in the building. The gallery had moved into the 1927 provisional Parliament House because there was nowhere else to go in the frontier town of Canberra and the ministers also had their permanent offices in the building. (It had originally been envisaged that ministers would work in their departments, but most of the departments were in Melbourne in the early years of the Parliament being in Canberra.)

Snedden's idea was for the media to erect a separate building accommodating the gallery nearby and linked to the permanent Parliament House by a walkway.

Like so many other politicians who have slid down the slippery pole, Snedden blamed the gallery for Fraser overthrowing him as Opposition Leader. Most politicians and particularly prime ministers or those who see themselves as prime ministers want the gallery in Parliament House.

Nobody was more confident of becoming Prime Minister than Paul Keating and nobody cultivated the gallery as keenly and successfully. He told me that when the key decision came before the committee on the question of gallery accommodation, Snedden was overseas. Keating lobbied joint chair Senator Laucke hard and warned him that if the gallery was not to be within the parliamentary building, the media proprietors would turn against the building and harness public opinion against building it. Hence the gallery now occupies the entire top floor of the Senate building on the western side. Canberra is unique in Westminster parliaments at least with both the Cabinet and the press gallery, complete with TV studios, accommodated in the parliamentary building.

As completion of the permanent Parliament House came closer, work slowed. The hundreds of union members working on the building would have to find work elsewhere. The unions had been able to bluff none other than the Chief Justice, Sir Garfield Barwick, over the building of the High Court. The Parliament decided that the High Court would come to the national capital and its new building would be on a key site in the parliamentary triangle, alongside the National Gallery on the southern shore of Lake Burley Griffin, near Kings Avenue Bridge. Architecturally, it balances the National Library to the west, which is also on the lake and close to Commonwealth Avenue Bridge.

The justices of the High Court were less than enthusiastic at the prospect of setting up in 'the bush capital', as Jack Lang described Canberra. Completion of the building drew near, with 26 May 1980 set for the official opening by the Queen. The unions adopted time-honoured go-slow tactics. It was feared the building might not be finished in time for the opening ceremony, unless the Government met union demands for more money. In a panic, Barwick pushed the Fraser Government to agree to unions' demands and the building was finished on time.

Similar demands for more money were made on the Hawke Government as the new Parliament House neared completion, and the threat of go-slow tactics was implicit. Again, it seemed the building might not be ready for the Queen to perform the opening ceremony on the appointed day of 9 May 1988.

The unions pressured Ralph Willis, Hawke's Industrial Relations Minister at the time, for more money. Willis told them bluntly he would not agree to the conditions they demanded and the Queen would open the building on the appointed day, whether or not it was finished. Willis won. Finally, the great day came and the Queen opened the permanent Parliament House on 9 May 1988—exactly the same date in May that the first Parliament in Melbourne and the provisional Parliament in Canberra were opened. On this sunny autumn day, politics changed forever.

17. New House, New Rules

Television and the move to the permanent Parliament House completed the demolition of the centrality of the House of Representatives in political life. Where once the contested issues of the day were fought out on the floor of the house, now the debate is conducted, via the electronic media, in the lounge room, car, office, or even on the street, with miniature devices providing everything that can be received anywhere else. Whether or not this is a good thing in a modern democracy should be a matter for some public debate. The absence of such a debate is largely because the changes wrought have been gradual and public interest in politics has declined. Most gallery journalists know nothing of the change, few having sat in the house or Senate to listen to a debate.

Only a small minority has worked in the Old Parliament House and most, since coming to the gallery, have known no prime ministers other than John Howard, Kevin Rudd and Julia Gillard. The permanent Parliament House is massive by any standards, dwarfing the provisional Parliament House at the foot of the northern slope of Capital Hill. During the 1980s, the permanent Parliament House was the largest building under construction anywhere in the world. Long corridors separate the gallery, MHRs, senators and above all ministers. There is no equivalent in the permanent Parliament House to the mixing bowl of King's Hall in the Old Parliament House.

During the Hawke Government, the Speaker, Leo McLeay, banned smoking in the building and the non-members' bar in the new Parliament promptly died for want of patronage. Aussie's coffee shop, on the ground floor at the northern end of the building, is the only social gathering spot in the building. Journalists might bump into an MP walking through the gallery corridors for a TV or radio interview, but that is about all. MPs have their own dining areas, the staff canteen caters to all occupants of the building and there is a separate canteen for tourists. The proceedings of the house and the Senate can be seen on screens in the offices of all MPs, hence, apart from Question Time and some debates on matters of great public interest, MPs watch proceedings in their offices.

When tourists enter the impressive space of the House of Representatives chamber, sitting in the visitors' gallery, they must be puzzled at the small number of MPs—often there are less than six—in attendance in the chamber. A fractious opposition occasionally calls quorums only when it thinks there could be some political point to be made by dragging ministers into the chamber. Only during Question Time, or a debate of special interest, is there a decent attendance of journalists in the three-tiered press gallery above the Speaker's chair. Mostly AAP covers proceedings in the chamber for all the major media outlets and its journalist is the only occupant of the press gallery. Barring a government with a wafer-thin majority, the Lower House is irrelevant.

Since the introduction in 1948 by the Chifley Government of proportional representation for Senate voting, governments have mostly lacked an upper house majority. Without the numbers, they must negotiate with the Opposition and/or independents and minor parties such as the Australian Greens. Debates in the Senate give an indication of whether a particular piece of government legislation will pass or be amended, hence the interest of the gallery in Senate debates.

Compared with the provisional Parliament House, the permanent building is a dream for publicity-hungry politicians. Every TV network has studios and offices in the gallery and TV crews are on hand for interviews or press conferences in the parliamentary courtyards or committee rooms. For politicians, radio and TV journalists, the news cycle each day begins with snatched interviews with MPs at the entrance to the house, Senate and ministerial wings of the building. A new phrase has entered the lexicon of politics: 'the doors'—the spot where morning interviews are given to gallery members.

A 'presser' is the term for the more formal press conference for which notice is given. Although the decline of Question Time in the house began during the Fraser Government and has now hit rock bottom, the gallery still takes the farce of Question Time seriously. The purported purpose of Question Time is to allow MPs to question ministers on urgent matters relating to the administration of their portfolio. Instead, it has become an opportunity for a slanging match between the Opposition frontbench and ministers. With the Speaker belonging to the same party as the Government, no matter how independent the Speaker tries to be, the Government has the edge. What should be one of the most important of the Standing Orders relates to the requirement for relevance to the question asked when ministers reply.

They rarely are. Ministers need only make some passing connection between what they want to say and the question put to them. Opposition MPs raising points of order on grounds of relevance know full well that the Speaker rarely rules a minister's answer irrelevant. The very meaning of the word has been lost. The real purpose for raising points of order is to highlight to journalists the fact that the minister is avoiding a question. Repeated points of order are designed to throw the minister off his or her stride in answering the question, although Opposition MPs then run the risk of being ejected from the chamber by the Speaker.

In the Senate, the President is more likely to direct a minister mouthing irrelevancies to return to the substance of the question. Opposition MPs in the Senate have the advantage of following up an answer to a question with a supplementary question, which, skilfully worded, can highlight the minister's failure to deal with the original question.

Ministerial statements were once a feature of parliamentary procedures. They are supposed to provide an opportunity for ministers to announce some new or changed policy, or report on an important topic, such as foreign affairs. Menzies would carpet ministers making a statement outside the Parliament that he believed would have been more appropriately dealt with in a ministerial statement. Beginning with the Hawke–Keating Governments, ministerial statements became less frequent and they disappeared almost entirely during the Howard Government, before making somewhat of a return with the arrival of the Rudd Government.

As ministerial statements must be debated in Parliament, governments do not like the idea of giving the Opposition an opportunity to attack. Therefore it is far better to deliver the message on television or radio, without the inconvenience of the Opposition immediately having a say. John Howard in 2003 announced the decision to go to war at a press conference in the Prime Minister's courtyard before announcing it to the house. In my newsletter, *Inside Canberra*, I noted no ministerial statement was forthcoming from Howard to mark the fourth anniversary of the Iraq war in March 2007. Instead, he arranged an invitation from the Australian Strategic Policy Institute (which receives most of its revenue from the Government) to address it on the war in the parliamentary theatrette. Howard then made his speech on a day the house was sitting 50 m away. Howard announced on the ABC—not in Parliament—an inquiry into possible corruption by Santo Santoro, the Minister for Ageing, in allocating bed licences to a friend's company.

There was no ministerial statement on: the Murray–Darling water plan, involving a change of constitutional arrangements between the Commonwealth and the States; a security agreement with Japan; the federal takeover of NT Aboriginal communities; or Howard's greenhouse gas abatement measures (including nuclear energy). This is by no means a comprehensive list. Howard announced all these initiatives outside the House of Representatives by way of speeches or interviews. Most members of the gallery do not regard ministerial statements as an issue and take for granted the dominance of the electronic media in political discourse.

The Senate is the true bastion of democracy in the Parliament. It may modify or block the excesses of the Prime Minister—an elected dictator who has a handy rubber stamp in his pocket to apply to the votes of the Lower House.

As the relevance and importance of the house have diminished, those of the Senate have risen. Prior to the Chifley Government introducing proportional representation, the system that existed from 1919 gave the winner of the most votes in any State all the Senate seats for that State. Hence, occasionally one side of politics held all the Senate seats.

Proportional representation has given smaller parties and independents a chance of winning Senate seats; hence governments generally lack a majority in the Upper House. Without a majority in the Senate, governments have to deal with all the other senators to get their legislation through. I was, for many years, a supporter of the Labor platform—long since properly abandoned—of abolition of the Senate. It was, in any case, unachievable, as the smaller States would never pass a referendum to abolish the Senate. The founding fathers saw the Senate as essential to counter the dominance of NSW and Victorian MPs in the Lower House.

Indeed, it is difficult to imagine how the six States would ever have agreed to Federation without the Senate. Paul Keating once referred to the Senate as 'unrepresentative swill'. True, the Upper House is not 'democratic' in that, irrespective of the size of the population of the various States, each has the same number of senators (currently 12), yet this was not the intention of the founding fathers. The election of senators within each State by proportional representation is far more democratic than the house, the members of which are elected on the preferential system of voting, allowing parties to come to office with less than 50 per cent of the two-party preferred vote (after primary voting preferences have been allocated). In the 1998 election, the Beazley-led Labor Party received 2 per cent more of the two-party preferred vote, yet still lost the election to the Coalition, led by Howard.

It is often claimed the Senate long ago ceased to be a chamber guarding the interests of the States, and rigid discipline of the major parties forces senators to vote the party line. This, the argument goes, prevents senators from representing the interests of their State. This is true to a point, yet government senators, on issues of importance to their State, have frequently crossed the floor, or have threatened to do so—often achieving the same result. Most importantly, with the smaller parties and independent senators so often holding the balance of power, benefits to various States are wrung from the Government in return for votes.

Tasmanian Senator Brian Harradine, since the war perhaps the most controversial independent in the Upper House, had millions of dollars showered on Tasmania by governments anxious for his support. Harradine, with his adherence to Catholic values, was able to achieve acceptance of a number of policies he promoted. One such was the Howard Government's decision ending overseas aid that included advising women in recipient countries of abortion procedures—a policy abandoned by the Rudd Labor Government in 2009.

Irrespective of whether or not the Government had a Senate majority at some particular time, but for the Senate guarding the interest of States, Australia might be very different today. We might not have, for example, a car manufacturing industry in South Australia, the Ord River Dam (and many other dams), or generous subsidies to ferries to Tasmania if the Senate was, like the House of Representatives, a rubber stamp for the Government.

The Senate committee system has opened the administration of the executive government to scrutiny and is the enduring gift of the Senate to Australian democracy. Apart from housekeeping committees covering such matters as procedure and senate publications, there are standing committees looking at the big issues: economics, education, workplace relations, the environment, communications, foreign affairs, defence and trade, rural and regional affairs, and transport regulations and ordinances. When examining budget spending, senators in estimates committees question public servants on how, when and why the Government is spending taxpayers' money in the policy areas covered by each standing committee. Thus, the Foreign Affairs, Defence and Trade Standing Committee, as the estimates committee in this area, questions officials of the Defence, Foreign Affairs and Trade Departments.

Sadly, there has been a steady decline in the standing of politicians among voters and deep public cynicism about politics. Revelations by senate committees have contributed to this, and the media is ever on the prowl for stories of ugly behaviour by politicians, their wives or children. Politicians in the broad have themselves to blame. Prime ministers have been transformed into celebrities, competing for media space with sporting heroes and show-biz personalities. Any launch of an event important enough to have TV coverage is more than likely to show the ever-smiling Prime Minister's visage. Prime ministers are eagerly sort by a range of TV shows, where they are often asked to do silly things by someone such as Kerri-Anne Kennerley. They are frequently shown on the news waving as they enter their own RAAF VIP jet on departure for something important somewhere. The catering on the jet is invariably not up to scratch, hence Rudd was so angry at the food provided on one flight that he reduced a RAAF hostess to tears.

Prime ministers were not always celebrities. Alan Ramsey came across a wonderful Chifley story he included in his weekly *Sydney Morning Herald* Saturday column on 23 June 2001. That year was marked by celebrations for the centenary of Federation and the founding of the Commonwealth Public Service. Guided tours of the administration building were conducted and Dr Michael

McKernan, a historian, was one of the guides. The administration building foundations had been dug in 1930 but the Depression and World War II halted further work until 1949. The supervisor of the building construction told McKernan that Chifley would often call in on the building site for a natter and would invariably ask the supervisor, 'How's it all going, son?' The supervisor also recounted another story to McKernan, reported on by Ramsey.

Like all prime ministers, Chifley had a private phone on his desk—the number known only to his wife, senior colleagues and advisers. It was, of course, a silent number, but apparently was only one digit removed from the number for the butcher shop in the nearby suburb of Manuka. Occasionally, the phone would ring and when the Prime Minister of Australia answered, he would find a housewife calling, wanting to leave her meat order for the weekend. And what would Chifley do? Of course, he would simply take the order for the chops, the leg of lamb, or whatever, saying nothing to the caller except, 'Yes, madam', then when she had rung off, he would phone the butcher himself and say 'It's happened again' and repeat the order.

These days, it is impossible to imagine anyone getting through, by accident or not, to the Prime Minister unless first vetted. David Day[1] records that Ben Chifley, even as Prime Minister, drove himself between his home in Bathurst, NSW, and Canberra in his own Buick—his pride and joy. It was not even considered necessary that a bodyguard should accompany him on this journey. Jim Snow, former Labor MP for the southern NSW federal seat of Eden-Monaro, told the author that on Chifley's drives between Canberra and Bathurst he sometimes changed his route and went through the small town of Crookwell, lunching at a café. On one occasion, he asked for steak and onions, but the waitress told him, 'I'm sorry, Mr Chifley, we have no onions'. 'Well', said Chifley, thrusting his hand into his coat pocket, 'here's one', and he produced an onion.

In Canberra, home for Prime Minister Chifley was a single room in the Kurrajong Hotel. Menzies, as Leader of the Opposition, had to finance his own trip abroad in 1948, the year before he defeated Chifley and considered raising money writing newspaper articles. Fortunately, Menzies' wealthy friend Arthur Sims, a leading pioneer of the New Zealand frozen meat trade, came to his assistance.[2]

These days prime ministers automatically approve overseas travel expenses for the Opposition Leader being met by the Government. When Menzies retired, he could not afford to purchase his home in Melbourne, and the Melbourne business community financed it. The Brits, at that time, were far tougher on their parliamentarians. In 1981, Margaret Thatcher's Deputy Prime Minister, Willie Whitelaw (later First Viscount Whitelaw), visited Australia and, as President of

---

1   Day, *Chifley*.
2   Martin, *Robert Menzies*, vol. 2, p. 85.

the National Press Club, I sat alongside him while hosting a lunch at the club in his honour. He told me he had recently seen Harold Wilson, twice Labour Prime Minister of England and then a backbencher in the Commons, standing at a bus stop in Westminster. Whitelaw told me he was stunned and went to Thatcher, pleading, successfully, 'Can't we have a government car for Harold?' Wilson was then a Knight of the Garter and, on leaving the Commons in 1983, was created Barron Wilson of Rievaulx, after Rievaulx Abbey, in the north of his native Yorkshire.

Contrast this with the lavish lifestyle of John Howard, the first Prime Minister to insist on the taxpayer providing him with two homes: the Lodge and Kirribilli House. Labor hardman the late Eddie Ward asked Menzies in the house on 23 April 1958: 'Is it a fact that the Prime Minister now regards Kirribilli House as his official residence?' Menzies replied that Kirribilli House was for Commonwealth Government guests: 'It is a very good thing for this country that we should be able to give distinguished visitors from overseas, in the largest and senior city of this country, accommodation appropriate to them', Menzies declared.

Howard appropriated Kirribilli House without any authority from the Cabinet or the Parliament. His initial explanation was that his children's education required him to live in Sydney. When his children reached adulthood, his new excuse was that he saw it as an advantage to live in a major city. The Howards were big on the Sydney social scene, and Kirribilli House was a much more desirable address than the Lodge.

Every elected prime minister, except Scullin, Chifley and Howard, has lived at the Lodge since Canberra became the capital. Senate estimates committee probing revealed that Howard enjoyed an expensive and well-stocked wine cellar, kept in shape by a taxpayer-provided wine consultant. He had his own RAAF 34 (VIP) Squadron Boeing 737—a private aerial taxi for the short hop between Sydney and Canberra. The Air Force had purchased a smaller and more economical Bombardier Challenger executive jet to make these trips, but Howard liked the comfort of the bigger 737.

When overseas, only the very best hotels would do for the Prime Minister. During the debates on a republic, Howard, having at first promised to keep out of the debate, came in on the side of the monarchists and declared the Constitution had served Australia well. The Constitution is silent on where the Prime Minister should live, but the founding fathers obviously intended that the Prime Minister reside in the capital, otherwise why would the Lodge have been built? This aspect of the Constitution, 'which has served Australia well', did not suit Howard. Prime Minister Kevin Rudd moved his family into the Lodge, yet Kirribilli House is not always available for its original purpose—as a guesthouse for VIP overseas guests of the Commonwealth.

In the 26 years the Federal Parliament sat in Melbourne, seven prime ministers were in power. Two of them, Alfred Deakin and Andrew Fisher, served on three separate occasions. In the 61 years the Parliament sat in the provisional Parliament House, 17 prime ministers sat in the chamber of the House of Representatives. All served only once, except Robert Gordon Menzies. Only Menzies, the longest-serving prime minister, twice led the government: 26 April 1939 – August 1941 and 19 December 1949 – 26 January 1966. Stanley Melbourne Bruce was the first prime minister to sit in the provisional Parliament and the last was Robert Lee Hawke.

Menzies, Gough Whitlam (5 December 1972 – 11 November 1975) and Hawke/ Keating (Hawke: 11 March 1983 – 20 December 1991; Keating: 20 December 1991 – 11 March 1996) were the three (four) outstanding achievers during my term covering politics in the Old Parliament House. (I exclude two who are widely regarded as the greatest prime ministers—Curtin and Chifley—who were out of office before I arrived in Canberra.)

Menzies' and Whitlam's greatest achievements were as leader of the opposition, not as prime minister. Menzies revived and unified the moribund conservative side of politics by sinking the old and failed United Australia Party and replacing it with the Liberal Party of Australia. The conservative forces were in the wilderness for eight years before Menzies achieved his hard-won success at the 1949 election. Menzies' much-criticised foreign policies were a product of his times and the Australian experience flowing from the Cold War and his well-founded concern about the threat to the West from communism.

He found it hard to accept the anti-colonialism that swept the former empires of Britain and the European powers, hence his misreading of the Suez affair. Similarly, his enthusiasm and genuine belief in the strategic insurance policy provided by the ANZUS alliance led him to the foolish policy of refusing to recognise the reality of the Chinese Communist Government and his devious manipulation of public opinion, leading Australia into the Vietnam War.

Like Menzies, Whitlam's achievements were more impressive as opposition leader than as prime minister. He did not change the name of his party, but he brought about a revolution inside the Australian Labor Party. He put it back in the political game, after 23 years of failure, with his 1972 election win. This is not to put down the achievements of the Whitlam Government. His achievements in foreign affairs were considerable. Recognition of the People's Republic of China was the single most important initiative any government has made in the field of foreign relations since the war. Also of great importance was his role in achieving independence for Papua New Guinea by granting the former Australian mandated territory internal self-government.

Andrew Peacock, Foreign Affairs Minister in the Fraser Government, was responsible for Papua New Guinea taking the next step to full independence as a nation within the Commonwealth of Nations. Whitlam commented at the time that he would much rather be the father of Papua New Guinea than the midwife. He also ended conscription for the Vietnam War. His role in Indonesia's takeover of East Timor (Timor-Leste) in 1975 remains a controversial issue.

In one swoop—now almost forgotten—he slashed the Australian tariff by 25 per cent and fathered the economic reform of tariff reduction. Whitlam has been much criticised for his handling of economic issues. Yet it is instructive to remember that in the 1973–74 budget, when the Whitlam Government first had full control for the whole financial year, Treasurer, Frank Crean, turned in a cash surplus of $1.06 billion, or 3.1 per cent of gross domestic product (GDP: the measure of the size of the economy). The best since then was 2 per cent 1999–2000.

Further, tax receipts in that budget were a mere 20.1 per cent of GDP—still the best figure, as also were the low payments from the budget at 18.3 per cent of GDP. John Howard, as Treasurer in the Fraser Government, had four budgets—all in deficit. Rudd Government minister Craig Emerson[3] observed that at the peak of its social program, the Whitlam Government's spending constituted 22.2 per cent of GDP, whereas at the peak of the Howard Government's expansionary period in 2007, after 17 years of national prosperity, spending hit 24.2 per cent of GDP. The baseless myth that the Whitlam Government was the most incompetent economic manager has arisen because of the loans affair. It was the result of ministerial stupidity and Whitlam's slowness to knock it on the head, yet no damage resulted to Australia, no money ever changed hands and no-one was ever charged with an offence.

Whitlam's greatest domestic policy achievement was to push Medibank—the forerunner to Medicare—through the Parliament. As in the United States today, then there was much dissatisfaction with the voluntary health insurance scheme. Medibank provided a compulsory national health insurance scheme applying to everyone and financed by a special income tax levy. The Senate rejected legislation for Medibank in the Whitlam Government's first parliamentary term and it was one of the major issues for the 1974 double-dissolution election campaign. Whitlam won the election narrowly and the Senate again refused Medibank, which was finally passed by Parliament at the historic joint sitting of both houses. John Howard, who entered Parliament in that double-dissolution election, voted unsuccessfully with the Liberal and National Party MPs against Medibank at the joint sitting and yet, decades later as prime minister, he had the temerity to claim his government was the greatest friend Medicare ever had.

---

3 *The Australian*, 24 January 2009.

Other important advances achieved by the Whitlam Government have been forgotten, but were important. The bureaucratic dead hand of the old Postmaster-General's Department was ended, with its two man functions split up into Telecom and Australia Post—both overseen by commissions. Whitlam's Attorney-General, Lionel Murphy, achieved national, no-fault divorce reform and put clout into the *Trade Practices Act*. Whitlam also legislated for uniform pay for women, which is still a long way from reality. In the face of fierce opposition from the churches, Whitlam removed the sales tax from the contraceptive pill for women ('the pill' as it became known).

Keating shares Hawke's successes, since Hawke could not have achieved the reforms of the Australian economy without Keating in his dynamic role as Treasurer. All the groundbreaking economic reforms of Hawke/Keating were accomplished while they were in the provisional Parliament House. Hawke spent a little more than two years in opposition and 20 days as Opposition Leader before winning the 1983 election. Labor had been out of power for eight years. Keating had been in Parliament for more than 13 years before he became Treasurer. He had the hard slog through opposition and was a junior minister at the fag end of the Whitlam Government.

In opposition, his powers of persuasion and vigour had much to do with the modernising of thought in the Labor Party from its protectionist history. The Hawke/Keating team reshaped the Australian economy and shook it free from many of the governmental constraints imposed since Federation. Keating's crowning achievement was to do what would have seemed impossible before and since: rising to leadership of the Labor Party by defeating on the floor of Caucus the most successful leader the party ever had, in Hawke—a winner of four successive elections: 1983, 1984, 1987 and 1990. A majority of Caucus believed Keating was more likely than Hawke to win the 1993 election. Whether this was good for the ALP let alone Australia remains a matter of debate.

A consequence was nearly 12 years of Howard—in the author's opinion, the worst, most divisive Australian prime minister. Bill McMahon was hopeless, but at least he did not damage the nation. Howard wasted the avalanche of revenue from the resources boom; fostered paranoia, xenophobia and racial hatred among Australians; and, in foreign relations, caused the rest of the world to view Australia not as an independent and proud country, but a subservient puppet to George W. Bush's imperialism. Howard's most costly failure might yet prove to be his scepticism about climate change—unshaken until almost the last year of his reign.

In the first year of the Rudd Government the press gallery had three or four more times the number of journalists compared with the situation in the provisional Parliament House, and 50 or more TV technicians and camera operators, both

TV and still. Today's gallery journalists are better educated, and they need to be as governments grow bigger and ever more complex, as do the issues faced. Above all other issues looms climate change. Then there is the endless challenge of economic and social issues: from health to coal loaders, infrastructure needs expansion; fostering skills training to match the demand of the export industries serving the growing economies of China and India; federalism is crumbling; efforts to lift the Indigenous community from poverty and match the life expectancy of the rest of us are insufficient and disappointing; foreign policy is more confronting and difficult.

Since the Parliament moved into its permanent building, the gallery has become the central information point of the nation. Information from all over Australia and the world pours into the gallery through press conferences, media statements, pamphlets, seminars, phone calls, emails—the whole menu of information exchange systems—with all the public and private pressure groups seeking to attract attention, be it the National Farmers' Federation, the Australian Medical Association, various think tanks, the Australian Conservation Foundation or the Canberra offices of the European Union, and hundreds more. This continuous flow of information has to be dealt with every day in the gallery—and is not always done successfully.

The myth of a gallery rat pack arises almost every time a big political issue surfaces, be it a scandal or a crisis. Those injured or feeling badly served by the media reports complain of bad treatment by the gallery rat pack, the inference being that the gallery acts in unison and somehow, collectively, makes up its mind to adopt the same view on any big story. This is rubbish. The top gallery journalists and bureau heads are not conspiring together; they are in fierce competition, striving to get a different angle or turn up a new 'exclusive'. Newspaper and TV news editors do not want their Canberra representatives to all be singing from the same song sheet; they want something new.

There is an argument that, as the House of Representatives is a mere rubber stamp for the government of the day, and Question Time is pointless, it is a good thing ministers and prime ministers are available for face-to-face interviews with the media. The longer, more penetrating interviews conducted on Sunday-morning TV provide more information and important commentary than would ever come out in Parliament, yet their ratings are low. Polls consistently show that most people get their political information from the late-evening commercial TV news—a medium that demands, above all else, brevity. The newsy 'grab' from politicians is what TV and radio journalists are looking for. Politicians are aware of this and work on composing the 'grab', yet information from the 'grab' is limited.

Research has shown younger people largely ignore TV or radio news and information on day-to-day events does not appear to interest many of them, or even reach them. The affluence of successive 'what's in it for me' generations has produced a political 'dumbing down' of much of the population and the collapse of membership of the major political parties. An elite hierarchy controls the Liberal and Labor Parties with little or no input from the shrinking rank and file. There are encouraging signs: voters are now interested in the politics of global warming and this will continue for generations to come. Young people are beginning to pick up information on such popular web sites as YouTube, to the extent that in the 2007 election, both Howard and Rudd used the site to pitch to young voters. These and other sites are capable of turning every citizen into a reporter; all they now need is the device to enter cyberspace.

Whatever the attractions of the Web and the ability of anyone with a computer to become part of the media (and not just a media consumer), responsibility for reporting what is happening—both in Parliament and in the vast and increasingly intricate operations of the federal administration—rests squarely with professional journalists, basically, but not only, from the Federal Parliamentary Press Gallery. There are a number of journalists, former members of the gallery and not now residents of Canberra doing sterling work. It is the gallery, however, that carries most of the responsibility.

We take for granted the right of the media to say what it likes as long as it is within the law and not defamatory. In 2004, Michael Harvey and Gerald McManus, two gallery journalists, published a 'secret' document that caused great embarrassment to the Howard Government, revealing the Government had decided, without an announcement at that point, to reject the findings of an inquiry calling for additional benefits to war veterans, estimated by officials to cost $500 million. This was a serious embarrassment for Howard, who was ever ready to wrap himself in the Australian flag to put himself forward as the champion of Australian security with unbounded admiration for those who served, or are serving, in the Australian Defence Force.

A fifty-two-year-old public servant, Desmond Kelly, was charged with leaking the document. At Kelly's pre-trial hearing, Harvey and McManus were asked to reveal the source of the document and both declined, on the grounds they could incriminate themselves. Given immunity against self-incrimination by the Crown, they were again asked to reveal their source and both declined—this time on the grounds that revealing a source breached the journalists' code of ethics. They were charged with contempt of court, pleaded guilty and were fined $7000. Their employer, the *Herald Sun*, reimbursed them, but this still left the stain of a criminal offence on their records, automatically excluding them from any press party going to the United States to cover visits there of senior ministers, including the Prime Minister. Under US law, any foreigner guilty of a criminal offence is denied a visa to enter the country.

Ironically enough, no US Government would treat a US investigative journalist in the same way. Prime Minister John Howard had two bob each way. He described the pair as 'good blokes' and added: 'I think it is worthwhile preserving the principle that a government does have a right, in the public interest, of conducting some confidential discussions.'[4] He made no mention of the necessity, in the national interest, of journalists going about their work of scrutinising government and discovering what politicians wanted to keep from the public.

Despite the risk to their careers and Howard's for government secrecy, the affair has not halted the flow of leaks from government officials. In the author's experience, such leaks are, to a greater or lesser extent, invariably in the public interest and not in the political interest of the Government, and (more rarely) of the Opposition. Whether or not Australia should have a charter of rights embedded in the Constitution is a matter of contention. Nevertheless, the national interest would be enhanced if the media in Australia had the same freedoms enjoyed by media in the United States.

Another concerning aspect of the Australian media is a concentration of power in metropolitan newspaper ownership. Paul Keating approved the takeover by News Limited of the Herald and Weekly Times, and the report of the Foreign Investment Review Board on the takeover remains secret. As a result, News Limited commands 70–80 per cent of the circulation of metropolitan newspapers: *The Courier-Mail*, the only hardcopy newspaper in Brisbane; *The Daily Telegraph*, which has the largest circulation of any Sydney paper; the *Herald Sun*, which has the largest circulation of any paper in the nation; *The Advertiser*, the only paper in Adelaide; *The Australian*, a national daily; and Sunday papers in every mainland State capital.

John Fairfax, now controlled by J. B. Fairfax's Rural Press, has the *Sydney Morning Herald* and the *Sun-Herald* (Sunday) in Sydney; *The Age* and *The Sunday Age* in Melbourne; *The Canberra Times*; plus the *Australian Financial Review*, a national daily. The importance of the Internet in the media industry is growing rapidly and commercial radio and TV, plus the ABC, provide necessarily brief news services. Nevertheless, newspapers mainly set the issues of the day and obviously are able to cover any particular item in greater detail. The influence of newspapers on day-to-day politics remains profound.

---

4   Radio 3AW, Melbourne, 26 August 2005.

Governments leak items, such as an important new policy yet to be announced, or bits of the coming budget. The intention is to get an issue out in the public domain to test public reaction, allowing assessment of whether the official announcement needs to be altered. To attract major media attention, leaks are generally directed to major newspapers and are then immediately picked up by radio and talkback commentators, plus the all-important TV evening news. A bureau head out of favour will not be given the leak, which can lead to the editor demanding to know why a story in the first edition of a rival newspaper was missed. This form of media control is unknown to the public, but it is just one of the tools governments apply in their endless efforts to manage the media.

Holding the Government to account is the central role of the gallery and in the process journalists can and do inflict damage on governments. To a lesser degree, it is also the gallery's job to hold the Opposition to account, but the focus must be on the Government. Politics is about power and the objective of politicians is to gain power by winning government and staying there. The Government (at the taxpayers' expense) employs an army of journalists in government departments, instrumentalities and in ministers' offices to block bad news reaching the voters. The struggle between the gallery and the spin doctors continues.

Epilogue: Changing the game

The political system must be turned on its head. After nearly 60 years of observing politics from the gallery, I believe the system has lost its way. The competition for ideas is constrained as parliamentary colleagues of the Prime Minister or Opposition Leader are required to fall in behind whatever policies they hand down from on high. Before new policies are introduced, the political leaders give too much weight to the political advantage or disadvantage that might follow.

There is excessive attention devoted to market research and devising the best spin for new policies, and not enough to the intrinsic merits or otherwise of policies. The stranglehold on political power by the two major parties, Labor and Liberal, needs to be broken. We need more parties, not less, and a system that will encourage the participation of the grassroots of parties in policy formulation. Rigid party discipline and television have combined to transform the Prime Minister from a party leader to an elected dictator and celebrity. Few prime ministers or presidents in modern Western democracies are as powerful as the Australian Prime Minister.

Party discipline in the United Kingdom is not nearly as tight as in Australia and the occupant of 10 Downing Street can be forced by his or her party to bend. The American President needs the approval of Congress for legislation and Congress may initiate its own legislation, whereas in Canberra, once the Prime Minister has decided on a measure, it is rubber-stamped in the Lower House. There is the brake of the party room and it is more effective in the Labor Party than in the Liberal/Nationals party room. When Labor is in government, Caucus has a theoretical right to both scrutinise and reject legislation; this often happened during the Whitlam Government, but is rare now.

Caucus also elects the ministry. Since Whitlam, Labor prime ministers have assured voters that they alone decide the composition of the ministry. In truth, the factions work out in advance who will be in and out, although the Prime Minister may always insist on getting his or her way if they want particular MPs in the ministry who are not on the factional lists. The Prime Minister has the sole right to allocate portfolios to those chosen by Caucus for the ministry.

When R. G. Menzies wrote the rules for the parliamentary Liberal Party, he insisted that the leader alone would decide which Liberals would be in the ministry and allocate their portfolios. Liberal prime ministers, and particularly Howard, used this power to keep dissenters in the party room out of his ministry and to reward those who unquestioningly supported him. Ministers became 'yes' men and women. Since 1949, when in government, the Liberals have formed a coalition with the Nationals (the Country Party in Menzies' day), and the Liberal and Nationals leaders come to an agreement as to how many Nationals will be in the ministry and what portfolios they will occupy.

Fortunately, governments generally lack a majority in the Senate and when they do gain control of the Upper House, the result is invariably bad government, a lack of accountability and arrogance. The media, particularly the electronic media, has become a fixation for prime ministers, particularly at public events, putting them in front of the TV cameras, and they have taken over many of the traditional tasks of the Governor-General—an example being ceremonies marking the departure or return of troops from overseas service.

Election campaigns are increasingly presidential in style, with voters urged to ensure that the Prime Minister or the Leader of the Opposition runs the country after the election, not their party. Despite the central role in government of the Prime Minister, this summit of national government is not directly elected by the people, unlike the President of the United States and the heads of state in many democracies. Voter reaction to the removal of Kevin Rudd demonstrated that many imagined they had voted him in as prime minister, and were unaware of the fact that the party room decides on and disposes of the leader.

Leaders were just as central to politics in the Chifley, Menzies and Whitlam eras, but these three showed considerable respect to their party room. The fundamental change in politics of the past three decades has been the erosion of the numbers of rusted-on supporters of the major political parties who could be relied on to vote the party ticket, no matter who is the party leader. Maybe only 5 per cent of voters were 'swingers' in the Menzies era; now the percentage of 'swingers' is probably as high as 20 or 30 per cent. They vote on issues, of course, but also on their attraction or otherwise to the leader. (Much of the above changed with the hung parliament elected on 21 August 2010, but there will be a return to near normality once one of the major parties gains a clear majority at a future election.) Because of the swingers, party leaders are extremely cautious about policies and each policy must pass the test of support from swingers, rather than the first priority being the national interest.

I propose abandonment of the present system of one MHR representing each of the 150 divisions of the Lower House, with voting on a preferential system. Instead, there would be 30 divisions and five MHRs elected from each division, on a proportional basis, which retains the present size of the House of Representatives of 150. This could be accommodated in terms of Section 29 of the Constitution and would not require any change to the present senate numbers and system of voting.

Tasmania's constitutional right to at least five House of Representatives seats would be undisturbed. These divisions would be named federal, regional and metropolitan divisions. With five MHRs elected for each division, the small parties and independents would have a reasonable chance of picking up at least one seat in each division. A diversity of policy ideas would flow as a result. The Senate would continue in its role as the house of review, as well as the protector of the rights of the smaller States and regions in the States from the dominance of New South Wales and Victoria in the Lower House.

Something needs to be done about the mounting cost of election campaigns, which in turn drives parties in their unceasing search of large donations from unions and corporations. The donations amount to the purchase of the right to influence parties' policies. The political parties all deny this—a denial I do not accept and nor, I suspect, do most voters. It is difficult to devise a system that would deal with this unsatisfactory situation. An inquiry equivalent to a royal commission should examine this issue with terms of reference to examine and report on the funding of political parties and the cost of election campaigns.

There should be a specific reference to examining the need for an absolute ban on paid commercial advertising on television and radio by political parties, or by any entity on behalf of a political party. Pressure groups such as unions, farmers, gays and all the rest would be free to advertise and advocate whatever they liked, but not to advocate the election of a particular party. A problem is that the parties could set up 'independent' donor organisations to advocate the policies of political parties, without actually seeking votes for a political party.

The unions did this in the lead-up to the 2007 election by damning the Howard Government's WorkChoices legislation without actually urging voters to support the ALP. Alternatively, television and radio stations could be required to provide limited free time to political parties or the Australian Electoral Commission could recompense them.

Public funding of parties or individuals is provided for those that reach 4 per cent of the primary vote and could be doubled or trebled from the $2.31 per vote at the 2010 election, with both the Liberal Party and the ALP receiving about $21 million each. A total cost twice or three times this amount would be well spent if it produced greater competition in ideas and less dependence of the parties on outside donations. Compulsory voting would also be abandoned, requiring political parties to work to ensure their supporters turned up at the ballot box.

This would, hopefully, bring the parties in closer contact with the community. The parties' easy reliance on a presidential election, fought on TV by two political leaders, largely funded by pressure groups, would end. Hopefully, with a reduction or elimination of TV advertising, campaigns would return to the town halls, workshops and the streets, and grassroots membership would once again be important to the parties for donations and voluntary work. Private donations to political parties from any entity or individual of $1000 or more (indexed to the consumer price index) would be registered on a public register.

The system I am sketching here would automatically halt the rise of centralism. Both the Howard and the Rudd Governments fostered, or advocated, centralism in various policy areas, such as health, education and industrial relations. Howard succeeded in winning federal control of most of the area of industrial relations and Rudd welcomed this development and applied it in government. The Federal Government should return industrial relations powers to the States. Because it is easier to lobby one government rather than a number of State governments—and appear before a single, national industrial relations commission or court—employers and unions warmed to Howard's centralised industrial relations.

Tony Abbott is an unashamed centralist and in his book *Battlelines*, published before he took over the Liberal leadership, Abbott proposed that the Constitution should be radically altered to ensure the Commonwealth may always overrule the States. In an interview with the *Australian Financial Review*, Abbott argued that if the States would not refer unspecified powers to an Abbott federal government, he would seek the powers via a referendum. Before he entered Parliament and 10 years before he became Treasurer, Peter Costello was one of the founders of the anti-union H. R. Nicholls Society, established in 1986.

When John Howard revealed his WorkChoices industrial relations legislation—built around a centralised system—Ray Evans, President of the H. R. Nicholls Society, rejected the plan. Instead, said Evans, the Government should abandon Section 51:35 (the industrial relations power) of the Constitution and 'let the states compete with each other in providing effective labour market regulation (or freedom) as opportunity or political fashion afforded'. Evans continued: 'Regrettably we have a Prime Minister and Treasurer who are strong centralists and a Cabinet in which the number of federalists can be easily accommodated on the fingers of one hand.'[1] Evans was—as is the author—championing competition and diversity. To this end, I propose restoring the prewar income-taxing powers of the States to increase their independence and stop the swing towards centralism. It is madness for governance of a continent to be centralised in Canberra.

The Griffith University Values Survey of 2008 measured the views of those surveyed on the present three-tier system of government (federal, State and

---

1   *Inside Canberra*, 11 April 2006.

local governments) 20 years on. Only 31 per cent wanted to keep the system while nearly 66 per cent wanted 'reform'. When asked what type of reform, only 7 per cent suggested abolishing the Federal Government, while 30.5 per cent said abolish State governments, nearly 33 per cent wanted to abolish local government and the same percentage wanted to create regional governments. Yet this poll—apart from its value in showing support for change—is pointless. A referendum abolishing State governments would not even be put, let alone succeed.

What is possible, without any referendum, is a big improvement in the system. The local-government tier could be abolished by the States, yet this would be a mistake. It is the tier of government closest to the people—accurately described as 'local' government. Through State agreements, all existing councils and shires could be abolished and replaced with one council or shire responsible for each of the 30 federal regional divisions outlined above. This would be a worthwhile reduction in the present number of some 700 local-government organisations, while some existing local-government bodies, such as land councils in northern Australia, would be retained.

Because of the diversity of parties sending representatives to Canberra, the needs and ambitions of various geographical areas would have to be taken seriously. The Australian Electoral Commission would still be responsible for regular redistributions of House of Representatives divisions. Democratic countries, including federations, all over the world operate successfully with coalition governments of two or more parties.

The successful economies of Western Europe and Scandinavia have not been held back by their coalition governments. What I propose will mean changes in the outlook of the two major political parties. The Liberals will need to think about coalitions with other parties, apart from their traditional ties to the Nationals. Labor—convinced that it alone has all the answers—will be forced into coalitions (as it was after the 2010 election). Sometimes the system seems to fail—Italy, with chronic political instability, is a prime example, but that arguably has more to do with the culture of the country than the voting system.

I would favour four-year fixed terms of Parliament, but this would surely fail at a referendum. My alternative is a fixed three-year term, imposed by legislation. Lawyers point to a difficulty as Chapter 1, Part 1 Para 5 of the Constitution allows the Governor-General to dissolve the House of Representatives at any time. The legislation could be worded to provide for a fixed three-year term, while not denying the power of the Governor-General. Who would then want to challenge the legislation and who would be recognised by the High Court as having the necessary standing to mount a challenge? The fixed three-year term for the house would leave untouched the present fixed terms of senators, allowing for election of both houses on the same day every three years. Legislation for fixed three-year terms could, of course, be repealed, but once it came into operation, it would be a gallant government that attempted to abolish it. In short, big changes and improvements can be made to the system without difficult referendums.

I also propose a royal commission to inquire into an entirely new system of setting the salaries and allowances of parliamentarians, with the primary aim of lessening the profound cynicism of voters towards politicians. Perhaps the pay should be higher and the perks lower; the salary would have to be high enough to encourage capable people, not just the wealthy or party hacks. Various changes could be made. For example, the salary could be two or three times higher and MPs would be required to rent their electoral office. The $100 000 printing allowance provided by taxpayers should be abolished. My particular objection to this is that it gives an unnecessary advantage to sitting members at elections. The printing allowance is used exclusively to retain electorates for the incumbents and such printing costs should be carried by the political parties. The less advantage to the sitting MP the better.

In short, my proposals would enhance the power of the Parliament at the expense of the executive. The complexities of policy options and various shades of opinion on display in both houses would once again be adequately covered by the media. The obvious final problem is how to achieve change. The current ranks of politicians will not voluntarily change anything impinging on their power.

We need something like Rudd's Australia 2020 Summit on a permanent basis, and devoted entirely to reviewing the whole apparatus of parliamentary democracy. What to call it? Perhaps, the 'People's Democratic Assembly' (which sounds a bit like something in a communist state), or maybe the 'Australian National Democratic Assembly'. Whatever the name, it could perhaps meet at the beginning of each new term of Parliament following an election; annually might be a bit much. The chair would be the Chief Justice of the High Court and a small executive body—independent of government and political parties—would invite, say, 50 eminent Australians to each assembly and there would be appropriate representation from the Federal, State and Territory Parliaments. Maybe a political party might be formed—the 'Change Politics Party'—just to bring this all about.

Changes to the political system should be easy compared with dealing with global warming and putting a man on the moon. To borrow from President Obama's election campaign theme, YES WE CAN!

Bibliography

Abbott, Tony 2009, *Battlelines*, Melbourne University Press, Carlton, Vic.

Brawley, Sean 2007, *The Bondi Lifesaver: A history of an Australian icon*, ABC Books, Sydney.

Buckley, Ken, Dale, Barbara and Reynolds, Wayne 1994, *Doc Evatt: Patriot, internationalist, fighter and scholar*, Longman Cheshire, Melbourne.

Cabban, Peter 2005, *Breaking Ranks*, Random House, Sydney.

d'Alpuget, Blanche 1982, *Robert J. Hawke: A biography*, Schwartz in conjunction with Lansdowne Press, Melbourne.

Day, David P. 1999, *John Curtin: A life*, Harper Collins, Sydney.

Day, David P. 2001, *Chifley: A life*, Harper Collins, Sydney.

Dobell, Graeme 2000, *Australia Finds Home: The choices and chances of an Asia Pacific journey,* ABC Books, Sydney.

Faulkner, John and Macintyre, Stuart 2001, *True Believers: The story of the federal parliamentary Labor Party*, Allen & Unwin, Crows Nest, NSW.

Frame, Tom 2005, *The Life and Death of Harold Holt*, Allen & Unwin, Crows Nest, NSW.

Freudenberg, Graham 2005, *A Figure of Speech: A political memoir*, John Wiley & Sons, Milton, Qld.

Golding, Peter 1996, *Black Jack McEwen: Political gladiator*, Melbourne University Press, Carlton South, Vic.

Grattan, Michelle (ed.) 2000, *Australian Prime Ministers*, New Holland, Frenchs Forest, NSW.

Hartcher, Peter 2009, *To The Bitter End: The dramatic story of the fall of John Howard and the rise of Kevin Rudd*, Allen & Unwin, Crows Nest, NSW.

Hill, David 2007, *The Forgotten Children*, Random House, Sydney.

Howson, Peter 1984, *The Howson Diaries. The life of politics*, Don Aitkin (ed.), Viking Press, Ringwood, Vic.

Kelly, Paul 1984, *The Hawke Ascendancy*, Angus & Robertson, North Ryde, NSW.

Lloyd, C. J. 1988, *Parliament and the Press: The Federal Parliament Press Gallery 1901–88*, Melbourne University Press, Melbourne.

Martin, A. W. 1993, *Robert Menzies: A life. Volume 1: 1894–1943*, Melbourne University Press, Melbourne.

Martin, A. W. 1999, *Robert Menzies: A life. Volume 2: 1944–1978*, Melbourne University Press, Melbourne.

Menadue, John 1999, *Things You Learn Along the Way*, David Lovell Publishing, Melbourne.

Oakes, Laurie and Solomon, David 1973, *The Making of an Australian Prime Minister*, Cheshire, Melbourne.

Page, Michael 1988, *The Prime Ministers of Australia*, Robertsbridge, London and Sydney.

Rattigan, G. A. 1986, *Industry Assistance: The inside story*, Melbourne University Press, Carlton, Vic.

Reid, Alan 1969, *The Power Struggle*, Shakespeare Head Press, Sydney.

Reid, Alan 1971, *The Gorton Experiment*, Shakespeare Head Press, Sydney.

Royal Canberra Golf Club 1977, *Royal Canberra Golf Club Jubilee History 1926–1976*, The Club, Canberra.

Ryan, Susan and Bramston, Troy (eds) 2003, *The Hawke Government: A critical retrospective*, Pluto Press Australia, North Melbourne.

Sparke, Eric 1988, *Canberra: 1954–1980*, AGPS, Canberra.

Whitlam, E. G. 1965, *Labor and the Constitution*, Victorian Fabian Society, Melbourne.

Whitlam, Gough 1985, *The Whitlam Government 1972–75*, Penguin, Ringwood, Vic.

Whitlam, Gough 2005, *The Truth of the Matter*, Melbourne University Press, Carlton, Vic.

Woolcott, Richard 2003, *The Hot Seat: Reflections on diplomacy from Stalin's death to the Bali bombings*, Harper Collins, Sydney.

Name Index

Kerr, Sir John 73, 109, 161, 186-7, 190-3, 195-6
Khemlani, Tirath 187-8
Killen, Sir James ('Jim') 63, 66, 92-6, 133, 139
Kirby, Tui 4

Lang, Jack 7, 17, 162, 218
Latham, Mark 164
Laucke, Sir Condor 217-8
Lawson, George 54
Lawson, Valerie 86
Lazzarini, Bert 38
Leonard, Reginald ('Reg') 122
Lees, Meg 196
Lewis, Tom 189
Lloyd, Clem 21-22, 79, 115, 168-70, 193
Lloyd, John 74
Lloyd, Owen 175
Lloyd Jones, Lady Hannah 46-7
Louis, Joe 7
Love, David 62
Love, Les ('the Lapper') 23, 62, 64, 89-90, 112, 119, 129
Lynch, Sir Phillip 142, 188, 195-6, 199, 204
Lyons, Dame Enid xi
Lyons, Sir Joseph xi, 35, 56-7, 67, 76, 154

MacArthur, Douglas (General) 43
MacCallum, Mungo 21-22, 40, 47-8, 94-5
McClelland, Doug 212, 216
McClelland, Robert 212
McClintock, Eric 153
McDonald, Leo 26
McEwen, Sir John ('Black Jack') xi, 55, 60-1, 67, 136, 142, 146, 147-55, 195, 197
McEwen, Lady Mary 151
McFarlane, A.B. ('Tich') 136
McGregor, Gregor 97
McKell, Sir William 40, 89
McKenna, Frank 76
McKernan, Michael 225-6
Mackerras, Malcolm 27
Macklin, Michael 194

McLaren, Bill 125-6
McLeay, Leo 221
McMahon, Sir William ('Billy') 49, 93, 98, 120, 128-9, 136, 142, 147, 149-50, 153, 154-5, 157-8, 166, 167, 174, 179, 184, 195, 213, 215, 230
McManus, Frank 105
McManus, Gerald 232
Macmillan, Sir Harold 58, 151
McNicoll, David 46-9,
Macphee, Ian 199-201, 207, 216
Malan, Daniel 123-4
Maley, Jean 126
Maley, Ray 26, 78, 79, 122, 125-6
Mannix, Daniel (Archbishop) 108
Marina, Princess (Duchess of Kent) 126
Martin, Alan W 28, 36, 38, 46-8, 51-2, 91, 124
Martin, Ray 139
Mathews, Race 214
Mathieson, Laurie 173
Mayne, Stephen 122
Meeking, Charles 41, 122
Menadue, John L. 164, 166-7, 172, 188, 190-1, 200, 210
Menzies, Belle 36
Menzies, Frank 36, 37, 49
Menzies, Heather 50
Menzies, Ian 50
Menzies, Les 36, 37, 49-50
Menzies, Sir Robert Gordon xi, 17, 19, 23, 24, 27-8, 31-2, 33, 35-52, 53, 55-9, 61-3, 67, 69, 75, 77, 78, 79, 81-5, 86, 90-1, 92-3, 98, 100, 105, 106-7, 109, 111-2, 113, 117-8, 119, 121-31, 133, 135, 137, 141-3, 147-8, 151, 153, 155, 161, 164, 168, 175, 178, 184, 186, 196, 201, 211, 213, 217, 223, 226, 228, 236
  resignation as prime minister 36, 67
  failing to enlist in WWI 36-7, 68
  leadership and oratory 38-9, 52, 63-4, 66-8, 72, 119, 120, 130, 228, 235
  affair with Fairfax's wife 46, 61
  economic management 61-3, 65
Menzies, Dame Pattie 125, 128, 129

Subject Index

www.ingramcontent.com/pod-product-compliance
Lightning Source LLC
Chambersburg PA
CBHW061244270326
41928CB00041B/3403